WOMEN IN THE LABOUR MOVEMENT

WOMEN IN THE LABOUR MOVEMENT: the British experience, ed.
by Lucy Middleton. Rowman and Littlefield, 1977. 221p bibl index
76-54160. 13.50 ISBN 0-87471-942-9. C.I.P.
Women's history is well represented by this volume of short essays.
The major theme is the efforts of British middle- and working-class
women to initiate social reforms, become politically involved and fran-
chised, and influence governmental policy. Women, as these authors
point out, were and are an integral force in the Labour party. Part I
contains six essays ranging in subject matter from the early years of
labor politics and trade unionism to women's involvement in social
services and internationalism. "The early years" is followed by three
essays, "The movement today," which effectively describe women's
contemporary role in the Labour party, trade unions, Parliament, and
government. The essays are well researched, well written, and present
new material for assessing the impact of women upon British politics.
Eight appendixes provide statistical data such as listing of women
M.P.s, Labour peers, ministers, office holders, trade union officials,
etc. In addition there are biographical notes and a bibliography. All
levels of undergraduates and graduates will find this book interesting
and useful.

WOMEN IN THE LABOUR MOVEMENT

THE BRITISH EXPERIENCE

Edited by LUCY MIDDLETON

Foreword by RT. HON. JAMES CALLAGHAN

117208

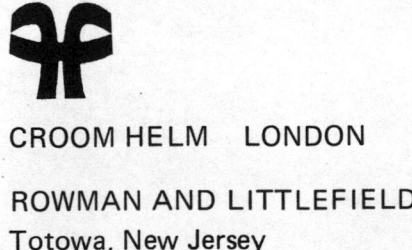

CROOM HELM   LONDON

ROWMAN AND LITTLEFIELD
Totowa, New Jersey

© 1977 Lucy Middleton

Croom Helm Ltd,
2-10 St John's Road, London SW11

ISBN 0-85664-472-2

First published in the United States 1977
by Rowman and Littlefield, Totowa, N.J.

Library of Congress Cataloging in Publication Data

Main entry under title:

Women in the labour movement.

    Includes index.
    1. Women in politics — Great Britain — History —
Addresses, essays, lectures. 2. Women in trade-unions —
Great Britain — History — Addresses, essays, lectures.
3. Labour Party (Great Britain) — History — Addresses,
essays, lectures. I. Middleton, Lucy.
HQ1597.W57 1977   301-41'2   76-54160
ISBN 0-87471-942-9

Printed and bound in Great Britain by
Redwood Burn Limited
Trowbridge & Esher

CONTENTS

ACKNOWLEDGEMENTS

We would like especially to acknowledge the help and encouragement given us by Miss Betty Lockwood, lately Chief Woman Officer of the Labour Party, and now Chairman of the Equal Opportunities Commission, whose idea the book first was, and to her staff, also to her successor, Mrs Joyce Gould, to Mrs Wagner, Labour Party Librarian, and her staff for their unremitting help, and to Mrs Dora Segall for her assistance in proof-reading. Other special acknowledgements will be found after individual chapters, but to all who helped and encouraged us, we are deeply grateful.

FOREWORD

by The Prime Minister

It is with great pleasure that I write this foreword to Labour Women. It is a source of pride that this Labour Government has put on the Statute Book the Act outlawing discrimination on the grounds of sex, as well as bringing to fruition the Equal Pay Act, passed by the previous Labour Government in 1969. But I think we all recognise that these Acts only provide the framework within which women have the opportunity to play a fuller and more effective role in our national life.

Throughout its life the Labour Party has been closely identified with the advancement of women's rights. Keir Hardie gave help and advice to the early Suffragettes. Margaret Bondfield became Britain's first woman Cabinet Minister in the 1929 Labour Government. The post-war parliaments saw women such as Edith Summerskill, Jennie Lee and Peggy Herbison at the very heart of party and government. More recently Barbara Castle and Shirley Williams have taken major governmental responsibilities.

I hope that the work of the pioneers described in this book will encourage a new generation of Labour women to build on the achievements of the last three quarters of a century. Women must become more fully and truly represented, not only in parliament, politics and government, but in the economic and industrial life of our country. There are still far too few women in parliament. We still do not make full use of women's skills and talents in industry or in the professions. This is not only damaging to individual girls, it is a waste of a great national asset.

So my message to the new generation of women reading this book and contemplating playing an active part in Labour politics is that there is still much to be done, but in the following pages you will find much to inspire you.

James Callaghan

CHRONOLOGY OF EVENTS

1883   Formation of 'Women's League for the spread of Cooperation' was announced.

1884   The League's name changed to Women's Cooperative Guild.

1888   The Matchgirls' Strike.

1889   Emma Paterson's Protective and Provident League becomes Women's Protective and Trade Union League.

1905   Railway Women's Guild requests formation of a National Women's Labour Committee.

1906   Inaugural Meeting of Women's Labour League at 3, Lincoln's Inn Fields.

1909   Women's Labour League granted affiliation to the Labour Party.

1911   Deaths of Margaret MacDonald and Mary Middleton.

1916   Formation of Standing Joint Conference of Industrial Women's Organisations.

1918   New Labour Party Constitution under which Women's Labour League becomes the Women's Section of the Labour Party.

1918   Marion Phillips appointed Chief Woman Officer.

1918   A limited Parliamentary franchise for women operated in 1918 General Election for first time.

1921   Two seats for women reserved on General Council of the Trades Union Congress.

1923   Election of first three Labour women members of Parliament.

1924   First British woman delegate to League of Nations appointed by the Labour Prime Minister.

1926   International Socialist Women's Bureau established.

1928   Parliamentary franchise granted to women on the same terms as men.

1929   Margaret Bondfield becomes Britain's first woman Cabinet Minister.

1931   ILO Convention on Equal Pay adopted.

1945   Family Allowances Legislation reaches Statute Book.

1958   Appointment of first women Life Peers.

1962   Sara Barker appointed first woman National Agent of Labour Party.

1967   Labour Party set up Study Group on Sex Equality.

1970   Equal Pay Act passed (to be fully operational by end of 1975).
1972   Publication of Labour's Green Paper on Discrimination Against
        Women.
1975   International Women's Year.
        Sex Discrimination Act becomes law.
        Equal Opportunities Commission set up.

To the memory of
JIM MIDDLETON
whose faith in Labour women never faltered

NOTE

Where names appear in the text marked with an asterisk the reader is referred to the Biographical Notes p.208.

INTRODUCTION

Sheila Lochhead

Britain, at the turn of the last century, was changing very rapidly in industry, economics and politics, but the emergence of women into public life was to prove the greatest change of all.

In 1900 the British Labour Party was born. Six years later political Labour women commenced to organise alongside the men. Already trade unionism for women was an accomplished fact growing slowly but steadily, and already women, as consumers, had established a network of branches of the Cooperative Women's Guild. So the forward march of women in the labour, trade union and cooperation movements had begun and there was no turning back. The story of their struggle and their achievements, their frustrations and their victories over the past seventy-five years will be the theme of this book.

Let us look first at the life of the great majority of working-class married women around 1900. The housewife was busy from early morning till late at night with household and family duties. She was washing, cooking, cleaning, mending, shopping, feeding the baby, minding the children, all tasks that were in those days more laborious than today, for scarcely any of the labour-saving devices which we take for granted were then invented, let alone available to working-class people. Imagine trying to keep your house clean without the help of vacuum cleaners and detergents, with the dust from the nearby factory blowing in, with rain dripping through the leaking roofs. Imagine trying to keep up with the endless wash, without quick drying fabrics or laundry gadgets except the corrugated scrubbing board which wore one's hands; or trying to cope with the constant sewing, before sewing machines were common and when candles, paraffin lamps and occasionally gas, were the brightest lighting.

No wonder that women suffered from anxiety and ill-health. Bearing so many babies was a strain on the hardiest of them, but when child-rearing was coupled with undernourishment and weariness, then the pleasing charms and the liveliness of the young mother steadily withered away. Illness abounded. The insanitary conditions, particularly in the towns but also in the country, brought fevers and a host of ailments. Accidents, so prevalent in the early days brought both sickness and often disablement, besides a desperate loss of earnings.

15

As for her intellectual life, what chance, quite apart from the lack of time and energy, had these women of understanding the stirring in the industrial, the political and the social scene around them? Beyond partial simple schooling — often none at all — the educational world was almost closed to them. Few informal occasions for gathering information and discussion were available, as women for the most part did not join clubs or go to pubs, nor were they expected to take part in chapel organisation, though chapel going with its nonconformist thinking and self government might have helped. All these were a man's world. Even conversations with the family, or with neighbours over the yard wall were restricted because women simply were not expected to join in economic and social affairs.

Still another factor weighed down on their enterprise — women's own acceptance of their traditional role of subjection. So many of them believed — and indeed still believe — in their own inferiority, and saw no point in trying to change. Unfortunately, many of their menfolk staunchly encouraged them in this view and men must take their full share of responsibility for keeping women unthinking and diffident.

The women who went out to work form a group distinct from the wholly housebound women. It has been estimated that the number of working women over 15 years old was approximately 4 million, which was well over one third of the total female population. Of these nearly 2 million needed to be self-supporting. The rest were supplementing a family income. Job opportunity was despairingly restricted. Those who became domestic servants experienced a whole range of living conditions from utter degradation to being a cherished friend of the family; and for those in the sweated industries, the House of Lords 1890 Select Committee on Sweating pronounced that its evils could 'scarcely be exaggerated'. Both domestic and sweated labour were too scattered to be able to organise themselves, nor did they dare protest for fear of victimisation.

The position of women factory workers was somewhat different. They too often worked in disgraceful conditions; long hours, stifling workshops and child labour were commonplace. Notwithstanding, particularly in the textile trades, they were beginning to be organised and were gradually gaining valuable experience of industrial problems. It must be remembered, however, that a large proportion of them were very young, and consequently their work loyalties were too temporary and their outlook too immature for responsibilities. Nevertheless the factory workers were the ones in the best position to undertake leadership in the women's movement, and the following chapters will show how ably they took up the challenge.

Such a brief sketch cannot make a properly balanced picture. The term 'working class' includes people ranging from the utterly poor to the moderately comfortable. In 1880 Charles Booth estimated that in London 30 per cent of the population were living below the poverty line. Nevertheless, a sense of working-class solidarity was emerging. The Labour movement was beginning to rouse an exciting spirit of comradeship. When Keir Hardie spoke on socialism women left their baking and their scrubbing to listen. They would gather at factory gates to hear trade union leaders explain unemployment. News filtered through to them of Labour women's efforts to bring the true facts about sweated workers to public notice. And they began to feel very much involved.

Turning now to the leisured women, what were their lives and opportunities like? They had huge advantages. First and foremost they possessed time — time to think and time to act. And they had money. They employed servants to take the place of our labour-saving gadgets.

They were beginning to have considerable opportunities in formal education. It became acceptable for leisured women to attend meetings of learned societies with their menfolk. Books and pamphlets on all kinds of advancing subjects — scientific discoveries, social research, Darwinism and others — introduced exciting discussions on such fundamental issues as individual determinism, environmental influences and the question of social structure and behaviour. Of special importance was the extraordinary output of novels featuring social conditions, many of them written by women. These drew women readers' attention to the realities of living conditions.

Women's religious and humanitarian interests were also developed. The nineteenth century religious sentiment stirred people's consciences and responsibilities, and here we can see the influence of the Christian Socialists. Many leisured women pursued charitable works but most would only sympathise with the conditions of poverty not the aspirations of the poor. However for others social work was the means of bringing them into direct contact with working-class people and conditions. They became deeply anxious about what they found. Was charity alone enough? Overstepping the mere charity motive, some of them joined with the Labour movement in upholding the view that only a radical change in society could bring about massive and lasting betterment.

On the very different question of women's rights and equality with men, opinions split. Here was no altruistic concern for others but a hard-headed demand for justice, and the controversy continues to this day. Many women, particularly of the leisured classes, worked fervently for 'the cause' especially with regard to the suffrage, whereas on the whole Labour women concentrated their attention more on needs than on rights. Theirs was a practical rather than a theoretical approach.

Perhaps this sketch of upper-middle class attitudes has overstressed their leanings towards Labour. Were not conservative minded women, however progressive, alarmed by the prospect of socialism? In *The Edwardians* by V. Sackville West, a young lady voices this anxiety: 'Aunt Clemmie explained it [Socialism] to me. Everything we believe in would go by the board. All decencies. All ʼrinciples.' The nineteenth century had already proved Aunt Clemmie inaccurate. The twentieth century was to prove her downright wrong. We shall be reading how women of all classes were learning to respect and to like each other, but whether their ideas would continue to harmonise depended a good deal on what the Labour movement chose to stand for. The choice was crucial. The movement chose moderation.

Another dimension of the Labour women's programme helped to attract wide support. From the earliest days it believed in international cooperation, and was concerned with the welfare of colonial peoples. It was indeed an idealistic movement. Some cynics deny that Labour women fought for more than their own material benefits. Who would blame them for this, living as they did? But their efforts far outstripped the goal of personal gain. They believed sincerely in the brotherhood of man.

The names in this book are the names of women from all walks of life. Surely this is a cornerstone of the strength of the Labour women's movement. Friendships such as Julia Varley and Mary Macarthur, Mary Middleton and Margaret MacDonald, brought immeasurable warmth and inspiration, as well as wisdom, to the whole cause. Throughout the book we shall see how in all spheres the educational evangelism of dedicated imaginative women was steadily transforming the understanding of the rank and file. As Lucy Middleton writes, 'The happy association of working-class women with leisured women is a motif that runs throughout the story of Labour women right up to the present day.' Without this mutual, often affectionate, understanding the latter might well have gone on keeping themselves to themselves and the former taken a much longer time to gather confidence and knowledge for their tasks.

Special fields calling for women's attention were glaringly obvious.

In the first place, family welfare matters had always been traditionally the woman's concern. What the women did was to apply this traditional role more widely. Besides caring for their own families they began to care for those throughout the country. Sometimes groups of women worked alone; sometimes in cooperation. For example, we shall read how the Women's Labour League worked for infant medical care, which was also part of the Women's Cooperative Guild programme; or how the pit head baths agitation starting with the miners' wives (not without resistance from miners) was taken up by Labour women's groups. The book is full of accounts of how individual groups supported each other's work, almost invariably leading to more and more united action.

The treatment of women in industry was another obvious field where women themselves could take action. Reading the trade union chapters one realises how complicated this problem was. Sweated labour involved social welfare. Women's trade union recognition introduced all kinds of economic factors, and their demand for equality of treatment brought in the controversial question of women's rights. Whereas in social welfare women stepped in almost by default of the men, in industrial matters they had to fight for their position. They had to convince their male colleagues as well as the government.

It is difficult to get the attitude of men into proper perspective. Certainly many did not approve of women's independent tendencies, holding firmly to the dictum that the woman's place was in *his* home. They were evasive, if they were not being resistant about the vote. But we must remember that by no means all the feminist agitation took place within women's organisations. Much happened through joint efforts. That was true of the Labour Party as well as among individuals like Sir Charles Dilke, Keir Hardie and Pethick Lawrence, who staunchly supported the women. The battle had to be fought on two fronts, against unwilling men and apathetic women.

The majority of Labour women too, realising that social and industrial unrest must move into political unrest in order to get satisfaction, recognised that for their rightful share of control they must win the vote and a place in Parliament. But they tended to stress adult, rather than female, suffrage, and thought of equality not so much in terms of the emergence of women as of the women taking their full part with men in the emergence of a better society. Therefore we find many different Labour women's groups campaigning for the policy which resulted in the 1906 Leicester Women's Labour League (WLL) Conference Resolution. Nor were they content merely to win the vote. They foresaw that in order to be fully effective they had to share in the country's administration.

Less remote than Parliament was local government. Whilst Westminster might decide national policy, it was local government which carried it out and which decided local matters. The issues involved corresponded closely to women's traditional interests — creches, school boards, maternity benefits, sanitary inspection — and both working-class and leisured women were able to participate in local government more easily. It was the constant exertion of informed female public opinion through meetings, deputations and strikes, which influenced policy. Pressure more than facts moves governments.

The themes running constantly throughout this book show, above all, the eagerness of the women to learn, the strength of their mutual encouragement and the importance of good organisation. This last point was, and is, vital. It was clearly extremely difficult to keep alive unwavering interest and to build up a strong organisation. Emma Paterson and Mrs Ellis led to Mary Macarthur, Anne Godwin and Ethel Chipchase. Gradually, albeit not without failures, e forts were united, without loss of individuality. As time went on, women became more and more accepted as an integral part of public life, winning their recognition not only because they were women demanding equality with men, or on grounds of the equality of the sexes, but on the far more valid ground of equality of ability. Perhaps now our focus must concentrate more on psychological equality than on the political and social standing we have virtually succeeded in achieving, for full equality appears almost within our grasp, with more women — though still not enough — sharing responsibility with men, in all fields and at all levels from the smallest community upwards.

By dint of immense effort and comradeship the almost impossible has been achieved in a remarkably short space of time. The women knew their goals would be hard to reach but would be worthwhile. As Margaret MacDonald said: 'We expect to find more Paradise and more difficulties as we go on.'

PART I   THE EARLY YEARS

1 WOMEN IN LABOUR POLITICS

Lucy Middleton

There were women supporters of the Labour movement twenty or more years before the modern Labour Party was born at the turn of the century. Helen Taylor, a stepdaughter of John Stuart Mill took the chair at a meeting in support of the *Radical* newspaper in 1881, which in its first issue deplored the small number of representatives of working people in the House of Commons. She worked with H.M. Hyndman in the Democratic Federation even before it became the Social Democratic Federation (SDF) and she gave a printing press for the production of posters when *Justice* was published and helped to sell that paper in the streets. Eleanor Marx, daughter of Karl Marx and wife of Henry Aveling, worked both in the SDF and later in the Socialist League. She was a very effective speaker, much in demand at socialist gatherings. Margaret Harkness, who wrote socialist novels under the nom de plume, 'John Law', gave £100 to Keir Hardie's by-election fight in Mid Lanark in March 1888. Most people know something of Annie Besant's work for the striking London match-girls in 1888. She was a feminine tour de force both as an orator and as a writer and organiser.

When the ILP was formed in 1890, it was able to draw on a number of important women activists. Among them were Katharine St John Conway (later Mrs Bruce Glasier), Carolyn Martin (who founded the Socialist Sunday Schools) and Enid Stacey, a beautiful and intelligent Cambridge graduate. She lost her post as a high school mistress in Bristol because middle-class parents were outraged that a teacher of their daughters had her name taken by the police while speaking at a prohibited meeting in one of the city's parks. From then on, until her death in 1903, her time and her talents were devoted to the advocacy of socialism.

Henry Pelling, writing of that period of ILP history, expressed the view that 'the "New Woman" was almost as important an element in the leadership as the "New Unionism" '.[1]

These and many other less prominent women took part in the struggle for working-class representation before the TUC decided at its Plymouth Congress in 1899 to take steps to set up an organisation for getting Labour representatives into Parliament who would be independent of the existing political parties. The Labour Representation

Committee (in 1906 renamed the Labour Party) which resulted from
that decision was born at a conference of trade unions and socialist
societies at the Memorial Hall, Farringdon Street, in London on
27 February 1900. There were no women delegates at that Conference.
The shop assistants, on whose behalf Margaret Bondfield had spoken
eloquently at the Plymouth Congress in support of the resolution of the
railway servants that such a conference should be called, were not
represented. But at the first Annual Conference of the LRC held in
Manchester on 1 February 1901, there was one woman delegate. She
was Annie Lee, and she was one of a delegation of two from the
Workers' Union. It would be interesting to know more about this first
woman delegate to a Labour Party Conference, but unhappily only her
name and address are recorded.[2]

From the 1903 conference onwards, the ILP seems to have followed
a policy of including some women in their delegation. That year Miss
Isabella O. Ford was one of their representatives.[3] Miss Ford is an
interesting character. She came from a middle-class Quaker background
and was a close friend of Edward Carpenter (author of *Towards
Democracy* and *England Arise*), and of the American poet, Walt
Whitman. When Whitman's complete works were published in one large
volume, he sent two copies to Britain, one for Carpenter and the
other for Miss Ford and her sister.[4]

Isabella Ford was the first woman to speak at a Labour Party
Conference. She seconded a resolution of the Burnley weavers at the
1905 conference asking for the extension of the franchise to women
'on the same basis as that allowed for them for parochial purposes',
and in her speech expressed the view that there ought to be a woman
on the Executive Committee of the party.[5] In 1904, when she again
attended the Annual Conference, she had become a parish councillor,
probably the first Labour woman parish councillor in Britain. When in
1918, a limited parliamentary franchise was, at last, extended to
women, Miss Ford was invited to fight a seat for Labour; but she
declined.[6]

Isabella Ford's fellow woman delegate to the 1904 Conference was
Miss Julia Varley, who was at that time secretary of the Bradford
branch of the Weavers' and Textile Workers' Union and who later
became an organiser for the Transport and General Workers' Union.
The happy association of working-class women, often with bitter and
wretched experience of the fight against poverty, with leisured women
of ample means with eyes to see the wretchedness and injustice that
existed around them, is a motif that runs through the story of Labour

women right up to the present day. Isabella Ford and Julia Varley were one of the earliest of many examples of that kind of comradeship.

At the next LRC Conference (1905), Miss Ford was joined in the ILP delegation by three other women. One of them was Ethel Annakin (later to become Mrs Philip Snowden), who was undoubtedly in her day one of the foremost women orators. The other was Emmeline Pankhurst, later of suffragette fame.

During these years at the beginning of the century there was a growing desire among women for a real part in politics, and, in Labour circles, for an increasing opportunity to know more about Labour's struggle and for a larger share in the work for Labour emancipation. This was a period of grave concern especially for trade unionists and their families. During the previous decade the 'new Unionism' or the development of trade unions among unskilled workers, posed many problems. The antagonism of the employers to the organisation of non-craft workers in the general unions during these years was hard on the men who joined the new unions and even harder for their wives struggling in the home often against unemployment and desperate poverty. Then in 1901 came the Taff Vale judgement imposing damages of £23,000 on the Amalgamated Society of Railway Servants, a craft union, because of a strike on the Taff Vale Railway. This House of Lords decision seemed to undermine the whole system of collective bargaining upon which trade unionism depended. Again, not only the men were affected but also their wives and families. So it is really not surprising that the demand for women to have a chance to know more of Labour politics should have come initially from two trade union sources — from the wives of railway workers and from a docker's wife in Hull, where the 'new Unionism' had been most viciously attacked by the employers.

Mrs Mary Fenton Macpherson was a London journalist, who wrote a regular column for women in the *Railway Review,* and was for many years the honorary secretary of the Railway Women's Guild doing much speaking for them. She was well aware both of the problems railwaymen faced and of the need for working men's wives to know more of the problems of trade unionism and of Labour politics. She seized the opportunity, which her work for 'railway women' offered, to persuade them that they had a right and a duty to get to know more about the struggle of their menfolk and all the political problems associated with it. Thus it came about that a resolution was carried at the Railway Women's Guild Conference in 1905 in these terms,

This meeting is strongly in favour of the true principles of Labour
representation on our local governing bodies and in the House of
Commons and pledges itself to do all in its power to return direct
representatives of Labour and that this Conference requests the
National Labour Representation Committee to form a National
Women's Labour Committee.[7]

About the same time Mrs Cawthorne*, the wife of a dock labourer
in Hull, who had seen the same problems and who felt that women had
a right to know what their men were fighting for, wrote to the
secretary of the NLRC (J. Ramsay MacDonald) asking that an
organisation of Labour women should be set up. Ramsay MacDonald
and his assistant, J.S. Middleton, discussed the letter and decided to
seek the advice of their wives, Margaret MacDonald and Mary '
Middleton.[8]

It emerged from these two initiatives that, on 9 March 1906, a
meeting was held at the MacDonald home, 3 Lincoln's Inn Fields,
London, which resulted in the formation of the Women's Labour
League with Margaret MacDonald as its President and Mary Fenton
Macpherson as its Secretary.

It is worth recording here that Mrs Cawthorne who sent that letter to
Ramsay MacDonald had never been to school. She had learned to read
and write by persuading her children to teach her what they had
learned at school when they came home in the evenings.[9] It is hard to
believe, in these days of so many educational opportunities how
difficult it was for girls, especially, to get the very minimum of
education such a relatively short time ago.

The decision taken on 9 March 1906 to form an organisation of
Labour women and to call an inaugural conference resulted in a
conference at Leicester on 26 June 1906. By the time the conference
met, eleven local groups were already working and their delegates
attended, together with a number of interested observers. Margaret
MacDonald in her opening speech described the objects of the new
organisation thus:

We want to show the wives of trade unionists and cooperators,
particularly, what they have not yet fully discovered, that the best
way of looking after their homes is by taking an interest in the life
of the community . . . that to improve their conditions it is

* See Biographical Notes.

necessary to take up their cause with earnestness on the same lines as men have done and if it is to be anything the Labour Women's Movement must be international.[10]

Eventually, after considerable discussion, a resolution was passed 'to form an organisation to work for Independent Labour Representation in connection with the Labour Party and to obtain direct Labour Representation of women in Parliament and on all local bodies'. The resolution was moved by Mrs Hawkins (Leicester) and seconded by Mrs Philip Snowden (Central London). Thus, the Women's Labour League was brought into existence.

It is interesting to have a look at the other subjects discussed at that Leicester Conference and to realise how far-sighted many of their plans must have been in the circumstances of those days. Inevitably they discussed hours and conditions of labour for women workers. In education they demanded the provision of school meals and of medical inspection in schools, and were of the opinion that education should be free, compulsory and secular with a school leaving age of 16. (It has taken more than sixty years to achieve that school leaving age and even now, in 1977, some opponents of the measure are striving to put the clock back.)

They decided that the full rights of citizenship 'for all women and men' should be one of their objects, and throughout the women's suffrage campaign during the next decade, this continued to be the suffrage policy of Labour women despite a few attempts to modify it so as to get a limited franchise for certain classes of women. In the year 1905 the question of women's franchise had been discussed at the Conference of the Labour Representation Committee (LRC) — now named the Labour Party — and a resolution proposing a property qualification for women voters had been defeated. So the general organisation of the Party and the women's organisation were both committed to work for manhood and womanhood enfranchisement.[11] Probably the most surprising decision was to support the principle of treating the native populations of colonial territories with justice and of not forcing them, 'by taking away their land to labour for landowners and capitalists'. There can be little doubt that with a programme such as this those first organised Labour women knew where they were going and were determined to get there.

Undoubtedly that Conference and the organisation it founded owed much to the idealism and leadership of Margaret MacDonald. She was a remarkable woman by any standards and those who had known her

spoke of her long after her death in tones of admiration, deep respect
and affection. She had never known poverty. Her family were well-to-
do, but with a sense of public responsibility in the use of their
resources. When the young Margaret met the young Labour candidate
Ramsay MacDonald and they fell in love, his very different background
created no barrier between them, nor did it deter her from entering
fully into the work of Labour politics. Her greater experience of wealth
and influence as well as her fine mind were tools to help forward the
causes they served together. A story is told of how, when she found
that some working-class women were wary of speaking in her presence
lest they made mistakes and 'disgraced' themselves, she helped them to
overcome their hesitations by making her own mistakes and then
quietly apologising and correcting her errors. In one of the tributes to
her after her death, it was written:

> One of the reasons why Mrs. MacDonald was so wonderful was her
> power of 'making diamonds from dust'. She would take the unknown
> woman and set her to work in a good cause bringing out
> unsuspected talents of organisation or speech. . .Her capacity for
> fitting jobs to people has been one of the greatest assets the Labour
> Party and the women's cause ever had.[12]

Undoubtedly the Women's Labour League owed much in those early
years to her high standards of public service and even those who never
had the privilege of meeting her still speak of her with gratitude and
admiration.

After a very few months Mary Macpherson was obliged to resign
from the secretaryship of the League and the new secretary was Mary
Middleton, wife of J.S. Middleton. Mrs Middleton was the eldest
daughter of an Ayrshire miner and his wife. Before her marriage she had
been in domestic service. It is difficult to describe the splendid
comradeship that developed between her and Margaret MacDonald, or
the complementary gifts and experiences they brought to the work of
the League; but in the five years they worked together, they, with their
colleagues, built an organisation that withstood the devastating impact
of the First World War and laid the foundations on which the finest
political organisation of women in Britain was later built — one more
instance of an understanding that transcends the boundaries of
education, of experience and of social class.

What sort of women were these pioneers of Labour politics bringing
into the organisation and where did they come from? The best answer

is found in a description of the work of the League and of the women
who joined it written by Margaret MacDonald and published in the
Internationalist in January 1909. She wrote:

> The League makes a special effort to enrol the wives and daughters
> of Trade Unionists and Socialists, since it recognises the weakness
> and danger where the wife is not in sympathy with her husband's
> Labour politics. Then we have among us many professional women,
> teachers, nurses, doctors, inspectors, post office clerks, etc. The
> facts of life have driven them to make common cause with the wage
> earners and they see in our movement the only hope for real social
> reform.

From the first there was the closest possible cooperation and
support for the work of the League from the Labour Party but until
1909 no direct representation of the League within the party was
possible, since an amendment of the constitution was necessary to
provide for this. Long before that date, however, the League had
proved its great value politically in by-elections and in constituency
activities, especially in constituencies where there were Labour
candidates. In January 1910, for instance, the report for 1909 states
that Miss Dorothy Lenn* who organised for the League had 'helped
in election campaigns at Taunton, Croydon, Attercliffe, Bermondsey
and Portsmouth and her time had been mapped out for the forthcoming
General Election, while a number of members of the Executive had
helped on several election occasions'.

The amendment admitting the League to membership of the party
was the first matter discussed after formal business at the Portsmouth
Conference of the Labour Party in 1909, and immediately this was
passed Margaret Bondfield took her seat as the first League
representative at a Labour Party Conference. She seems to have had a
very good time, with three resolutions in her charge, on the Break-up of
the Poor Law, the New Reform Bill and Boy and Girl Labour.[13]

In these years the WLL was constantly widening its horizons. In
1907 and 1908 League members were campaigning about sweated
industries. They staged a Sweated Industries Exhibition at the
Bishopsgate Institute in London in connection with the Clarion
Handicraft Exhibition. This included examples of work done in sweated
industries, together with a catalogue of time taken, prices paid and kind

---

* See Biographical Notes.

of work done, and afterwards the Exhibition went on tour to provincial centres for 'only the price of postage'. The next year, in association with other interested organisations, they went on a deputation to Prime Minister Asquith about the scandal of sweated labour, especially women's labour.

They campaigned for women jurors and magistrates and for higher education for all men and women who desired it. Under the leadership especially of Katharine Bruce Glasier they took up the subject of industrial dirt, particularly mining dirt, and were among the earliest and foremost advocates in Britain of pit head baths.

From its inauguration the WLL did not overlook the importance of the printed word. At that very first Leicester conference Mary Macpherson announced that five leaflets for propaganda purposes had already been printed dealing with 'Feeding of School Children', 'Why Women Want a Labour League', 'Labour Laws for Women', 'Women and the Unemployed' and 'Health and Education'. As occasion demanded leaflets were reprinted or new ones published. In 1910, there was a demand for a regular *League Leaflet* conveying news and views to members all over the country. This was supplied monthly at 6d for 24 copies, post free, and proved an excellent means of knitting the branches into a closer unity. Its publication continued until 1913, when it made way for a larger and more comprehensive monthly periodical, *Labour Woman*, which continued until 1971. Another fascinating and most useful early publication was the League cookery book entitled *My Favourite Recipe, by Women of the Labour Party*, which sold in many thousands at 6d each.

From its inception the League was active in the international field, making and building up contacts with like-minded women all over the world. As early as 1907, Margaret MacDonald and Mary Macpherson represented the League at a Socialist and Trade Women's Conference in Stuttgart and from that gathering came the International Women's Bureau. A later chapter tells the story of Labour women's work in the international field. Here it is only necessary to record that the basis of international friendship and solidarity laid that summer in Stuttgart has remained unbroken through two world wars, right up to the present day.

The year 1911 was a tragic one for the League. On 24 April, Mary Middleton, only 40 years old, died of cancer after a long illness. Her friends in the League, under Margaret MacDonald's leadership, decided to found a baby clinic in Kensington in her memory, but on 8 September Margaret MacDonald too died, of blood poisoning. She was just 41 years old, and the memorial which she and the League planned for Mary Middleton became a memorial to them both.

In the League's Annual Report for 1911 there is this tribute to the two women

> All Mary Middleton's public work was done for the League, and in Margaret MacDonald's full and varied life the League was, since its formation, her chief thought in working for the progress of the Labour Movement. The place of these two women can never be filled by others. we can only catch what we may of their inspiration. . .in giving our whole strength to the making of a world where men and women shall have the chance of happiness of freedom and the comradeship of equals.[14]

The story of the memorial clinic founded as a tribute to these two women pioneers — the first such clinic to be established in Britain — is told in the next chapter of this book, but it is impossible to leave this period in Labour women's history without mentioning the names of some of the many who worked so hard, some for thirty years or more, for the success of the clinic and later the Baby Hospital. One remembers especially Margaret Bondfield, Mrs Despard, Mrs Elkin*, Katharine Bruce Glasier, Nancy Gossling*, Mary Macarthur, Margaret McMillan, Mary Macpherson, Minnie Nodin* (and her husband Philip) and Marion Phillips. But, above all, Dr Ethel Bentham who 'for over twenty years took the Clinic and later the Baby Hospital under her guidance bringing health and healing to the young children of North Kensington'.[15]

Perhaps the greatest contribution to literature in the history of Labour women is found in Ramsay MacDonald's memoirs of his wife *Margaret Ethel MacDonald*. This went into six editions and was reprinted nine times. The paperback edition at 2s 6d per copy was especially printed for Labour women and must have sold in many thousands of copies throughout the country. *John o' London's* reviewer wrote: 'It is a beautiful touching memorial. It has a sweetness and a nobility which stir the depths of human love and sympathy.' And another reviewer said of it: 'The finest tribute ever paid to his wife, by a British public man.'

After a brief period during which Margaret Bondfield tried to add the secretaryship of the League to all her other work and fell ill in

consequence, Marion Phillips took it over in 1913 and continued to give
unstinting service until 1915. When she resigned Miss Mary Longman
was appointed, but the many references to Marion Phillips in the reports
of the League and in *Labour Woman* show clearly how she kept in
touch and the leadership she so willingly gave throughout the troubled
period just before and during the First World War.

This was a time of considerable development in the field of local
government and in the 1913 report a list is published of WLL women
elected to local authorities. It included four London municipal
councillors, Dr Bentham, Dr Phillips, Miss Turnbull and Miss   alters,
and nineteen members of boards of guardians, while many more
women served on education bodies and care committees. These figures
had risen during 1913 to five borough councillors, one rural district
councillor and thirty-one members of boards of guardians. This pattern
of local representation remained pretty constant throughout the years
of war except that it was added to by Labour women members of
munition tribunals, insurance committees, local pensions committees
and school managers.

There was a great increase in the number of Labour women
representatives in local government in the years immediately following
the 1914-18 war, especially in London and the larger provincial cities.
It would be impossible to name all those women who in the decade
1914-24 gave valiant and effective service in local government, for the
work done in this field increased immeasurably. But in London the
pattern was set, and some of the women serving there were known all
over the country, women like Sister Kerrison, Alderman Mrs Lowe*,
who became the first Labour woman chairman of the LCC, Mrs Ada
Salter*, who served both in Bermondsey and on the LCC, Miss Agnes
Dawson* and Mrs Barbara Drake*, and, in Cambridge, Mrs Clara
Rackham*, all of whom, with others too many to name, rendered great
service to local government. Since the First World War there has been
considerable improvement in both the percentage of Labour women
standing in local government elections and in the numbers of successful
candidates, though there is, even today, a long way to go to achieve
parity with men.

The years of the First World War were not easy ones for the Labour
Movement, which was split on the issue of the war itself. There were in
its ranks pacifists, anti-militarists, moderate supporters of the war effort
and some who wanted the war pursued to the bitter end. The task of

guiding such an organisation through those times of doubt and difficulty was not an easy one — easier perhaps in the WLL than in the Party generally. The struggle was to preserve unity without sacrifice of principle and in that task the War Emergency Workers' National Committee (WEWNC) was both a great unifier and a great force for social justice.[16] In this work the League cooperated to the full and, indeed, many of the problems with which the committee dealt were essentially women's problems — like housing and rents, separation allowances, rationing, profiteering and the price of food, women in trade unions and the conditions in munition factories where increasing numbers of women were employed. But while campaigning with the WEWNC on these essentially wartime problems the general work of the League was not forgotten and conference resolutions show that concern for the elderly, for education and the needs of children, health and sanitation was as strong as ever.

Indeed so impressed was the Party Executive by the work the League was doing that in 1916 a request was sent out to all local parties asking them to help the League's work by:

1. the provision of rooms for meetings,
2. making the League's work the nucleus of women's work in the areas, and
3. pointing out the importance of supporting the League and of using its publications.[17]

Undoubtedly the coming of some degree of women's Parliamentary franchise had already had its impact, as well as the recognition of the excellence of the work women in the League were doing.

The year 1916 saw the beginning of a further development in the organisation of working women. Throughout its history there had always been the most cordial relationships between the League and other organisations which catered for working women, as trade unions, groups formed for the womenfolk of trade unionists and cooperators. But the impact of the war upon the employment of women made possible, indeed necessary, the drawing together of Labour and industrial women's organisations into a central consultative committee. So, in February 1916, the Standing Joint Committee of Industrial Women's Organisations (now known as the National Joint Committee of Working Women's Organisations) was brought into existence and has continued to watch over the interests of working women ever since. The first task the SJC undertook was the preparation of a register of names of working women who could be suggested for service on various administrative and other committees. The second task it set itself was to draw up a report on what the position of women in industry would be when the war ended.

After considerable protest to the authorities that questions concerning the employment of women were being discussed officially with no working women present, and often no women at all, the Standing Committee at an early date won recognition as the body best able to speak for women in industry and as an integral part of the Labour Movement.

A major struggle with the authorities was successfully concluded in 1919. The Rt. Hon. George Barnes, who had served in the later years in the wartime Cabinet, was appointed by Prime Minister Lloyd George as British Representative on the International Labour Legislation Commission. The SJC impressed upon Mr Barnes the importance of the representation of women at the International Labour Conference to be held in Washington that year and it was agreed that women 'advisers' should be appointed when items on the agenda dealt specifically with women's interests.

An account of the successful struggle which took place to establish, internationally, the right of some workers to be represented by their own sex is told on pp.84-93. It is interesting to note that the conference where that struggle took place was also responsible for bringing into being the International Labour Organisation (ILO), the only section of the 1918 peace settlement that has lasted until the present day and is still doing useful work.

The SJC was from its earliest years deeply interested in equal pay and in 1919 took part in a deputation with the National Union of Teachers to the Minister of Education urging equal pay for men and women teachers. This subject remained a foremost concern of the SJC and of Labour women generally. In 1928 the subject of equal pay again thrust itself into the foreground of discussion by the appointment of the Royal Commission on the Civil Service and the SJC prepared a report on equal pay in the Civil Service. This was presented to the Commission and the SJC campaigned with the Civil Service Equal Pay Committee at that time. But it was about twenty-three years later (1931) that, at long last, the ILO adopted Convention 100 which urged member countries both to ratify the Convention and to make statutory provision for equal remuneration for men and women workers for work of equal value.

Happily there were two British women among the workers' delegates to that ILO Conference, Florence Hancock and Anne Godwin, both of whom had struggled for the recognition of equal pay through long years of trade union service and who played a notable part in securing the adoption of the Convention. But while in 1931 the International Labour Conference listened to the arguments of these two experienced British women among others and adopted the Equal Pay Convention, it has taken a much longer time, indeed, until 1970, to persuade the people of Britain of the justice of the case for equal pay for work of equal value.

These are only a few of the many topics about which the Standing Joint Committee had taken action in the earliest years of its existence but they serve to show the serious social and industrial tasks in which it became immediately engaged.

To return to the WLL (whose chief officer has always acted as Secretary of the SJC) and take up its story again in 1916 with attention largely concentrated on the domestic problems war conditions had produced: 1917 saw the birth of a new Franchise Bill following the report of a Speaker's Conference. This recommended that men over 21 years of age should be enfranchised on a six months' residence qualification and that the Parliamentary franchise should be extended to women over 30 years of age on the old occupancy basis that used to apply to men. The Bill passed the Commons in December 1917, and came into force in June 1918. So manhood suffrage had been granted but younger women and those older single women who had no occupancy qualifications had to wait until 1928 before they could vote on equal terms with men.

The fact of this partial enfranchisement of women led however to a new status for Labour women. The WLL was merged with the party; special representation of women on the party executive was provided for; a Women's Advisory Committee was appointed and the *Labour Woman* was taken over and became a party publication. Provision was also made for individual membership of the party and a new party constitution was introduced. The woman who had been the leader of Labour women ever since 1912 except for quite a short interval, Dr Marion Phillips, was appointed Chief Woman Officer in control of Labour women's work throughout the country.

This is an appropriate moment to look at the great services Marion Phillips gave to Labour women so unstintingly until her death in 1932. She had been born in Melbourne, Australia, where she graduated and was awarded several scholarships. A Rhodes scholarship brought her to London to the London School of Economics where she gained her D.Sc.(Economics). Later she worked with the Webbs and as a special

investigator appointed by the Poor Law Commission to enquire into
the working of the Poor Law. Later still she joined Mary Macarthur in
the Women's Trade Union League.

Marion Phillips became Secretary of the WLL in 1913 and she was
appointed Chief Woman Officer at the party conference in Nottingham
in 1918. Under the new constitution adopted at that conference, women
members of the party were given the right to create Women's Sections
for special work among women electors. In the next fourteen years
Marion Phillips and her small band of women organisers had established
2,000 sections in Britain. In 1932, at the time of her death, Arthur
Henderson wrote of Marion: 'She constructed the most formidable
organisation of politically conscious women in Britain — probably in
the world.'

Nothing was too small, nothing too large for her genius. Many older
women will remember her in the early days coming to area conferences
carrying a secretary's kit and demonstrating how best to use a card
index, how to draft minutes or to keep section accounts. But they will
also remember her great work for the miners in the Lockout of 1926
when she raised more than £300,000 for miners' wives and children
and, too, her fine oratory founded always on facts that were flawless.
By any standard Marion Phillips was undoubtedly one of the great
women of the Labour Party and of the women of her generation.

For Labour women the 1918 general election was a disappointment.
Four women candidates stood but none was returned, not even the
redoubtable Mary Macarthur on whom so many hopes were pinned.
The 1922 election was even more disappointing. Ten Labour women
were candidates and again none was returned.

Meanwhile, in Europe the aftermath of the war was causing widespread misery and destitution, especially among the children of the
defeated countries. Many people were appalled at the constant reports
of hunger, starvation and death, but felt powerless to help. There was,
however, one British woman who was determined to rouse the
conscience of the nation to save the children from the suffering which
war had brought in its wake.

She was Eglantyne Jebb, a Labour supporter and a sister-in-law
of Charles Roden Buxton (later, Labour MP for Accrington). She
determined to start a fund to save the lives of starving children in
Europe. Even her well-wishers, who were prepared to help as far as they
could, regarded the campaign on which she was embarking as a lost
cause before it had even started. Internationalists like F.W. Pethick
Lawrence told her she would be fortunate to get £100. But nothing

daunted Eglantyne Jebb and one of her greatest early assets was an invitation from the Executive Committee of the Labour Party to plead her cause from the platform of the Labour Party Conference. This was in 1920 and is the only time in the entire history of the Party when someone not a delegate to the Conference, nor a fraternal delegate, nor a Labour Minister, has had such an invitation — and Eglantyne Jebb used it to good effect. A few days later Robert Smillie, at that time Chairman of the Miners' Federation, handed her a cheque for £10,000 for her fund and soon the miners increased this contribution to £35,000 — apart from all the other contributions from individuals and organisations that her speech and her other activities evoked.

The 'Save the Children Fund', the organisation which Eglantyne Jebb founded, and for which she pleaded so effectively that day, saved thousands of needy children all over Europe at that time, and many millions since. Over the years it has raised well over £20,000,000 for work among suffering children. The unique opportunity granted to Eglantyne Jebb to plead the children's cause at the Scarborough Conference in 1920 was both a tribute to a fine woman and a great asset to the work in which she was so gallantly engaged.

Meanwhile another election opportunity was approaching. In 1923 fourteen Labour women fought the election of that year, and three were returned. Maybe others, like myself, can remember their excitement of 6 December 1923, when the news came through that Susan Lawrence had won East Ham North, and later, when during the weekend Margaret Bondfield's victory in Northampton and Dorothy Jewson's in Norwich were announced. At last, the women of the Labour Party were on the way: but few can have realised in that hour of early success how long and arduous the road to economic and political equality and social justice would continue to be.

Notes

1. Henry Pelling, *The Origins of the Labour Party 1880-1900*, Macmillan, 1954, p.164.
2. *Labour Party Report 1901*, p.24, Labour Party Library.
3. *Labour Party Report 1903*, p.8, Labour Party Library.
4. J.S. Middleton, *Memoirs* (not yet published).
5. *Labour Party Report 1904*, p.47, Labour Party Library.
6. Melville Currell, *Political Woman*, Croom Helm, 1975, p.10.
7. *Conference Report 1906, Women's Labour League*, p.2, Labour Party Library.
8. J.S. Middleton, *Memoirs*.
9. Mrs N. Kneeshaw, letter to *Labour Woman*, July 1956, p.102.
10. *Conference Report 1906, Women's Labour League*, p.2, Labour Party Library.

11. *Labour Party Report 1905*, p.55, Labour Party Library.
12. E.J.N., *League Leaflet*, September 1911, pp.1 and 2, Labour Party Library.
13. *Conference Report 1909, Women's Labour League*, p.31, Labour Party Library.
14. *Conference Report 1912, Women's Labour League*, p.2, Labour Party Library.
15. *Labour Party Report 1931*, p.64, Labour Party Library.
16. *Conference Report 1916, Women's Labour League*, p.11, Labour Party Library.
17. *Labour Party Report 1916*, p.20, Labour Party Library.
18. *Labour Party Report 1920*, p.141, Labour Party Library.

2 LABOUR WOMEN AND THE SOCIAL SERVICES

Sheila Ferguson

By the turn of the twentieth century women had still not made much headway in their fight for Parliamentary suffrage but they had already proved that they could make a valuable contribution as elected members of public bodies. Women had been members of school boards since 1870. In 1888 women householders were among the electors of the newly created county council. Though to begin with they could not stand as candidates, they could be coopted on to council committees. In 1894 the Local Government Act abolished the property qualification for members of boards of guardians and many working men and women were immediately elected.

The impact of women on the boards was swift and effective. They raised the standard of efficiency, humanity and courtesy. And since they were free from personal financial interests, such as for example those of some members who manipulated contracts for workhouse supplies for themselves, they helped to achieve a new level of financial probity. On the governing boards concerned with the running of workhouses, women had the direct opportunity to remedy some of the ills that were overlooked by all male administrations. Some women, who were willing and able to do this voluntary work formed a considerable proportion of the membership of the boards of guardians. The plight of orphans, young babies, widows, unmarried mothers and destitute old couples, which had received scant sympathy from previous 'Dickensian' guardians, now had at least some leaven of womanly understanding and working-class solidarity. Even women like the Countess of Galloway, who deplored the aspirations of the women's rights movement for political careers for women, admitted that as members of school boards and as guardians of the poor, 'their special characteristics of sympathy and love of their fellows make their presence and work most useful'.

There was indeed a pressing need for social reform and for a stirring of the national conscience especially in the field of child health and maternity and infant welfare. During the nineteenth century, a variety of improvements and advances in medicine had led to a fall in the general death rate but in 1899 an unenviable record was achieved when out of 1,000 children born that year, 163 failed to reach their first

birthday. 'The tens of thousands of infants who died of diarrhoea, in
that year', wrote one commentator forty-five years later, 'can claim the
posthumous honour of having started a movement to ensure that such a
holocaust shall never occur again.'[1] The alarming infant mortality
statistics coincided with a great upsurge of interest in public well-being.
The uneasiness aroused by the work of such social investigators as
Charles Booth and Seebohm Rowntree deepened when recruiting for
the Boer War revealed evidence of widespread malnutrition and disease.
A Royal Commission and two government committees produced further
disquieting information which led to a burst of legislation widening the
functions of local authorities. The emphasis at first was on the age
group that was most easily reached — children of school age; among
other things, authorities were empowered to provide free school meals
for under-nourished school children and were obliged to organise the
regular medical inspection of all the children in their schools.

Many of the women who served on the public boards responsible
for various social services were also active campaigners for the vote and
many were involved in the trade union and Labour movements. Mrs
Emmeline Pankhurst, for instance, first entered into the public service
as a Labour nominee to the Manchester Poor Law guardians; later she
was a member of the Manchester school board. Two other examples
were the young Margaret McMillan who became a member of the
Bradford school board in 1894 and Sister Edith Kerrison, a prominent
figure in the Labour women's cause, who was elected to the West Ham
board of guardians in 1897.

Edith Kerrison was born in Welshpool in 1850 into a wealthy
family; her father, a minister of the church, saw no need for her to be
educated because she was a girl. Determined to become a nurse, she was
not allowed to go to Florence Nightingale's nurses training school at
St Thomas's Hospital, in London, but was eventually allowed to go as a
paying pupil to the Great Ormond Street Hospital for Sick Children.
She became a Sister and then nursed at the much less well equipped
Seamen's Hospital at Greenwich. Although Edith Kerrison loved
nursing, she hated the 'red tape' of hospital work and, by now an
ardent socialist, she wanted to take part in political life.

Sister Kerrison was inspired by hearing Keir Hardie speak in West
Ham and got to know him well. She ran a cooperative home for young
working men, providing cheap and comfortable accommodation, decent
food and educational and cultural activities. In 1894 she joined the ILP
and in 1897 she was elected to the board of guardians in South West
Ham, where she worked especially to improve the lot of the sick, and of

children, for the next twenty years. She became the first woman
member on the West Ham council where she gave much attention to the
physical care of children, school clinics, the feeding of needy children
and the provision of maternity and child welfare centres.

Both Sister Kerrison and Margaret McMillan joined the Independent
Labour Party which began in 1893 but they were rather isolated as
individual members of their boards and were soon aware of the need for
a common policy and organisation for women with socialist sympathies.

The Women's Labour League

When the Labour Representation Committee became the Labour Party
in 1906, the need for a complementary organisation for Labour women
was recognised and in the same year the Women's Labour League was
established. 'Members of the Society', stated its constitution, 'will work
with the Labour Party locally and nationally. . .They will educate
themselves on political and social questions. . .They will take an active
interest in the work of the Poor Law Guardians, Educational bodies,
Distress Committees. . .They will work to secure the full rights of
citizenship for all women and men. . .They will waken the interests
of working women in their own neighbourhood, and strive, where
possible, to improve their social and industrial conditions.'[2]

At the first Annual Conference of the Women's Labour League held
in Leicester in June 1906, the Chairman, (Margaret MacDonald)
declared that women in the Labour movement had always had equality
with men. They would not restrict their activities to limited domestic
matters but they had a special contribution to make on the many
questions on which women's knowledge was more extensive, such as
the feeding of children, women's work, old age pensions and many
things which closely affected home life. 'In the old crusades', she
declared 'men did the fighting, and women watched and waited
but now they wished to fight side by side. . .to make more progress
in the new crusade against the evils of society.'[3]

Already by the second Annual Conference of the Women's Labour
League in 1907, it was clear that during the eleven months since the
League had been founded a considerable amount of work had been
done to increase the membership and to bring pressure to bear on
society to raise the standard of the welfare services. Much of the social
legislation so far was permissive; it therefore became a major function
for Labour women to press their own local authorities to adopt the
reforms and to do the maximum allowed rather than the least possible.
Two resolutions from the second Annual Conference illustrate this

point: the first urged members to see that their local authorities passed
strict by-laws to limit the labour of school children out of school hours
(under the Employment of Children's Act), and that this should be
viewed as a step towards the total abolition of child labour; secondly,
the Conference urged its members to bring pressure to bear on their
local authorities to adopt and enforce the Feeding of School Children
Act and agreed to request the Labour Party to promote a Bill making
the present Act compulsory instead of permissive. It was pointed out
by the Chairman (Margaret MacDonald), however, that progress must
be made not only through the activities of women able to take an active
part in public affairs; 'the great majority of women whose first duty an
and responsibility is to their home and children are learning that they
cannot fulfil their charge without taking part in the civic life which
surrounds and vitally affects their home life.'[4]

During the years between the formation of the WLL and the outbreak
of the Second World War, Labour women played an increasing role in
public affairs, adding now to work on the boards of guardians, membership on insurance committees, local councils and council committees,
labour exchange committees, school managers and care committees,
distress committees and mental deficiency committees.

Feeding Needy School Children

The fight for the implementation of the Feeding of School Children
Act is a recurring theme throughout branch reports of the Women's
Labour League. In Leicester, for instance, in 1908, Miss Bell of the
National Executive reported on two large demonstrations which were
organised and a petition signed by over 1,000 women which was sent
to the council. But the council's reply was to agree that meals for
needy children should be organised but to entrust the work to charitable
bodies instead of paying for the service out of the rates. Central
London, Jarrow, Leeds, St Pancras and Westminster branches took
similar action that year and throughout the next few years this pressure
was kept up throughout the country. The Annual Conference passed
resolutions in 1909, 1910, 1911, 1912 and 1913 urging the
government to make the provision of school meals compulsory instead
of permissive, to abolish the halfpenny rate limit on the service and to
permit authorities to feed the children during school holidays. Sister
Kerrison said she was one of the West Ham education committee who
had been surcharged £462.01 for feeding the children during the
holidays; she could afford to pay the fine but did not propose to do
so!

Dr Ethel Bentham argued that meals were not only necessary but should be of decent standard. She knew of a school in London where the children were sent out to a little eating house where they got their tea out of a pail and a lump of stale bread. This was not what was needed. 'Starving children', said Mrs Simm of Benwell, 'do not touch the stony hearts of our councillors' — the children were fed by charities and got half a glass of milk and a stale bun one day and a plate of porridge the next. In the first edition of the League's monthly journal *Labour Woman* of May 1913, some facts and figures on child malnutrition taken from the report of the chief medical officer of the board of education for 1911, were quoted to support the case. In Staffordshire, for instance, 19.2 per cent of children aged 13 medically inspected were found to be below normal and 'bad' in nutrition but no meals were provided for needy children by the authority; in Westmorland the figure was 16.4 per cent and in Gloucestershire 15 per cent. Many towns like Wolverhampton, Southampton, Carlisle, Darlington, Blackburn and Brighton had figures of 16 per cent and over but they at least provided a small amount of free meals. In 1914, a further Provision of Meals Act extended the powers of local authorities.

During the First World War, though most authorities cut down their arrangements for feeding school children, as a result of the full employment of wartime, there were certainly much smaller numbers of necessitous children, reported *Labour Woman.* But now there was a class of children for whom the education authorities had to provide meals, whose parents were not poor and were willing enough to pay; these were the children whose mothers were employed in war work and were unable to cook dinner for their children and were even compelled to lock their children out all day. So the Labour women's campaign became one for school meals for all, not just for the needy, an objective which was not to be fully achieved until the Second World War.

The first Labour woman to address the House of Commons was Susan Lawrence who intervened on the Address in reply to the King's Speech in January 1924. The subject of her maiden speech was objection to the government's cutting of expenditure on the provision of meals for needy children.

Medical Inspection of School Children

One of the first actions of the first Executive Committee of the new Women's Labour League was to send a deputation to the Minister of Education to talk over with him the necessity for adding a clause to the

Bill currently in progress to provide a more thorough system of medical inspection in schools. They were able to report to the second Annual Conference in 1907 that they had been able to put forward some facts not previously appreciated 'which could only be explained by women with a sympathetic insight and knowledge of the daily lives of the children in the schools', and that the following day the Minister made a favourable statement in the House of Commons which they could claim, without flattering themselves, had resulted from the case they had put before him.

But soon, Labour women were pointing out that medical inspection in itself was of little value if it was not followed up by proper treatment. Dr Ethel Bentham, for instance, told the 1909 Annual Conference that 60,000 London children needed treatment for eye conditions while 90 per cent needed attention to be given to their teeth. 'Medical inspection without treatment was a farce', she declared, 'and treatment could not be provided by poor parents.' Dr Bentham was supported by Miss Margaret McMillan, who urged that Labour women school managers or those on care committees should demand proper facilities for the treatment of disease, including sanatoria and open-air schools. At the 1910 Conference it was unanimously resolved that school clinics were the best method of dealing with children's ailments and that they should be free and compulsory. A year later Miss McMillan quoted some impressive figures about the efficiency and economy of school clinics. In Deptford a case that had been unsuccessfully treated at hospital for five years was cured in two months at the clinic; the cost of hospital treatment averaged 20d while at the clinic it was 14d; five small clinics could deal with more cases than seventeen large hospitals.

An article by Dr Ethel Bentham in *Labour Woman* of October 1916 commented on the appalling state of school children's health as revealed in the reports of the chief medical officer to the board of education. Of the six million children in elementary schools he reported that a quarter of a million were 'seriously crippled or disabled' and one million were 'so far defective or diseased as not to be capable of getting "reasonable benefit" from their education. Thus one in six children will probably be unsuccessful in life and more or less a burden to society', declared Dr Bentham.[5]

The 1907 Act which had required local education authorities to provide for the medical inspection of all children on entering school and on other occasions as directed by the board of education, also *enabled* authorities to provide for medical attendance, recovering the cost from parents able to pay and giving varied other powers. But as usual the national pattern of provision was very uneven and Labour women were able to press in their localities for the best and most comprehensive services.

Baby Clinics

The school medical service often felt that it was fighting a losing battle. Four in every ten of the new entrants to the elementary schools needed medical attention at the very outset of their school careers, and most of the defects — the results of poverty, ignorance and neglect — could have been prevented. The school medical officer of the LCC said that the school medical service was in fact 'a receiver of damaged goods' and was forced to spend time and energy patching them up.

The early development of services for children below school age was left to voluntary workers and a few enterprising local authorities. Some municipalities such as Battersea, St Helens, Liverpool and Woolwich opened milk depots for mothers and children. Food and clothing were provided for mothers in poor districts and many of these depots developed into clinics where advice was given on feeding, clothing and hygiene. Babies were kept under regular supervision with weekly weighing and supplied with sterilised milk and some authorities also organised home visiting. Labour women were frequently involved in this voluntary work. In 1910, for instance, the Woolwich Branch of the WLL reported that a milk depot initiated when the Labour Party was in control of the council had been closed down now that the composition of the council had changed even though the medical officer of health had reported favourably on the good work of the depot. They planned to start it up again when they did better at the elections.

In 1911 the Women's Labour League decided to open a Baby Clinic at North Kensington to commemorate the work of Mary Middleton and Margaret MacDonald who had both died that year. 'We shall not be satisfied', declared the first Annual Report of the Clinic, 'until Baby Clinics have sprung up in all other parts of the country, and until they have become part of a fully organised public medical service, owned and controlled by the people themselves.'

The membership of the Clinic's first general committee reads like a roll call of famous Labour women — it included Margaret Bondfield, Katharine Bruce Glasier, Charlotte Despard*, Mary Fenton Macpherson, Margaret McMillan, Mary Macarthur, Ada Salter, Marion Phillips and Dr Ethel Bentham.

Dr Bentham, a pioneering woman doctor, voluntarily gave her time and skill to the medical work of the Clinic and later the Baby

Hospital from the days they opened until her death in 1931. She did her medical training in Dublin and on the Continent and was impressed from an early age by the hardship and bitterness suffered by working-class families as a result of poverty and ill-health. She had first a successful practice in the north of England where she was also active in the Women's Suffrage campaign and the Labour movement and then moved to London where she played a prominent role in the WLL. Dr Bentham was convinced that the pre-natal months and the years of early infancy were the most vital time for future progress so that when the idea of the Memorial Baby Clinic came to be discussed she was especially enthusiastic.

A typical afternoon session was recorded by a reporter from the *Daily Citizen* in 1913:

> That afternoon Dr Bentham saw 72 patients. Between 2.30 p.m. and 6.45 p.m. I watched her deal with 69 of them. To each was given the same true sympathy and womanly kindness that they would be expected to receive in a private consulting room.

> Up to that day Ethel Bentham had been the name of one of our woman leaders, who was to be honoured for her ability — and her good comradeship — I went away with a new understanding and a new kind of admiration for the one, a little of whose work I had been privileged to study that day.

As well as regularly working in the Clinic, Dr Bentham was for many years an active member of the National Executive Committee of the Labour Party. She served for a time on the Kensington borough council and on the Metropolitan Asylums Board. After three unsuccessful attempts to enter Parliament, on the fourth occasion she became the MP for East Islington in 1929. She was now nearly 70 but she entered into duties in the House of Commons with the same practical earnestness that had always characterised her work. She served on the Select Committee on the Abolition of Capital Punishment and introduced a private member's Bill to enable British women who married aliens to retain their own nationality.

The North Kensington Baby Clinic was an example of a sound local medical service and a model for others to imitate. In 1913 the League decided to launch a national campaign for baby clinics. There had been a rumour that schools for mothers were likely to be eligible for grants-in-aid in the next Education Bill, so they thought there might be a chance of also getting baby clinics included. Within four months 245 trade unions and branches of socialist organisations had passed resolutions in favour of the establishment of baby clinics by municipal authorities supported by grants from national funds.

The Women's Labour League sent out letters to medical officers of health and school medical officers describing the work of the Baby Clinic at North Kensington and asking them to say whether there was need for further provision of this nature for pre-school-age children, whether the officers would advocate grants-in-aid of such institutions and whether they favoured the establishment of baby clinics by local authorities as part of a preventive medical service. A large number of medical officers replied to the letters giving full support to the proposal. There was, however, some division of opinion about whether baby clinics should be closely linked with the school clinics, which would take over when the children started school and thus fall under the board of education or whether they be the responsibility of the health authorities.

The second Annual Report of the Memorial Baby Clinic pointed the way to an ideal kind of service. Any child under 5 years of age resident in Kensington was admitted free of charge to receive advice and treatment from a doctor or nurse; dental treatment, minor operations and medicines were also provided. During the year there had been 5,382 attendances at the Clinic and treatment had been given ranging from the removal of tonsils and adenoids, bone setting and the lancing of abcesses to treatment of rickets, diarrhoea, bronchitis and skin diseases. Help was also given to mothers on the feeding of their babies and the need for hygiene. The report concluded that 'this work of life and health saving' cost £452 that year, including drugs, cod liver oil in vast quantities, ointments, dressings and the salaries of the staff, rent, gas and cleaning. 'So small an expenditure' encouraged them to hope that there might soon be '1,000 clinics in a country where today we have but one'.

In 1914 the goal was achieved in that grants could be made by the Treasury for baby clinics, schools for mothers and baby consultations, though the League was disappointed about the division of work between the local government board and the board of education which they feared might seriously hamper progress. Nevertheless, the granting of the money was a tremendous gain and there could be no doubt that the 'model' Baby Clinic at North Kensington had provided an inspiration and guide for the new public service. The WLL had every right to be proud of having been the first organisation to realise the importance of giving a practical demonstration of the work of saving the lives of babies and keeping little children healthy and well.

There had been an important development at the Baby Clinic. The work had been extended to cover expectant and nursing mothers who could now get advice and treatment for themselves. Already there was a marked improvement in mothers' health and in that of their babies though the Clinic was disturbed about the 'terrible need of dental treatment amongst the mothers'. The Clinic received a grant from the local government board for its work for mothers and babies. It was emphasised that it was now up to branches of the League to prevail upon their own local authorities to set up similar maternity and child welfare clinics in their districts.

At the end of the war the Maternity and Child Welfare Act, 1918, gave very wide powers to county councils. Grants amounting to half the expenditure on various services for maternity and child welfare could now be made by the Treasury to local authorities and a number of new services could also be provided, including home helps, the provision of food for expectant and nursing mothers and young children, day nurseries and convalescent homes. The Women's Labour League had played a vital role in achieving the acceptance of these important reforms. The League had pressed for home helps during discussions on the National Health Insurance Act and Margaret Bondfield, with the Central Committee for Women's Employment, carried out a scheme for training women in this work. Invaluable work in medical care and the training of young children had also been done by Margaret and Rachel McMillan and Margaret Llewelyn Davies with the Women's Cooperative Guild.

In 1919, the Baby Clinic extended its scope when a Baby Hospital for in-patients was established nearby which needed at least £2,000 a year to be raised by voluntary effort. This was done by Labour women holding knitting guilds and sewing parties, bazaars, concerts, parties, etc. and by donations from public funds. In 1927, a Star Matinee was organised by Miss (later Dame) Sybil Thorndike, for the funds of the Clinic and the hospital. In 1936, the Clinic was handed over to the Kensington Borough Council to be an integral part of the infant welfare services of the borough and in 1937 Queen Mary became the patron of the Baby Hospital. In 1948, history seemed to repeat itself. Just as in 1936, the Clinic, having achieved its pioneering purpose, was integrated into the Borough Council's Welfare Services, so the Baby Hospital passed into the care of the Ministry of Health when in 1948 the National Health Service was established.

Nursery Schools

Once the fight for government financial aid for maternity and child welfare services had been won it was the duty of Labour women to press their local authorities to make the most of the permissive powers. Although the early emphasis had been on services for poor and deprived families, it was recognised that the maternity and child welfare provision was essential for *all* mothers and young children. But there were some young children who needed more specific and detailed care in nurseries of some kind either for health or social reasons. Two of the great pioneers in the field of nursery education were Margaret and Rachel McMillan, members of the WLL from its inception.

In the nineteenth century large numbers of children under five attended the ordinary schools, whether in the Dames' Schools, the National Schools or the new Board Schools. Very many married women were out at work and their children needed some form of shelter during the day. However, after 1905, the peak in the number of under-fives accepted in the ordinary schools had passed, though voluntary day nurseries were increasing. The National Society of Day Nurseries was founded in 1906 by enthusiasts, including many Labour women, who were interested in some thirty nurseries. The aim was to define standards and encourage further progress. A new type of nursery provision also made its appearance about this time — the nursery school, which was concerned with both health and education. In 1910, Rachel and Margaret McMillan opened their nursery school at Deptford, in south-east London, which was to be an inspiration and pattern for much future development.

Margaret and Rachel McMillan were born into a comfortably off home in Westchester, New York, within fifteen months of each other and remained very close all their lives. Both became convinced socialists in their twenties. For a time Margaret was a companion to a wealthy lady who encouraged her to train as an actress but they parted when Margaret became active in politics. She attended the great demonstrations of the dockers' strike and, with Rachel, sold Christian Socialist tracts at the dock gates. Margaret made her first public speech on May Day 1892 in Hyde Park.

Margaret went to Bradford in 1893 where she joined the new Independent Labour Party, lecturing, writing and organising full-time for no payment while the practical Rachel earned money to keep them both. In 1894, Margaret took one of the few opportunities for public service open to women when she was elected to the Bradford school board. She was appalled by the sight of children in every stage of illness

and neglect — children with adenoids, rickets, curvature of the spine
and diseases due to filth. She fought for baths for school children in
Bradford arguing passionately 'How can you educate a dirty child?'
She also campaigned for the medical inspection of school children, for
the feeding of needy school children, for the abolition of half-time
education for children of over eleven and for better ventilation in
schools (leading her later to advocate open-air schools). In 1902,
Margaret, who was ill having exhausted herself working in Bradford,
joined her sister in Kent where she was working as a teacher of hygiene.
Her colleagues in Bradford were sad to see her leave — 'She was a
pioneer whose influence had been greatly felt in the city', said the
chairman of the school board. No member of the board had ever shared
her interest in the physical development of the children. Starting out as
a political propagandist she had become an authority on the care and
education of children. 'Many of her ideas', said the Rev. Rhondda
Williams, 'despised and rejected of men, have become corner stones of
the educational edifice.'[6]

From 1902 to 1917, when Rachel died, the sisters lived and worked
together. Margaret fought strenuously for many causes including
medical inspection and treatment of school children. It was a period of
constructive work resulting in the Children's Clinic at Bow, and then
the Clinic, Camp Schools, Open-Air Nursery School and Training
College at Deptford. Margaret was determined to justify remedial and
preventive medical treatment in a properly run clinic, but the terrible
home conditions of many of the patients undid her work, so she created
a night camp for girls at Evelyn House and a night and day camp for
boys in St Nicholas Churchyard. The next problem was that many
children were damaged in their pre-school years so she devised her
Open-Air Nursery School where young children could stay for nine
hours a day thus having better resistance to the 'foul forces' of the
slums. Margaret's final triumph was the creation of the Training
College, named after Rachel, in Deptford. There students, who used
the Nursery School as a centre, were trained in the McMillan
principles of education and nurture and so her ideas and methods were
spread further afield. The college is still training teachers in south-east
London today.

During the First World War, nursery provision expanded as women
were needed in the factories in unprecedented numbers, and publicly
provided nurseries were a partial answer to the problem of releasing
women with young children. At the end of the war public nursery
provision was placed on a new and permanent footing. Two types of

nursery were distinguished. First, day nurseries taking the children of working mothers under the age of five, staffed by nurses and being mainly concerned with the health of the children. Under the Maternity and Child Welfare Act 1918, the new local welfare authorities were empowered to make grants-in-aid to voluntary nurseries. Secondly, nursery schools and nursery classes in the public elementary schools who took children between two or three and five and whose aims were mainly educational. Under the Education Act, 1918, local education authorities were empowered to establish nursery schools or classes and to aid voluntary nursery schools. As the legislation was permissive, there was an obvious duty for Labour women to bring the maximum pressure they could on their local authorities to take the opportunity to provide or help in the provision of both types of nursery. However, before much progress could be made, an economy drive in 1921 (the Geddes Axe) to be repeated in 1931, hit nursery development. Between the world wars, day nurseries actually declined in numbers though nursery schools grew slowly from 19 in 1919 to 118 by 1938.

Margaret and Rachel McMillan saw as an immediate priority the need to provide nurseries for the 'special case' disadvantaged children in slum districts but in the long run they recognised that nursery schools should be a part of the mainstream of educational development. They had too much to offer to *all* children to be allowed to degenerate into what Professor Tawney called 'a way-side concession to charity'. Margaret McMillan wrote:

> The Nursery School should make a new Junior School possible because it will send out children who are equipped for a much easier and more rapid advance than is the average child of today. The modern world of interest and movement and wonder will be ajar for him already.

> In short, if it is a real place of nurture, and not merely a place where babies are 'minded' till they are five, it will affect our whole educational system very powerfully and very rapidly.

> The Bastilles will fall at last — by the touch of a little hand.[7]

Unfortunately progress in nursery schools has not been as fast as the Labour pioneers would have hoped.

Milk

In June 1921, an article by Miss (later Dame) Mabel Crout, a member of the public health committee of Woolwich Borough Council drew the attention of Labour women to a new Ministry of Health circular which ordered drastic economies in the provision of free milk to expectant and nursing mothers and to children under five from poor families. This provision under the terms of the Maternity and Child Welfare Act, 1918, could receive a 50 per cent government grant. But now most stringent regulations prohibited its supply to almost all children between three and five years and reduced the amount for babies. Moreover, the government grant was to be reduced to 5 per cent of the expenditure. This would mean in Bermondsey, for example, if they continued to feed the needy babies, that the council would lose something like £2,000 on the half year, or nearly ½d on the rates, thus putting the burden of healthy infancy on the shoulders of ratepayers of the poorest areas.

An official campaign was launched by the Labour movement, especially by Labour women. Deputations were organised to local authorities and local MPs, public meetings and conferences were held and Maternity and Child Welfare Committees were urged to make a united protest. The result of this strong action taken by Labour women and the Labour movement generally was a great victory. The government withdrew the circular and agreed to pay the 50 per cent grant for the next six months. However, this was only capitulation for six months and Labour women were urged to carry on a vigorous agitation to secure the babies' food. Sir Alfred Mond, the Minister of Health, was surprised at the volume of public opinion against his milk policy and agreed to consider the advice of his Consultative Council on General Health Questions, on which there were several Labour women. Early in 1922, the Standing Joint Committee of Working Women's Organisations asked the Chancellor of the Exchequer to receive a deputation from them, the Labour Party, the Trades Union Congress and the Cooperative Party to urge the case for making no reductions in the supply of milk to mothers and babies, nor in maternity and child welfare work. The Chancellor replied that 'despite the present financial difficulties, they propose to make adequate provision for its continuance and no reduction is contemplated'.[8] Having won the day the deputation did not take place but the Standing Joint Committee said that the matter would be very carefully watched and prompt action would be taken again if necessary.

The Poor Law

One of the earliest ways in which Labour women were able to contribute as citizens was on the boards of guardians, though their function was to try and make a system, of which they strongly disapproved, work as painlessly as possible. At the second Annual Conference of the WLL in 1907, Miss Margaret Bondfield moved a resolution recommending the abolition of the Poor Law and the substitution of such reforms as universal old age pensions, public provision of work for the unemployed, municipalisation of hospitals and the maintenance of necessitous mothers and children. The following year the conference gave its support to the Minority Report of the Poor Law Commission and urged immediate measures to prevent 'the vast amount of unnecessary starvation that exists in all parts of the country'. Sister Kerrison, a Poor Law guardian in West Ham for fourteen years gave details of how badly a widow with children or the family with an invalid father fared with outdoor relief.

After the First World War, Mrs Clara Rackham* of Cambridge urged more Labour women to stand for election as Poor Law guardians. 'A Labour majority on the Board of Guardians', she declared 'can make the whole difference to the happiness, health and standard of life of all those who for any reason come into contact with the Board. We want . . .men and women who know first-hand the needs and lives of the workers, who realise to the full the harm that results from the continued underfeeding. . .when inadequate allowances are given.'[9] Labour women could press for good nursing for the sick, for the kindly and humane care of the aged, for the best education and the greatest freedom for the 'children of the State' and for individual attention and care for the infants, she said. Labour people were not obsessed with keeping down the rates; they knew that money could never be better spent than in raising to a better level the poorest and most helpless members of the community.

'Women are working in the Labour Party to secure for the disinherited some of those advantages to which their labours for the community fully entitled them', argued a leading article in the *Labour Woman* of April 1925. 'The work of the Poor Law guardians is like housekeeping for a very big and difficult family and we want women's help to run this publicly-managed household.' Children needed 'mothering' and women with Labour ideals were needed to see that each child had a good start in life, not as a machine but as a human soul. A good training for future employment should be given. For instance, 'a Labour woman is not likely to send all girls indiscriminately into domestic service. Labour women would be sympathetic to the unmarried mother and the widow with children applying for outdoor relief; they would be invaluable in insisting on a high standard of nursing, good food, light and air in the infirmary. In a word, concluded the article, 'they will treat the poor as brothers and sisters, not as "paupers".'[10]

Pit Head Baths

The Women's Labour League took an active part in the campaign for baths at the pit head. This began in the Miners' Union but as it so deeply concerned miners' wives and their families, the League gave its enthusiastic support to the proposal and published a pamphlet by Mrs Katharine Bruce Glasier which was widely circulated in industrial areas. The pressure resulted in Clause 77 of the Coal Mines Act, 1911, which stated somewhat grudgingly that:

> where a majority ascertained by ballot, of two-thirds of the workmen employed in any mine. . .desired that accommodation and facilities for taking baths and drying clothes should be provided at the mine and undertake to pay half the cost. . .the owner shall forthwith provide sufficient and suitable accommodation.

The owner could not, however, be bound to provide the baths if the estimated cost of maintenance was more than 1½d per week for each workman involved. Where the facilities were provided all the workers at that mine would have 1d per week deducted from their pay. This clause, said Mr Robert Smillie, President of the Miners' Federation of Great Britain, was 'sorrowfully weaker' than in the original draft of the Bill and it placed the onus for the adoption of baths on the miners who had to make the first move.

A Home Office Departmental Committee set up to consider the whole question of baths for miners reported early in 1913. They visited France, Belgium and Germany to see various kinds of baths and concluded that the spray bath in a private cubicle was the best arrangement. They also favoured comfortably heated dressing boxes and heated buildings generally and hot air drying of pit clothes. They did not feel, however, that the 1½d per week per head was enough to provide a service that was 'sufficient and suitable'.

'Let our Women's Labour Leagues in mining districts bestir themselves now as never before', exhorted Katharine Bruce Glasier in the *Labour Woman*. 'Where the Act is weak it can be soon amended —

only let a start be made and the victory we have so long worked for is ours.' Many of the miners were a bit conservative about a change in their routine; it was up to the wives to see that the provision was implemented as widely as possible. A miner's wife from South Wales wrote of her satisfaction about the prospect. Boiling water on the kitchen fire for men to bath in a tin bath in front of the fire made miners' wives 'more like slaves than women'. 'Think of the man working in a wet place and perhaps having a two mile walk home! I've seen them come in with *icicles* hanging to them.' She was sure that the baths would be 'a great help in bettering the home-life of the miner, easing the burdens of his wife and making his children healthier. They will make him a better, stronger man — and help in the work of social reorganisation that we are striving for.'[11]

The war naturally held up progress though it was ironic when a soldier in the trenches on the northern front wrote home expressing delight at the comforts his battalion was enjoying. They happened to be stationed near a large colliery which was properly equipped with baths for miners and they were happy to have 'shower drill' every morning.

In May 1919 during sittings of the Coal Commission hard things were said about miners' wives opposing pit head baths and accepting poor housing conditions rather than pay more rent. Aspersions were also cast on their extravagance and low standards of cleanliness in their homes. Dr Marion Phillips challenged these views on behalf of Labour women and asked that some miners' wives should be called to give evidence before the Commission. Three wives, one each from Scotland, England and Wales were selected and gave a vivid picture of the home conditions of miners and families. A large number of miners' homes in Wigan, said Mrs Hart, were back-to-back with no water supply and no wash boilers. Mrs Andrews* reported a large number of underground cellar dwellings in her part of South Wales. Sanitation did not exist in Bellshill, Mrs Brown told the Commission, while Mrs Hart said the conveniences were totally inadequate to the number of houses and commented on the stench, particularly in summer. All three women who had experience in local politics and committee work dwelt on the effects on infant mortality, premature births and female ailments, of the heavy lifting of tubs and boilers necessary under the present housing conditions. They urged the provision of baths, both in the homes and at the pit head. They denied that miners' wives had low standards of cleanliness and quoted examples of deputations to press for pit head baths. 'I have known of cases where there were children and a baby

lying in a cot by the fire', said Mrs Brown, 'and three men's clothing drying round the fire and that baby lying ill with pneumonia, and it was detrimental to the baby's health to have that nuisance there.'
Mrs Andrews told the Coal Commission that she hoped the mine owners would move very rapidly in this question 'because otherwise I am afraid the miners' wives will adopt unconstitutional methods by going on strike'.

At last in 1924, came the vital breakthrough. A Labour Government with Mr Emanuel Shinwell as Secretary for Mines, promised to introduce a Bill making the provision of pit head baths *compulsory within three years.*

Other Causes

Just a few of the welfare causes pursued by Labour women have been selected as examples of the contribution they were able to make towards social progress both locally and nationally. Among the other causes that they discussed and in which they proposed reforms were various aspects of education, the employment of children, housing, pensions, lunacy services, birth control, VD, health services, domestic servants, the abolition of capital punishment, conditions in prisons, clean milk and the drink trade.

Just as only a few topics could be selected in this brief account of the early achievements of Labour women in social welfare, it has also only been possible to mention a few of the names of the participants. Reading through the annual reports of the WLL and the articles in *Labour Woman*, many names reappear, having taken up a cause or reporting a success in one of the many issues so vital to women and their families. From among the hundreds of Labour women of this period who were active and tireless in their work to improve society, the few whose names have been quoted are representative of their comrades whose joint efforts had a powerful influence in the progress made towards a better society.

Notes

1. *Medical Officer*, 1945, Vol.LXXIV, p.197.
2. *Conference Report 1906, Women's Labour League*, pp.6 and 7, Labour Party Library.
3. Ibid., pp. 1 and 2.
4. *Conference Report 1907, Women's Labour League*, pp. 8 and 9. Labour Party Library.
5. *Labour Woman*, October 1916, p.68.

6. Albert Mansbridge, *Margaret McMillan,* J.M. Dent, 1932.
7. Margaret McMillan, *The Nursery School,* J.M. Dent, 1927, pp. 93-5.
8. *Labour Woman,* February 1922, p.19, Labour Party Library.
9. *Labour Woman,* April 1925, p.53, Labour Party Library.
10. K Bruce Glasier, *Baths at the Pit Head,* pamphlet in volume of *Labour Women's League, Annual Reports,* 1906-16, pp. 1-16, Labour Party Library.
11. *Labour Woman,* July 1919, pp. 83-4, Labour Party Library.

3 THE CONTRIBUTION OF THE WOMEN'S LABOUR LEAGUE TO THE WINNING OF THE FRANCHISE

Margherita Rendel

When the Women's Labour League was founded in 1906, its object was 'to form an organisation of women to work for Labour Representation in connection with the Labour Party'. At the first Conference held in June 1906, the following sentence was added, thus stressing the importance attached to the franchise for women: 'and to obtain direct Labour Representation of women in Parliament and on all local bodies'.

The amendment was moved by Miss Isabella Ford, a delegate of the Leeds ILP and a Guardian of the Poor and seconded by Mrs Pethick-Lawrence. The other methods of the League relevant to the franchise were set out as follows:

The members of the Society will work with the Labour Party locally and nationally, and will help Labour candidates in local and Parliamentary elections.

They will educate themselves on political and social questions by means of meetings, discussions, distribution of leaflets, etc.

They will take an active interest in the work of the Poor Law Guardians, Educational bodies, Distress Committees, Town, District and County Councillors and Members of Parliament.

They will work to secure the full rights of citizenship for all women and men.

They will watch the interests of working women in their own neighbourhood, and strive where possible to improve their social and industrial conditions.

The story of the League's foundation is told in another chapter. This chapter is concerned with the work of the League for women's suffrage. While most attention is given to the Parliamentary franchise, women's access to the local government franchise is discussed, and relationships with other suffrage organisations indicated. Because the chapter is about what the women did, little is said about the role of men who also fought for women's suffrage. Sources not used by previous researchers, such as the *League Leaflet, Labour Woman* and some of the Minute Books of the Women's Labour League have been used.

Working women had long been active in politics. They had been active especially during the Civil War, but little is known about their activities in the eighteenth century. However, in 1739, a pamphlet was published entitled 'Woman not Inferior to Man: or short and modest vindication of the natural Right of the Fair Sex, to a perfect Equality of Power, Dignity and Esteem, with the Man', by 'Sophia, a Person of Quality' whose identity is unknown. In 1792, Mary Wollstonecraft, who lived on what she could earn by writing, published *A Vindication of the Rights of Woman.* From the turn of the century, as cartoons, for example, show, women were demanding reforms, rights and equality. The Great Reform Act of 1833 enfranchised a relatively small number of men, 'rationalised' the franchise and introduced a statutory bar to women by conferring the vote only on 'male' persons. In the 1830s and 1840s, women's sections were an important part of the Chartist movement and individual Chartists, such as R.J. Richardson, strongly claimed votes for women.

Throughout the nineteenth century and the early years of the twentieth, the struggle for women's rights became of ever-increasing importance. In 1867, the first suffrage societies were founded; and from 1870 until 1914, there was a Bill to enfranchise women before Parliament in all but seven of those forty-four years. But historians have given only a limited attention to the struggle for the emancipation of half the population and in particular the role played by Labour women has been largely ignored.

The attitude of the Women's Labour League was early demonstrated. When women electors became eligible to serve on town councils in 1907, the *League Leaflet* No.8 appealed to women to serve. Some quotations will show the nature of the appeal:

Women are needed badly for our *Municipal Housekeeping. . .*

Let us use our *women's brains and women's hearts* to help guide the Labour policy on matters where we have knowledge and experience which the men cannot have.

We women know the waste of precious time and health due to insanitary, crowded surroundings. Let us claim for ourselves and our children *decent homes to live in!*

Then we need to secure the appointment of well trained and properly paid *women sanitary inspectors.* They can visit in the homes and in

the women's workrooms and shops, and give help and advice as no
man inspector can do.

. . .the *women teachers,* who are paid so much worse than the men,
need to be championed by their fellow-women.

The *Leaflet* mentions other issues of especial concern to women,
such as infant mortality, the administration of the Midwives' Act, the
provision of baths and washhouses, hospitals, parks and playgrounds
and the provision of meals for needy schoolchildren.

The vote and the right to sit were not just to have, but to use, as
Marion Phillips later wrote. The Labour movement took for granted the
equal citizenship of men and women and was from the beginning
committed to universal adult franchise on a short residential
qualification. It was over priorities and tactics that different views were
held. There were three major issues; but first it is necessary to explain
briefly who had the vote and for what at the turn of the century. Only
63 per cent of men and *no* women had a Parliamentary franchise.[1]
Those men who were owners or occupiers of property of £10 annual
value or ratepayers were entitled to vote, but the rules were complicated
and anomalous. For the local government franchise, some men and
fewer women were entitled to vote, and a distinction was sometimes
drawn between married and single women. Married women could
qualify only in respect of property different from that of their husbands.
Thus married women of the property-owning classes were more likely to
qualify than married women who were less well off. To have the
qualifications was not sufficient: would-be electors had to apply to be
included on the Register, and anyone receiving poor relief was
disqualified from voting.

During the first ten years of this century, it was thought that the
winning of votes for all men was outside practical politics. The first
issue which arose was this: should some women be enfranchised in order
to establish the principle of votes for women? Some more people with
property, in this case women, would be added to the electoral register.
Also some well-propertied men might confer some of it on their wives
and daughters in order, as they would think, to increase the voting
power of their class, but there has never been any evidence that well-
propertied men are so generous to, or trusting of, their female relatives.
Among those less well off, only widows and spinsters would be likely
to benefit.

The second and third issues arose directly from the adamantine hostility of the Prime Minister, Asquith, to any form of female enfranchisement. The second issue was this: should the Labour movement oppose any measure for further enfranchisement of men or electoral reform that did not include a measure of enfranchisement for women? The third issue arose as a result of Asquith's repeated prevarications and after about 1912: should Labour MPs oppose *all* government measures until women were enfranchised? This would have meant opposing many social measures to which the Labour movement was committed.

Manhood suffrage was opposed on class grounds by Conservatives and some Liberals, and by no means all suffragists and suffragettes were committed to the principle of *universal* suffrage.[2] After the 1906 General Election had brought more Labour and trade union MPs to Westminster, it was clear that demands for greater social and economic equality could be effectively sustained. There was everything to be gained for those hostile to Labour policies by setting middle-class against working-class women, working women against working men and the needs of the working class against the most important means of emancipating half that class. This chapter tells how these three threats to the solidarity of the movement were handled.

One of the most important functions of the Women's Labour League was to politicise women, to make women aware that they could help themselves. Mrs L.E. Simm, the wife of the Organising Secretary of the North-Eastern Federation of the ILP, was the organiser for the Women's Labour League in Northern England and Southern Scotland. In 1908, she described the difficulties of rousing the women from the hopelessness into which poverty had plunged them. 'It is an awful task trying to rouse some of the women in the mining districts [around Newcastle and Gateshead], but it seems more awful that they should be left as they are.'[3] It was not only despair on the part of women that made difficulties for Mrs Simm. 'Some old trade unionists are afraid', she wrote, 'that we should spoil the homes by taking women out to meetings!' She seems to have overcome their fears as she reported at the same time that she had been able to arrange a number of special women's meetings.[4] But the men in some districts, for example Bishop Auckland, were anxious that the women should be organised as they valued the contribution the women made to election work.[5] The women in the League did not confine their activities to electioneering on behalf of the men.

Throckley Branch is already notorious. They sent a resolution to the local Council urging them to provide a recreation ground, and as such a suggestion from a *women's* organization caused quite a sensation, the branch got quite a show in the papers.[6]

At all times, women in the Labour movement were concerned with social issues such as school meals and school medical services, with economic matters such as sweated labour and female unemployment, and with foreign policy — demonstrations were organised against the visit of the Tsar in 1908 — and with the risk of war.

Womanhood suffrage was advocated as a means of ensuring women's participation in the struggle for better conditions. Mrs Cooper, a delegate from the ILP at the Fifth Annual Conference of the Labour Party in 1905 said she was speaking on behalf of thousands of women textile workers; women were as clearly alive to the needs of the people as anyone and if they had the vote they would be able to use it in the interests of reform. Mrs Cooper lived in Nelson, Lancashire, and was, with Eva Gore-Booth* and others, a signatory in July 1904 of a manifesto announcing that a committee of women textile workers had been formed in order to select a Parliamentary candidate who would be specifically committed to promoting women's enfranchisement and to finance the election expenses of some £500. The manifesto concluded:

> Anyone who wishes to better the position of her fellow-workers, and the thousands of women outside the ranks of the unskilled cotton operatives, who are being overworked and underpaid, should remember that political enfranchisement must precede industrial emancipation, and that the political disabilities of women have done incalculable harm, by cheapening their labour and lowering their position in the industrial world. What Lancashire and Cheshire women think today England will do tomorrow.

It began by explaining that the Labour Representation Committee had been formed with the object of gaining direct Parliamentary representation for the already enfranchised working men.[7]

The first Annual Conference of the Labour Representation Committee (subsequently the Labour Party) was held in January 1901. A resolution in favour of adult suffrage was carried unanimously. In 1902, in the education debate, opposition was expressed to any measure which would limit the opportunities for women to engage in public work; women were not then eligible to sit on county councils which, by the 1901 Education Act, had taken over the work of the school boards to which women had been eligible. In 1904, a resolution was adopted which proposed that women entitled to a parochial vote should also be entitled to the Parliamentary franchise and urged members of Parliament connected with the Labour Representation Committee to introduce a Bill to this effect. Isabella Ford, seconding, drew attention to the democratic nature of the proposal in that it did not distinguish between married and single women. The Labour movement was throughout concerned with obtaining the franchise for women on democratic terms. In contrast, the constitutionalist suffrage groups at the end of the nineteenth century were concerned primarily to establish the principle that women should have the vote and on the same terms as men. Thus the suffragists felt obliged to leave as they found them the disabilities to which married women were subject.

In 1905, and at the three subsequent Annual Conferences of the Labour Party, the democratic extension of the franchise to women was discussed from a different point of view. A resolution was moved approving the Women's Enfranchisement Bill introduced by Will Crooks and Keir Hardie in the previous session; this proposed the extension of the franchise to women on the same limited terms as men. The resolution was opposed on the grounds that it would enfranchise more of the propertied classes. The issue was argued, each side presenting its own estimates of the number of working women who would be enfranchised by the extension of the franchise on the same terms and each side guessing which way women already enfranchised for municipal elections actually did vote. In 1905, Mrs Emmeline Pankhurst quoted the results of the ILP investigations and suggested that 90 per cent of women who had the municipal franchise were working women, that is women without private means who had to earn their own living.

Those supporting a limited extension of the franchise to women stressed the importance of establishing the principle of women's right to vote — this was a 'thin-end-of-the-wedge' argument. They also pointed to the unlikelihood of obtaining complete manhood suffrage and to the likely difficulty of obtaining votes for any women once all men had been enfranchised. Their opponents stressed the importance of not increasing the anti-socialist vote. Each year the universal suffragists defeated the 'thin-end-of-wedgers'.

Women in the Labour movement were divided on the issue. Mrs Cooper and Mrs Pankhurst of the ILP supported the thin-end-of-the-wedge argument, but women trade unionists such as Margaret Bondfield of the Shop Assistants' Union (and of the Women's Labour League) and Mabel Hope* of the Postal Telegraph Clerks' Association were universalists. But not so all women trade unionists. Eva Gore-Booth (sister of Countess Marcievicz of Sinn Fein), the delegate of the Manchester and Salford Association of Machine, Electric and other Women Workers in 1908 said women trade unionists in Lancashire were tired of the controversy, tired of their claims being mixed up with the claims of other classes and wanted the vote to fight for their interests as a matter of the utmost importance.

At the Annual Conferences of the WLL held immediately before the Labour Party Conferences in 1907 and 1908, resolutions were passed accepting the division between the universalists and thin-end-of-the-wedgers as to the best tactics for obtaining the franchise but reaffirming the League's commitment to full adult suffrage and the importance of Labour representation. Universalists such as Mabel Hope urged acceptance of this resolution which enabled each to go her own way. At the 1908 WLL Conference, a delegate from Halifax, Mrs Willson, raised the problem of relations with the Women's Social and Political Union; she had worked with them and believed in their methods. But she was castigated by the chairman because the WSPU had asked its members to take no part in any affirmative work for the Labour Party. The WSPU was, by this time, a prominent and successful organisation and able to attract funds. Mrs Simm in a letter of 28 June 1908 complained to Mrs Middleton: 'I can't think how the Suffragettes get such a lot of money — it is certainly not from or *for* the class WLL is working to help.'[8]

In May 1908 shortly after Asquith had become Prime Minister, a deputation of sixty Liberal MPs waited on him to ask him to provide facilities for a women's suffrage measure. Asquith replied that he was contemplating a measure of electoral reform to be drafted in terms wide enough to permit of a women's suffrage amendment to the Bill and that this measure would be introduced during the current Parliament — but he did not say in which session. In September of that year, the Executive Committee of the WLL were asked by the secretary of the Women's Cooperative Guild, Miss Llewelyn Davies, to join with the Guild and as many other organisations as possible in signing a letter to be sent to the Prime Minister. After an exchange of letters about how far Mr Asquith's reply to the deputation could be pushed, the following letter was sent to him:

> You have announced your intention to introduce, during the present Parliament, an Electoral Reform Bill, and your willingness to accept an amendment giving the vote to women on democratic lines, if

passed by the House of Commons. We welcome this proof that you recognise the justice of women's claim to the vote. At the same time, we wish to point out that your announcement names no time for the introduction of the Bill and gives no indication that the Government would consider itself responsible for the carrying through of Women's Suffrage. For these reasons, we are unable to accept your announcement as satisfying our desire that the Government should enfranchise women. The introduction of your projected Bill will be subject to political accidents; and though the House of Commons has this year affirmed the principle of women's Suffrage by a very large majority, it is unlikely that the part of the Bill which would concern women could pass through all stages in both Houses unless the Government were prepared to insist on its retention.

Since you are willing to introduce a Bill so framed as not to exclude Women's Suffrage in its scope, and to accept the decision of the House of Commons on a Women's suffrage amendment you will, we trust, recognise that this admission of the justice of our claim gives us the right to ask you to consider in our favour the points which we regard as essential to the success of the Measure and to its obtaining the confidence of women. We do not think that the enfranchisement of women could be reasonably assured in the way indicated, unless the Government were prepared

(1) to introduce the Bill next session, and
(2) to emphasise the sincerity of their intention of giving votes to women by letting it be known that they would refuse to pass the Bill without the women's clauses, if these should be rejected by the House of Lords.
(3) We also wish to point out that in view of the attitude of the House of Commons to our claim there can be no reason why the Government, being themselves willing to accept Women's Suffrage, should not make it a part of their Bill as introduced. The unusual course proposed of offering the House of Commons the opportunity of inserting legislation on a subject of first-rate importance into a Government Bill by way of amendment, has given rise, in some quarters, to a doubt of the genuineness of the proposal, which we should be glad to see dispelled.
(4) With a view of securing the confidence of women, we regard it of importance that some clear indication should shortly be given of

the qualifications of women which would be compatible with your project of electoral reform.

We desire to ask you, with all the urgency in our power, to give your favourable attention to these points. The movement for political freedom amongst women is 40 years old: it has grown to great dimensions, embracing all classes, and has acquired a new strength from the wave of popular feeling to which the Government owes its power. The higher education and professional work of women, the increase of laws and of the demand for laws affecting, more especially, working women's lives, the development of women's political consciousness and their experience of public work, have given it solidity and force. There can now be no doubt of its strength and persistence, and as to its justice, we can appeal with confidence to Liberal principles.

The enfranchisement of women has been accepted as part of the programme of the National Liberal Federation, and has obtained the support of the organised Labour vote; resolutions in favour of Women's Suffrage having been passed by the Trade Union Congress, the Cooperative Congress, and the Annual Congress of the Independent Labour Party, while the Labour Party Congresses and the Social Democratic Party Congress have supported Women's Suffrage as part of Adult Suffrage.

Further, Great Suffrage Demonstrations, organised by women, are to take place this autumn in London and Manchester. The three demonstrations in London are being organised by the Women's Liberal Federation, the Women's Social and Political Union, and jointly by the Lancashire and Cheshire Textile and other workers' Labour Representation Committee and the Women's Trade Council (Manchester and Salford), whilst the Manchester Procession and Free Trade Hall Demonstrations are being organised by the North of England Society for Women's Suffrage (National Union of Women's Suffrage Societies) other Suffrage Societies, the Women's Cooperative Guild, and various political, industrial, and social societies are also taking part. At these Demonstrations we most earnestly desire to submit a favourable reply to the four points mentioned above, believing that the Enfranchisement of Women deserves the immediate attention of the Government.

Yours etc.

On September 19, 1908, Miss Llewelyn Davies sent the revised draft with a list of organisations that were signing. These were:

> The North of England Suffrage Society, Bristol and West of England
> Suffrage Society and the Glasgow and West of Scotland Suffrage
> Society, all affiliated to the National Union;
> The Lancashire and Cheshire Union of Women's Liberal Associations;
> The Lancashire and Cheshire Textile and other Workers
> Representation Committee;
> The Women's Trade Council (Manchester and Salford) and The
> Women's Cooperative Guild.

Miss Llewelyn Davies also expected the 'Liberal Forwards' and was nearly certain that the National Union of Suffrage Societies would sign. She was uncertain about the Women's Liberal Federation as Lady Carlisle, their President, thought it might not be expedient for the Women's Liberal Federation, although she was prepared to sign provided her Executive thought so. The Women's Liberal Association was thought to be unlikely to sign. Miss Tuckwell and Miss Macarthur, both leaders of the Women's Trade Union League, had already signed. On 21 September 1908 it was agreed that the full Executive Committee and the Secretary of the WLL should sign the letter.[9]

Thus the non-party suffrage associations joined the politically committed Cooperative Guild to press for the vote; that the Women's Labour League and trade union organisations should do so was to be expected. The adherence of the Liberal women was ambivalent, perhaps inevitably, although the Prime Minister had declared the issue an open question and the Chancellor of the Exchequer, David Lloyd George, was speaking openly in favour of women's suffrage. The Liberal women were admittedly in an awkward position in view of Asquith's hostility to women's suffrage, but they did pass a number of very strong resolutions at various times in favour of women's suffrage. The Primrose League (the organisation of Conservative women) had in 1889 determined that 'Habitations [local branches of the Primrose League] cannot take part in meetings for the promotion of women's suffrage'.[10]

The WSPU were unwilling to sign the letter because it was their policy to oppose the Liberal Government and all who supported it. The campaign of militancy had begun when Annie Kenney and Christabel Pankhurst asked Sir Edward Grey about the Liberal Government's policy on votes for women in the Manchester Free Trade Hall on

13 October 1905.* The campaign proceeded by way of many and varied demonstrations to window-smashing and ultimately to arson – of empty property. The WSPU opposed Liberal candidates at elections because only in this way, as far as they could see could they put pressure on the Liberal Government. The Labour Party on the whole supported the government because it was implementing at least some of the reforms the Party wanted. Furthermore, the Women's Labour League stuck throughout to constitutional action. In 1911, for example, the Executive Committee received with disapproval a proposal from the Women's Freedom League that women should boycott the census.

At the Annual Conferences of the League and of the Labour Party from 1910 to the outbreak of war in 1914, resolutions urging increasingly strong support for women's suffrage were submitted. The League remained in advance of the Party as a whole and on this issue acted as a pressure group within it. For similar reasons, the continued existence of the women's organisations within the political parties has been specifically safeguarded by Section 33 of the Sex Discrimination Act 1975.

At the Fifth Annual Conference of the Women's Labour League, in January 1910, Margaret Bondfield, representing the North Shields branch, moved the Executive resolution on the New Reform Bill to be presented by the government. The Resolution, which was carried unanimously, read as follows:

> Believing that the active participation of women in the work of Government is in the best interests of the nation, and in view of the Reform Bill promised by the Government, this Conference demands that the inclusion of women shall not be left to the chances of amendment, but that it shall become a vital part of the Government's measure; and further declares that any attempt to exclude women should be met by the uncompromising opposition of organised Labour to the whole Bill.

In seconding, Mrs Annot Robinson from Central Manchester stressed that the enfranchisement of women was a burning question for the country, for the race, for women and for children; no legislation could be wise or sane until the women of the country could express their views and they could not do so until a new franchise measure was

---

* Neale (1972) discusses just what question was asked and the participation of working-class women in WSPU.

introduced.

At the Labour Party Conference which followed almost immediately, Margaret Bondfield moved an identical resolution. At the request of Arthur Henderson, the words 'to the whole Bill' were dropped, but Mary Macarthur, representing the ILP, pointed out that as she and others had withstood the attempt to enfranchise some women only, it was for men to ensure that the women were enfranchised.

The League did not join officially in attempts to enfranchise some women only. This became a matter of especial importance from 1910 onwards because each year a so-called Conciliation Bill was moved in Parliament. The Conciliation Bills contained the amount of enfranchisement for women that all suffragists could agree on; this meant enfranchisement for those women whom Conservative supporters of the franchise were prepared to see enfranchised. H.N. Brailsford, the journalist, acted as Secretary to the Committee organising support for the Conciliation Bills. In July 1910, he wrote to the Executive Committee of the League asking for their support. Because the limited extension of the franchise was contrary to policy, the Executive Committee could not give official support, but it did offer to send a list of WLL Branches.[11] The Bill obtained a large majority on second reading, and was referred to Committee of the Whole House on 12 July; thus the government would have to find time for it. The Bill got no further.

At the next Annual Conference of the Women's Labour League in January 1911 an amendment to water down the resolution in favour of adult suffrage on the ground that this was not within the sphere of practical politics was defeated. The Cooperative Women's Guild supported the Conciliation Bill, but the rank and file of the Labour movement did not.

By the end of 1911, Asquith said that a Manhood Suffrage Bill — the measure he had promised in 1908 — would be introduced in the next session and that an amendment to include women, if carried, would be incorporated in the Government's Bill. The *League Leaflet* for November 1911, reporting this news, urged women not to let their enfranchisement depend on the chances of an amendment:

> Resolutions on these lines should be passed at every meeting we women of the League can hear of, resolutions which will hearten our supporters in the House of Commons and show them that no Bill will be acceptable to Labour which does not give a vote to every woman as well as every man.

In the next issue of the *Leaflet* in December, Marion Phillips in a stirring article, appealed to working men to ensure that women got the vote:

> No electoral advantages would outweigh the moral disgrace which would fall upon the working men, if at this crisis, their representatives in Parliament failed to gain the vote for women also.

She pointed out that an amendment for a limited enfranchisement of women would get rid of the anomalies in the qualifications for men only to introduce them for women, and ended by declaring: 'We rely on Labour MPs to make it clear that they will not support a Bill which comes to its third reading without including them.'

In December 1911, the League sent representatives to the Women's Suffrage Joint Committee of MPs and Societies. This was a coordinating committee which favoured granting the vote to women on a broad, *democratic* basis and allowed its members to interpret this phrase in their own way.

At the 1912 Annual Conference of the League, a resolution couched in stronger terms than previously, was passed calling upon 'the Parliamentary Labour Party to oppose any Government Bill for Electoral Reform unless it contains a clause enfranchising women'.

At the Labour Party Conference in January 1912, the Party strengthened its support for women's suffrage. Arthur Henderson, of the Friendly Society of Ironfounders, and Secretary of the Party, moved a resolution to the effect that a Franchise Bill which did not include women would be unacceptable to the Labour and Socialist movements. This resolution was opposed by Robert Smillie of the Mineworkers' Federation who urged that manhood suffrage should be supported if it proved impossible to include women in the Bill. Smillie's position was strongly attacked especially by Philip Snowden MP (ILP) and Millicent Murby (Fabian Society). Mary Macarthur (ILP) said the miners had been so helpful in the past, yet now they were prepared to take manhood suffrage and leave the women out; Labour women had refused to press for the extension of the suffrage to women on a property qualification only. It was for the men to stand by the women. Smillie's amendment must have seemed black ingratitude, for as long ago as 1906 the WLL had campaigned for Smillie when he stood as parliamentary candidate for Cockermouth.[12] Arthur Henderson's resolution was carried by 919,000 votes to 686,000 votes. Of the latter, 600,000 were those of the Miners' Federation.[13]

During 1912, the League and its branches were very active in the cause of women's suffrage. Branches held meetings, distributed literature, proposed resolutions at meetings of other organisations and the Bristol branch distributed 3,000 handbills to local trade unionists pressing them to send postcards to their MPs urging him that he *must* vote for the inclusion of women in the Franchise and Registration Bill on the *widest possible basis.* [14]

On the eve of the opening of Parliament, in February 1912, an adult suffrage meeting was held in the Albert Hall jointly between the Labour Party, the ILP and the Fabian Society. The speakers included Mrs Charlotte Despard, a member of the ILP and the WLL, and a leader of the Women's Freedom League, Mary Macarthur of the Women's Trade Union League and Miss Millicent Murby of the Fabian Society. The meeting voted a long resolution concluding:

> It assures the Government that no measure of Manhood Suffrage will be acceptable to the organised forces of Labour throughout the Kingdom, and demands a genuine measure of Adult Suffrage, conferring full rights of citizenship on all men and women. [15]

In March 1912, a great conference of working women in favour of womanhood suffrage was organised by the People's Suffrage Federation with the cooperation of the Women's Labour League, the Women's Trade Union League, the Women's Cooperative Guild and the Railway Women's Guild. In 1909, the WLL, like the Women's Cooperative Guild, had affiliated to the People's Suffrage Federation. The meeting, with Mary Macarthur in the chair, was attended by kitchen maids and school cleaners of the London County Council, shop assistants, tailoresses, ammunition makers, bookbinders, boxmakers, chocolate workers, laundresses, domestic servants as well as wives and mothers from the Women's Cooperative Guild and the Railway Women's Guild and twenty-seven representatives from the Women's Labour League. Two resolutions were passed, the first calling for

> the enfranchisement of every adult woman equally with every adult man as the only means of giving the workers of every class their due share in the government of the country, and in the reform of industrial and social conditions.

The second called for a Government Bill giving the vote to all adults on a short residential qualification. Several fiery and lively speeches were made from the floor. It had been said that women in Parliament would be dangerous because pretty women might exercise an unfair advantage over men. 'After all', continued Miss Price (WLL, Hackney) amidst laughter, 'even a pretty woman can have some sense, and after a short time she can even live down her prettiness.'[16] A comment as apposite now, alas, as it was then.

In March 1912, the Conciliation Bill failed by a majority of 147 votes to get a second reading — a failure commonly attributed to the members of the Women's Social and Political Union having broken a great many shop windows the previous evening. However, in 1910 and 1911 during the 'truce', when the WSPU suspended its campaign of violence against property, the Conciliation Bills had not got beyond a second reading. In May and June, the League was again pressing all its branches to pass resolutions to urge the immediate introduction of a Reform Bill that could pass through all its stages in that session and become law during the current Parliament under the provisions of the newly enacted Parliament Act even if the Lords voted against the measure, as seemed likely.

The Joint Campaign Committee for Women's Suffrage had already asked the Prime Minister to receive a deputation when the Government's long awaited Franchise and Registration Bill was at last introduced. Women were not included. Protests against the Bill were immediately organised. Two successive amendments would be needed: the first would be to delete the word 'male' in the first clause of the Bill and the second to introduce a clause granting votes for women. The League ran a campaign. The October number of the *League Leaflet* proclaimed:

WORKING WOMEN!
Less than one-tenth of the Women in Great Britain
have the Municipal Vote
NOT ONE HAS THE PARLIAMENTARY VOTE
Read our Publications and see how
many Reforms women want to gain.
JOIN THE WOMEN'S LABOUR LEAGUE
and
HELP THE LABOUR PARTY
to get
VOTES FOR WOMEN THIS YEAR

The November issue was a special suffrage issue. The Executive Committee joined the Women's Freedom League in October 1912 in adding the League's name to the scroll of societies supporting women's suffrage which was to be displayed at the Women's Freedom League's International Fair.[17] In November, the League sent a letter to all ILP Branches, Labour Representation Committees, Trades and Labour Councils and local Labour Parties urging them to support the Parliamentary Labour Party in pressing for amendments to enfranchise women:

> the exclusion of all women, simply as women, from the franchise is a continual weakness to the women's side of our movement. Adult suffragists though we all are, we fear that the grant of manhood suffrage and the refusal of votes for women would at this stage in our agitation give a setback to the women's cause which it would take years to retrieve. We are confident that you will feel with us in this, and therefore that you will be ready to forego more votes for men unless they are given to women also.[18]

Nearly all the recipients expressed approval both for the resolution and the accompanying letter.

In October the League agreed to take part in a great National Conference at the Opera House on 4 December organised by the Joint Campaign Committee. The Conference was addressed by MPs, members of the government and by Labour speakers. Sir John Simon, the Solicitor-General, assured the meeting that the Franchise and Registration Bill could be amended. Margaret Bondfield showed the close connection between the success of Labour and the growth of women's part in politics. Women had been politicised and politicised women supported Labour. Ramsay MacDonald declared without hesitation that to give votes to more men and not to women would be disgraceful and unfair. Societies represented at the meeting resolved that all their branches should organise deputations, letters and resolutions to MPs supporting the amendments to the Bill.

Seven weeks later, the Speaker gave his ruling: the amendments were out of order.

At the Annual Conference of the League on the next day, an urgent resolution was passed unanimously demanding that Asquith honour his pledge by introducing a government measure enfranchising women and according it the time necessary to ensure its passage under the Parliament Act.[19] Margaret Bondfield said that they must make the Liberal Government realise that any member of it who was opposed to women's suffrage was a menace to the Liberal Party, and must be sent to another place whether it was up or down. Mrs Chew, from the Rochdale Labour Party, said that it was not for women to modify their demands or to consider the difficulties of the Cabinet. There came a time when to be patient any longer was personally degrading for the individual or the organisation. She thought that point had now been reached in the women's suffrage movement.

At the Annual Conference of the Labour Party immediately following, an amended resolution was carried by an overwhelming majority. The amendment moved by Mr Dubery (ILP) and seconded by Mrs Simm, urged that no measure should be accepted which enfranchised more men but did not include women. Mr Sanders (Fabian Society) said that women felt they had been sold, that they were disillusioned with the parties and that a Bill which did not confer the franchise on women should be opposed.

The Speaker's ruling was a bitter disappointment to all who had laboured in the suffrage movement. Marion Phillips wrote in a moving article in the March 1913 issue of the *League Leaflet:*

> Some of us are sick and tired of the fight. Our work it is to drive home into the minds of the great slow moving public, that we are honestly and surely convinced that we could do much to better the home conditions of the nation if we could get political power into the hands of the mothers as well as the fathers. . .let us follow paths of right and justice. Let us still show and explain and persuade.

Nonetheless the government had to withdraw its Franchise and Registration Bill. Here was a justification of the policy of the Labour Party and of Labour women in refusing to press for a limited extension of the franchise to women and in insisting on universal adult suffrage.

The King's speech in March made no reference to votes for women. An amendment was put down by the PLP, but there was no time for it to be debated. The ILP condemned the government's failure immediately. Yet another Private Member's 'Conciliation' Bill was introduced. In May this failed on second reading, this time by a majority of 47 against it.

The struggle continued. Copies of the resolution passed at the WLL Conference were sent to members of the government, Asquith, Lloyd George and Edward Grey, to the People's Suffrage Federation and to the Labour Party. A deputation met a small committee of MPs to discuss tactics, but without finding immediate prospects for successful action.[20]

A handbill was ordered, printed and distributed from January 1913. The main points in it were:

> WORKING WOMEN
> Help your real friends, The Labour Party.
> Read what they have declared at their Conference:
> No more votes for men until women have votes as well.
> WHY DO YOU NEED VOTES?
> Because you want to hasten Social Reforms.
> Because you want a living wage, regular employment,
> healthy homes, a chance in life for your children.
> WORKING WOMEN, IT IS YOUR HELP THAT IS NEEDED
> The men cannot gain these reforms alone
> They have tried and failed.
> Come and help at once.

By the beginning of April, more than 36,000 copies had been distributed.[21]

In April, the League joined the Women's Cooperative Guild and the Fabian Women's Group in petitioning the House of Commons that a woman be heard at the bar of the House to advocate working women's claims. The petition was presented by Keir Hardie. A similar petition was at the same time presented by Lord Robert Cecil, the prominent Conservative suffragist, on behalf of the Actresses' Franchise League and other organisations.[22] The struggle continued throughout the year with further meetings, resolutions, deputations, letters, joint committees and more meetings and yet more resolutions.

In the handbill the League appealed both to working women and to women's family and domestic commitments. Much of the material published by the WLL stressed the need for the vote in order to safeguard woman's role as wife and mother.

> Our ideals of the good housewife, the ideal mother are changing fast. We are coming to see that it is only possible for the woman whose chief work lies in her home, to fulfill efficiently her mission there by uniting with other women under the same conditions and with the same aims. Like the men members of her household she must think and work *collectively* in order to help herself and those dependent on her *individually*.[23]

To appeal to women in their capacities as wives and mothers, and in their capacity as workers made, and still makes sound sense. Then, as now, women were brought up to believe they have, first and foremost, duties to parents, husbands and children and that they will find their satisfaction and fulfilments in life through the members of their family. This view implies that women have no claims in their own right, and married women especially often feel guilty about asking for anything for themselves. Such attitudes are of great value to the enemies of the Labour movement as they greatly assist the exploitation of all workers, men and women alike.

At the next Annual Conference of the League in January 1914, debate turned on what pressure Labour members should put on the government. Three resolutions on the subject were put. The first, which was carried, reiterated more strongly the demand that any Franchise Bill that did not include women should be opposed. The second resolution demanded that an amendment to the King's Speech be moved and pressed to a division. The third called upon Labour MPs to oppose all further government measures which did not deal with the enfranchisement of women. The second and third resolutions were both defeated, but they indicated the direction in which opinion was moving.

At the Annual Conference of the Labour Party in 1914, one Women's Suffrage Resolution was put to the Conference, that of the League:

> That this Conference re-affirms its previous decisions on Women's Suffrage and declares that the Government can only redeem the pledge it has given by bringing in a Bill to enfranchise both men and women and requests the Parliamentary Labour Party, in view of the unsatisfactory statements of members of the Cabinet, that Women's Suffrage cannot be dealt with in this Parliament, to raise the question of their enfranchisement at the earliest opportunity next session.

The WLL delegates subsequently reported that: 'Our resolution was then carried by a tremendous shout of Aye — against a single voice which cried No.'[24]

This was not quite the whole of the story. John Battle, a cotton spinner or textile worker,* spoke against the motion saying he had 'no substantial grounds for believing women as a body wanted the vote',

---

* In the list of Conference delegates, he is listed with the Operative Cotton Spinners' Provincial Association of Bolton; in the report, as a delegate of the United Textile Factory Workers.

and that his own members, mostly women, had refused to send him to a meeting in Bolton in favour of the suffrage. A resolution moved by Mr Sanders of the Fabian Society asked that no support be given to the Plural Voting Bill, which the Liberals wanted for their own political advantage, until a measure of women's suffrage had been introduced. Keir Hardie and, it seems, Ben Turner supported this means of putting pressure on the government, but the majority of the Parliamentary Labour Party, led by Ramsay MacDonald, thought that the Plural Voting Bill would help Labour to win more seats, by preventing those with property from voting in more than one constituency at general elections. (One speaker complained that the Parliamentary report, drawn up by Ramsay MacDonald, had omitted any reference to women's suffrage in spite of all the events of 1913.) Adult suffrage would have been potentially far more helpful to Labour, but the Plural Voting Bill was much more likely to pass. This then was a problem in priorities.

With the outbreak of war in August 1914, both suffragists and suffragettes declared a truce and turned their attention to the war effort. The WLL did not forget the problem. At the next Conference, held in January 1916, a resolution urged the government to include women in its special register to be introduced for the post-war elections, and the Executive Committee to press the matter. An opportunity soon arose. In the summer of 1916, ginger groups of the Conservative and Liberal Parties demanded a revision of the registration law to enable soldiers and sailors in the armed forces, perhaps from the age of 18, to vote in Parliamentary elections. Marion Phillips, the Editor of *Labour Woman,* stressed the anomalies and injustices such a measure would give rise to and pointed out that: 'For a nation fighting against the domination of a great military power. . .to establish a military qualification for the exercise of the vote would be to contradict the whole intention of the people.'[25]

She was right to draw attention to the dangers of a military qualification for the franchise. In a later debate in the House of Commons, opponents of women's suffrage argued that women, not having fought in the war and not possessing the physical force to defend the Empire, should remain voteless.[26]

In early October 1916, the Speaker's Conference, composed of representatives of all groups and parties in both Houses of Parliament, met in order to consider the post-war franchise. The suffrage societies were invited to give evidence. The procedure was rather like that for a Select Committee, the Conference sitting for several days each week. By the beginning of November, *Labour Woman* was able to report that eighteen out of the twenty-nine members were thought to favour women's suffrage,[27] but rumour had it that the Conference feared the effect of enfranchising at the same time significantly more women than men. It was thought that a higher age limit for women than for men would be imposed. Outside the Conference, more and more suffragists were supporting adult franchise.

At the end of 1916 Asquith, the anti-suffragist, was replaced by Lloyd George, the suffragist, as Prime Minister. Soon after, in February 1917, the Speaker's Conference recommended almost universal *man*hood suffrage; it accepted the principle of women's suffrage but proposed a minimum voting age of 30 or 35 and that the franchise should be based on the local government franchise but include the wives of voters. The effect of the age qualification, *Labour Woman* pointed out,[28] would be to exclude the majority of industrial women workers,* but the property qualification was more serious and would exclude many women workers who were neither wives nor occupiers.

A large Labour Conference, reported in the April issue of *Labour Woman*, agreed that legislation based on the recommendations of the Speaker's Conference should be supported provided women were included. The amendments of the women's organisations present strengthened this resolution to include women wage-earners and widows. The Miners' Federation wanted the Parliamentary Labour Party to support only a measure which would give the franchise to women on the same terms as to men. Regretfully and reluctantly many, including the WLL, voted against this resolution.

The Labour movement at this Conference committed itself to supporting a limited extension of the franchise to women, something which it had refused to do for more than a decade. Why did it change its position? Two circumstances had now changed. First, the principle of universal suffrage was now much more widely accepted. Second, the Prime Minister was no longer opposed to womanhood suffrage at any price. As long as Asquith was Prime Minister, it could be argued that even a limited extension of the franchise to women was not practical politics — and there is no point in compromising principles for nothing.

By June, the Bill based on the recommendations of the Speaker's Conference had been introduced under the 'Ten Minute Rule' and gone

---

* The majority of women at work at this period were young single women. The position now is completely different.

into Committee.* The Bill proposed to enfranchise women over 30 who were, furthermore, local government electors, the wives of local government electors or university graduates. The editor of *Labour Woman* commented:

> This means that if the Bill goes through we shall have to set to work again with the old agitation in order to bring in the younger women and to get the basis altered from occupation to residence.[29]

And so the Representation of the People Act, 1918, went through with manhood suffrage, but age and property or educational qualifications for women. The Lords did not, as some had feared, throw out the women's franchise clauses, but until the end of the debate the outcome was uncertain.

After the First World War, women in the Labour Party pressed for the extension of the franchise to women on the same terms as men. There were resolutions to this effect at most Annual Conferences before 1928. Women won both the Parliamentary and the local government franchise on the same terms as men in 1928, but universal suffrage in local government elections was not won until 1948.

This chapter has been devoted largely to the winning of the Parliamentary franchise because this struggle so vividly brings out the issues which confronted the Labour movement, but the WLL and the party were at all times concerned with the local government franchise and with the election of women to local government bodies. To recount fully the work put in by Labour women for women's civic rights in local government would require another long chapter. It is possible to point to some of the main differences in the two campaigns.

Issues did not arise in quite the same way, as it was not the local authorities but Parliament which controlled women's participation in local government. However, the WLL used the leverage it had to increase women's participation. The minutes of the Central London Branch meeting, for 7 November 1906, record that the following resolution from the National Executive was passed:

> That this meeting urges upon all the candidates put forward by the local Branches of the Labour Party for the Municipal Elections,

* The 'Ten Minute Rule' is the provision under which an MP can introduce a Private Member's Bill to the House in the first ten minutes of the business of the House following 'Question Time'.

Boards of Guardians etc. that members of the WLL are not
authorized to work for candidates who are not in favour of granting
equal rights of citizenship to women.[30]

Women's work at election times was much appreciated. The possibility
of its being withdrawn was therefore a sanction. When, after 1908,
women became eligible to serve on town and county councils, the
Central London Branch with the Women's Group of the Fabian Society
made determined and persistent efforts first to find seats for two of its
members, Margaret Bondfield and Dr Ethel Bentham, and then to get
them elected — efforts in which they were eventually successful. As and
when occasion offered, all the usual techniques of resolutions, and
letters and meetings were used to urge the cause of women's equal
participation in local government.

Local government was perhaps especially important in politicising
women, in making them aware of what could be done by their use of
political organisation and political power, whether it was to get a
playground, as in Throckley, or to run a milk depot as in Woolwich
(see Chapter 2). Much of the work of local government directly and
obviously affects women because local authorities provide services
which women need as a result of the roles which society traditionally
imposes on them. Fighting for the improvement of such services is of
direct value to husbands, children, elderly parents and others. Providing
such services costs money and liberates those who need and use them —
that is, women. Small wonder it took so long to obtain universal adult
suffrage in local government. This adds force to the perception of the
Labour movement that the extension of the Parliamentary franchise to
a limited number of women would not be swiftly followed by universal
suffrage. There was, in fact, a gap of 78 years between enfranchising
some women on a property qualification and granting adult suffrage in
local government.

The WLL, as a constitutional body, did not participate in militancy
and officially disapproved of illegal activities. For some members,
winning the franchise was the over-riding issue on which they wanted
to concentrate all their energies. For this reason, Ethel Annakin, the
wife of Philip Snowden, resigned from the Central London Branch of
the WLL in November 1906, as did Theresa Billington (later Billington-
Grieg). Mrs Despard did not resign but worked in the Women's Freedom
League — a militant body.[31] Mrs Pethick-Lawrence* was a member

of the Executive Committee of the Central London Branch in 1907 and all the Pankhursts were, for a time, members of the ILP.

Relations between the League and the Women's Social and Political Union were soured by the WSPU disruption of the meetings of Labour pro-suffrage candidates and members. By contrast, the constitutionalist suffrage societies, important in rallying non-militant opinion that was not Labour in political outlook, supported Labour candidates after 1913 as the only party which accepted women's suffrage as part of its official programme.

Hostility to the tactics of the militants was expressed openly only at the 1908 Annual Conference of the Labour Party. Harry Quelch of the London Trades Council said that the sober respectable Labour Party would not be impressed by:

> The Merry Andrew antics of these ladies who thought the best way to enhance the cause was to suppress the right of public meeting or of those others who had played the part of modern Andromedas in the prosaic surroundings of Downing Street.

Others thought differently. Victor Grayson MP (Independent Socialist) berated Mr Quelch for inconsistency in his revolutionary sentiments when he:

> Began to raise his revolutionary hands in holy horror because the ladies who had been fighting for the franchise had not been pretty, limp, submissive little things and asked beautifully for the vote.

Marion Phillips wrote a most respectful obituary of Emily Wilding Davison who, knowing the likely consequences of her act, ran into the path of the horses at the Derby in order to draw attention to the cause of votes for women, and was killed:[32] 'No nation can refuse respect to an act of such complete bravery. Every woman must feel her generous instincts stirred by the self-forgetfulness of this tragic figure.'

The WLL consistently and continuously opposed the Prisoners' Temporary Discharge for Ill Health Act, 1913. When suffragettes went to prison, they went on hunger strike. They were then forcibly fed with horrifying brutality, a process which they resisted. So that they should not die in the government's hands this Act, the 'Cat and Mouse' Act, authorised their release on licence, but rearrest as soon as they had recovered enough to be reimprisoned. In the first of a series of resolutions, the Executive Committee of the WLL called on the House of Commons to remedy the grievances of women rather than use coercion against militancy.[33] Such acts may seem timid compared with the heroism of some of the suffragettes. The Labour women worked on the tedious but necessary task of rousing the mass of women without which the franchise could not be won or used for securing necessary reforms when won. There was room for both tactics and a need for both tactics if women were to be free citizens.

The hostility to women's suffrage was noticed by Bertrand Russell when he stood as a Women's Suffrage candidate in the Parliamentary by-election in Wimbledon in 1907:

> It must be quite impossible for younger people to imagine the bitterness of the opposition to women's equality. When, in later years, I campaigned against the First World War, the popular opposition I encountered was not comparable to that which the suffragists met in 1907.

He goes on to describe the derisive shouts, the rowdyism, the rotten eggs and the rats let loose in public meetings which featured in that brief, arduous and unsuccessful campaign.[34] Bertrand Russell was not the only man to fight a Parliamentary election on a women's suffrage ticket. Thorley Smith had done so, also unsuccessfully, in 1905 as a Women's and Independent Labour candidate. He was supported in his campaign by the work and funds of the Women Textile and Other Workers' Representation Committee. The Wigan and District Trades Council withheld its support owing to the opposition of the miners.[35] George Lansbury's unsuccessful campaign in Bow and Bromley in 1912 is well known.

Russell was perhaps right in his view that 'the savagery of the males who were threatened with loss of supremacy was intelligible'.[36] But such an attitude is not compatible with Labour or Socialist principles, which are concerned with improving the position both of men and of women.

To improve the position of any women in substance as distinct from by way of exception to a general rule requires the improvement of the position of *all* women. Labour's universalist beliefs, though not always applied in practice by all members of the Labour movement, assist this understanding: I'm not all right, Jill, unless you are too. These principles, when applied to the suffrage, meant a universalist rather than a thin-end-of-the-wedge approach.

The leverage which Labour women could exert by giving or

withholding help for candidates who supported or failed to support women's suffrage has already been discussed as has the sheer numerical importance of giving the vote to all working women, whether working in the home or in paid employment. Women of other parties enjoyed the first of those advantages, but it is not clear that they used it. The response of the Conservative and Liberal women's organisations to the 1908 letter to Mr Asquith has been mentioned; nor do they appear to have been able or willing to use the machinery of their parties to support the claims of women as fully as Labour women did. Here the Labour women had one unmatched asset: the principles of the Labour Party did not permit of any argument about the principle of equal citizenship for all men and women.

The Labour Party has been criticised for its universalist position and hostility to the thin-end-of-the-wedge tactics, for example, by Constance Rover. Given Asquith's hostility, it seems a fair conclusion that no measure for women's suffrage could be successful as long as he was Prime Minister. Therefore, the only hope of the constitutionalist was to link women's suffrage with the extension of male suffrage, to which he was not so opposed, so that the one would not be obtainable without the other. Indeed, it was the Labour Party's official commitment to this policy which won for it the active support of the constitutionalist suffrage societies. The WSPU's militant tactics could be seen as an attempt to force the majority of the Liberal Party, who were, or claimed to be, sympathetic to women's suffrage, to force Asquith to change his policy or alternatively to force him out of office. If, as a result of the intervention of the militant suffragettes, the Liberal Party lost by-elections and general elections, Asquith would cease to be an acceptable leader able to carry through the other measures which the party wanted. Both tactics are comprehensible, but constitutionalists will prefer that of the Labour Party.

Notes

1. Neal Blewett, 'The Franchise in the United Kingdom, 1885-1918', *Past and Present*, (32), December 1965, p.31.
2. Constance Rover, *Women's Suffrage and Party Politics in Britain, 1866-1914*, London: Routledge and Kegan Paul, 1967, pp.23-4.
3. Report from Mrs L.E. Simm, Sept.1908 (WLL/90), Labour Party Library.
4. Report from Mrs L.E. Simm, May 1908 (WLL/93 ii), Labour Party Library.
5. Letter to Mrs Mary Middleton, 29 July 1908 (WLL/86), Labour Party Library.
6. Letter from Mrs L.E. Simm to Mrs Mary Middleton, 11 June 1908 (WLL/81), Labour Party Library.

7. R.S. Neale, 'Working Class Women and Women's Suffrage', *Class and Ideology in the Nineteenth Century,* London: Routledge and Kegan Paul, 1972, pp.153-4.
8. WLL/84 i, Labour Party Library.
9. WLL/128-31.
10. Quoted by Rover, *Women's Suffrage,* p.113.
11. *Minutes,* Executive Committee, 19 October 1910.
12. *WLL Annual Report,* 1907.
13. *Report of the WLL delegates to the Labour Party Conference,* 1912.
14. *Annual Conference Report,* 1913, p.11.
15. *Report of Executive Committee of the Labour Party to the Annual Conference,* 1913, p.16.
16. The *League Leaflet,* No.16, April 1912, Labour Party Library.
17. General Purposes Committee meeting, 4 October 1912.
18. The *League Leaflet,* No.24, December 1912, Labour Party Library.
19. The *League Leaflet,* No.25, January 1913, Labour Party Library.
20. *Minutes* of General Purposes Committee, 7 February 1913.
21. *Minutes* of Executive Committee, 4 April 1913.
22. Ibid.
23. *Annual Report,* 1914, p.47.
24. *Report of Conference Delegates, Report of Annual Conference,* 1914, p.6.
25. *Labour Woman,* July 1916, p.30, Labour Party Library.
26. *Labour Woman,* July 1917, p.172, Labour Party Library.
27. David Morgan, *Suffragists and Liberals,* Oxford: Basil Blackwell, 1975, pp.140-45.
28. March 1917, p.121, Labour Party Library.
29. June 1917, p.159, Labour Party Library.
30. *Minutes,* Central London Branch, 7 November 1906.
31. *Minutes,* Central London Branch, Executive Committee, 3 December 1906, 2 January 1907.
32. *Labour Woman,* July 1913, p.45, Labour Party Library.
33. *Minutes,* 4 April 1913.
34. Bertrand Russell, *The Autobiography of Bertrand Russell 1872-1914,* London: Allen and Unwin, 1967, pp.153-4.
35. Neale, 'Working Class Women', p.154.
36. Ibid., p.155.

4 LABOUR WOMEN AND INTERNATIONALISM

Mary Walker

In Britain towards the end of the nineteenth century, a few women had contact with like-minded radical women in Europe and in Australia but such contacts were on a personal level and there was no real structure for an exchange of views at regular international meetings. Although it is difficult to put a date on the true beginnings, the first account of a real contact occurred at the 1908 Conference of the Women's Labour League in a report of the preceding year.[1] A one day conference had been held on a Saturday in August 1907 in Stuttgart prior to a full meeting of the International and Trade Union Conference. The Women's Labour League were represented at this historic conference by Margaret MacDonald and Mary Macpherson and it was in Stuttgart that the International Socialist Women's Committee was founded. The International Socialist Women's Bureau was headed by Clara Zetkin* from Germany as secretary and Margaret Smith of Birmingham was confirmed at the 1908 WLL Conference as correspondent for the League with the International Bureau.

Delegates at the Stuttgart Conference drew great encouragement from their meeting with comrades from other countries and the need to intensify the fight for the vote emerged as the conference's main objective.

Regular contacts were established between the International Secretariat and the Executive of the WLL and news of activities of socialist women in Europe became a regular feature at meetings. A second international conference was held in Copenhagen on 26 and 27 August 1910[2] and again the need to strengthen the campaign for the vote was in the forefront of delegates' minds. The main outcome of this conference was the introduction of an annual women's day to further propaganda for the vote. The first International Socialist Women's Day was held on 19 March 1911 in the Flower Hall in Vienna with the slogan 'Equal rights for men and women'. The *League Leaflet* carried various commemorative messages and the event seemed to cement the first phase of international contacts between the pioneers of the women's Labour movement.[3]

With the coming of war in Europe the difficult task of maintaining international contacts was accomplished mainly through correspondence and the occasional visit to London of European socialist women. The *League Leaflet* became *Labour Woman* in May 1913 and this valuable publication served to keep British Labour women informed of the activities of comrades in the International socialist women's movement. The first issue printed a song of fellowship for May Day dedicated 'To all men and women who work' and there were notes from Mary Macpherson who was now international correspondent of the League. In the same issue there were further reports on the Finnish General Election of 1913, when one tenth of the elected MPs were women, and an article on pit head baths in France, Belgium and Germany by Jennie Baker. As if to reflect on the importance of the now well-established international contacts Jennie Baker wrote in March 1914 that 'the more we hear of the conditions and difficulties of working women in other countries, the more we realise that women have the same fight to wage all the world over'.

As the days grew darker in Europe, arms expenditure and the plight of women in other countries were frequently reported and commented upon. The war broke direct ties between socialist women and news was scarce. But the Women's International Council printed a message from the 'Working Women of Great Britain to sisters of other nations' signed by the Chairman, Marion Phillips and the Secretary, Mary Longman and in January 1915 a reply from German women signed by Clara Zetkin was printed. It is interesting that this reply reached London via Holland, Norway and Sweden.

During 1915 *Labour Woman* included a profile of Clara Zetkin, news of the sentence passed on Rosa Luxemburg,* and the arrest and then the release of Comrade Zetkin accompanied by a brief personal message of sympathy on the death of Keir Hardie. Continuing reports in the series 'Our Sisters Abroad'[4] emphasised the value of contact so that socialist women could lay plans when the war ended. Clara Zetkin wrote to the League and asked them to prepare information on the position of women in industry after the war with the idea of a conference in mind.

When peace came, the immediate post-war period was dominated by women's demand for the vote and there was less discussion of international affairs in *Labour Woman* or at Labour meetings in Britain. The established contacts remained between the International Committee and the League's Executive and, after 1918, with women's organisations in the Labour Party; but the close and personal links of the war years gave way to a greater emphasis on home affairs and there was a more formal, structured approach to international relations.

The major international event after the war was the Washington Conference of 1919. The Standing Joint Committee of International Women's Organisations published in *Labour Woman* a list of the demands with which Labour women had been identified and which they wanted discussed. The list included an end to sweated labour in all countries; hours of work and night work; health conditions in factories and workshops; child labour; industrial disease; employment of women in certain trades; and immigration and coloured labour.[5]

When it was announced that an annual conference would be held within the framework of the League of Nations to deal with labour legislation, Labour women saw their chance to press their views on the British Government. Representation was to be by four delegates from each country in the League of Nations – two government delegates and one delegate each from employers and workers. In addition delegates could be accompanied by advisers with a maximum of two for each item on the agenda. To quote the official provision 'when questions specially affecting women are to be considered by the Conference one at least of the advisers should be a woman'. This gave Labour women an added incentive to press for proper representation and they were even more keen to do so when the agenda was published. This covered five main items:

1. The eight hour day or a forty-eight hour week.
2. Problems of unemployment.
3. Women's employment.
4. Employment of children.
5. Extension of prohibition of night work for women and an end to the use of white phosphorus in the manufacture of matches.

The Standing Joint Committee joined the Labour women's organisation at a meeting in Caxton Hall on 4 September 1919 to decide 'how best to organise themselves so that the voices of women are heard in the deliberation of the League of Nations'. The object was to get women advisers included in the UK delegation and the two government delegates and the Prime Minister were told quite clearly what was expected of them. After discussions it was finally agreed that Margaret

Bondfield and Mary Macarthur would be included among the advisers. A pamphlet entitled *Labour women and international legislation* was produced and three SJC members contributed. Gertrude Tuckwell wrote on *Women's Employment,* Marion Phillips dealt with the employment of children and Susan Lawrence was asked to give her ideas on the prevention of unemployment. The pamphlet was widely read by delegates to the Washington Conference and by a conference of working women called by the National Women's Trade Union League of America. Margaret Bondfield and Mary Macarthur were also appointed as delegates to this conference, which allowed for an exchange of views on a wide range of subjects.

Both women were able to speak and vote at the Conference, as was Constance Smith who was also included in the Washington delegation as a government adviser. The decisions arrived at were to prove important in negotiating for Labour and trade union women in Great Britain and were constant reminders in the 1920s of the value of international decisions on labour legislation.

A general proposal was adopted limiting hours of work to forty-eight per week and eight hours per day with clauses limiting overtime. The Women's Conference went further and passed a resolution advocating a forty-four hour week. On the question of employing women before and after child-birth, it was agreed that women should not be allowed to work for the six weeks before birth and that maternity benefit should be paid. The details of an acceptable maternity scheme caused a great deal of controversy and the final agreed statement was a compromise.

On the matter of employing women at night, a resolution laid down the general principle that all night work should be forbidden; the use of white phosphorus in the manufacture of matches should be prohibited and the minimum age for the employment of children should be fixed at 14.

Until 1923 working women used the contacts made at both the Washington Conference and the American Women's Conference to further their aims on the international front. A second working women's conference was held in October 1921 the week before the International Labour Congress. Margaret Bondfield, Susan Lawrence and Marion Phillips were the British representatives. At this conference total disarmament was the main theme. Other topics included unemployment and the famine in Russia.

1923-24 were also important to British Labour women because of the appointment by the Labour Prime Minister, J.R. MacDonald, of the first British woman delegate to the League of Nations itself. She was Mrs H.M. Swanwick* and she attended the Geneva sessions as a substitute delegate. Mrs Swanwick had been an ardent and lifelong supporter of women's suffrage and student of international affairs. She was widely known for her work in the Labour movement and the Women's International League for Peace and Freedom. In 1929 when Ramsay MacDonald was again Prime Minister he followed up his earlier initiative by appointing Mrs Swanwick and Mrs Mary Hamilton, MP as full delegates to the meetings of the League of Nations in 1930.

The third meeting of international working women took place in Vienna in August 1923. Britain was represented by a dozen delegates from the TUC, various individual unions and the Labour Party. But the International Federation of Working Women only operated effectively from 1919-23 and only developed on the trade union side because of the constant financial difficulties faced in running an international organisation. Later it was absorbed into the International Federation of Trade Unions based in Amsterdam and a women's advisory committee met at regular intervals to sustain the interest and concern for the problems of working women.

The story of the international activity of Labour women entered another phase when the earlier international contacts were renewed. British Labour women were involved in international meetings in Bern in 1920 and in Berlin two years later but it was not until the formation of the Labour and Socialist International in 1923 that Labour women attended in strength. An international conference of Labour and Socialist women was held on 20 May 1923 in Hamburg, attended by eighty women from twenty-one countries. Britain was represented by Dr Ethel Bentham, Susan Lawrence and Mrs Sidney Webb: Marion Phillips attended on behalf of the International Federation of Working Women. Lucy Cox (later Lucy Middleton) was there as a fraternal delegate from the ILP. There was a wide ranging agenda but the most important question discussed was future organisation. The general view emerged that no permanent organisation of international Labour and Socialist women was desirable but that efforts should be made to get a woman representative on the Executive of the Bureau of the LSI.

British Labour women thought differently. They thought that an annual international conference was important, and that the necessary organisation should be established. At the Labour Women's Conference in 1925, Katharine Glasier urged British representatives to press for an annual international conference of women delegates from all bodies.

Opinions elsewhere changed and a conference was called in Marseilles
in August 1925. The British delegation consisted of Mrs Harrison Bell,*
Mrs Agnes Dollan* and Marion Phillips of the Labour Party, and
Margaret Bondfield, Miss Dorothy Jewson* and Miss Hinnie Pallister
of the ILP. Marion Phillips was chosen as one of the five Presidents of
the Marseilles Conference.[6] The women's conference agreed certain
procedures which were endorsed by the LSI and from the British point
of view the International Department of the Labour Party cooperated
very closely with Marion Phillips, the party's chief woman officer.

Although details have changed over the years, it is interesting to note
how little the structure and organisation has changed. The International
Advisory Committee of Women was to meet at least once a year and it
was to advise the LSI 'about the aims and methods of Socialist women
in various countries' and to organise an international conference to be
called at the same time as the International Congress. On the basis of
membership, the Executive Committee, or Bureau, consisted of Britain,
Germany, Austria and Belgium. The draft constitution was circulated,
discussions were held and a meeting took place in Brussels in early
December 1926.[7] Britain was represented by Susan Lawrence and
Agnes Dollan with Marion Phillips as a fraternal delegate. British women
were a little disappointed at the slowness of achieving international
contact and were a bit apprehensive at its formalised structure, but
Labour Woman published the constitution of the new international
body in January 1927 and reported that British Labour women had
three representatives on the Executive and one on the Bureau. Susan
Lawrence was the first Bureau member for Britain and the other
representatives were Agnes Dollan and Dorothy Jewson (ILP).

The first major event held by the International Advisory Committee
was a conference in Brussels in August 1928. An impressive number of
95 delegates attended from 16 countries and 11 fraternal delegates
were welcomed. The five Labour Party delegates were Susan Lawrence,
Agnes Dollan, Marion Phillips, Mrs Harrison Bell and Mrs Bell Richards
with Dorothy Jewson present for the ILP. The agenda was as follows:

1. Socialist demands including concern for:
   (a)   mothers and children;
   (b)   care of the sick, crippled and aged;
   (c)   women in industry.
2. Tendencies to mobilise women for war service.

The 1928 Brussels Conference was interesting because Susan Lawrence

and Agnes Dollan both submitted statements which became part of a
resolution adopted by the Conference. Susan Lawrence wrote and spoke
about the problem of mothers and children and proposed the
establishment of a free medical and nursing service for all mothers
before, during and after the birth of their children; maternity payment;
domestic help at the period of child-birth and free milk for mothers
and babies. Her other major proposal remains unachieved even fifty
years later — she demanded open air day nurseries for children from
2-6 years as part of the general education system. Agnes Dollan dealt
with the socialist approach to the care of the sick, crippled, invalid and
the aged and among other things proposed an adequate retirement
pension.

The International Advisory Committee was by now well established.
Susan Lawrence resigned from the Bureau and her place was taken by
Jennie Adamson. The Executive launched a campaign to secure the
right to vote and the eligibility of women as candidates in France,
Belgium and Switzerland and well-organised meetings were held in
those countries.

The next international women's conference was held in Vienna on
23 to 24 July 1931, before the LSI Congress. The Labour Party
delegates were Jennie Adamson*, Mrs Ayrton Gould*, Marion Phillips,
Mrs Bell Richards, Mrs Marie Anderson and Miss Mary Carlin* of the
Transport and General Workers' Union. The Conference theme was
'Women in the economic system' and the agenda was as follows:

1. Women in industry and commerce.
      (Speaker: Fanni Blatny — Czechoslovakia)
2. Women in Agriculture.
      (Speaker: Elizabeth Ribbins-Peletier — Holland)
3. Women in the Home.
   (a)   The Housewife;
            (Speaker: Isabelle Blume — Belgium)
   (b)   Domestic workers.
            (Speaker: Jennie Adamson — Great Britain)

The international activity of the International Advisory Committee
continued but political events in Europe, and, in particular, the rise of
fascism in Germany and Austria heralded the end of another phase.
The watershed was 1931; international contacts and activity continued
but to a more limited degree and it was not until the early 1950s with
the establishment of the International Council of Social Democratic

Women that the same level of activity enjoyed between 1926 and 1931 occurred again.

Despite the difficulties the International Advisory Committee continued its work. A project for a study week approved in 1931 was finally held in 1936 in Brussels. The theme was 'Women and Economic and Political Democracy' and eight lectures were given including one from Susan Lawrence on parliamentary institutions.

The years of the Second World War became a period when the relations of socialist women internationally would seem to have been completely severed. Formal ties were obviously impossible. Conferences and correspondence out of the question. But, in fact, in their place informal contacts were made and maintained in London and, under the stress of war, were perhaps as close, if not closer, than in any period before or since. So true internationalism was preserved throughout.

Nazism and the brutalities associated with it, brought many women comrades from Europe to seek refuge in Britain. Some had come before the war started: many others after its beginning. Women, some of whose names had been known for years, came to live in London — Fanni Blatny* of Czechoslovakia, Marthe Louis-Levy* of France, Isobel Blume* and Lucia de Brouckère* of Belgium, Marianne Pollak* and Emmy Freundlich* of Austria, Lidia Ciolkosz* of Poland, Maria Treves* of Italy, and Herta Gotthelf* of Germany (afterwards Chief Woman Officer of the West German SPD), to mention only a few.

At first they were lonely and isolated, but a tea party organised by the Labour Party Secretary's wife in her home, brought together many of them, from both Allied and enemy countries. From that gathering, a London International Socialist Group was formed and met as frequently as could conveniently be arranged. They discussed, not so much the war, but the problems they would face and the things they planned to do when the war was over.

The group consisted of colleagues from ten different countries. Dora Segall was the secretary and the Chair was taken by representatives of the ten nations in rotation. Never has there been a warmer and closer internationalism than in that *ad hoc* Women's International in London.

There may sometimes have been difficulties and errors, but, looking back over seventy years of service, the Labour Women's Movement can say with pride that they have lived up to the standard set for them by their first President, Margaret MacDonald, when she told the inaugural Conference at Leicester in June 1906, that 'if the Labour Women's Movement is to be anything, it must be international'.

The invasion of Austria and the rise of fascism saw the beginning of the end of organised international contact between women in Europe. With the collapse of the Labour and Socialist International in 1940, only the British, Swedish and Swiss parties survived.

The immediate post-war period was a time for rebuilding most socialist parties from the ashes of the war years. The official vehicle of contact was the International Socialist Conference based in London and gradually, as trust grew between comrades, activities were begun.

In June 1948 representatives of women socialists came from all over Europe to the first post-war Women's International Conference in Vienna. Alice Bacon spoke on the work of the United Nations and there followed conferences at Frankfurt, Milan and Stockholm. The Stockholm Conference of 1953 was in many ways a turning point following the setting up of the Socialist International in 1951 and two years later at the next Women's International Conference in London, the International Council of Social Democratic Women was established.

The last twenty years of international activity are well known to many women members of the Labour Party and that is why the emphasis in this chapter has been on the early pioneering years of British Labour women in the field of international endeavour. But there have been important changes in the international work of Labour women and the principles or 'statutes' of ICSDW laid down in 1955 hold the key to these changes.

For among other things, the 'statutes' lay down that the ICSDW should study questions concerning the work and status of women and the welfare of children and family life and should assist in promoting wider knowledge among women of the work of the United Nations and other international agencies on such questions. Further, its declared programme is mainly concentrated on educational activities 'to promote the full partnership of men and women in all fields and to raise the status of women in developing countries'.

Before 1955 international activity was concentrated in Europe; a new departure was the recognition given by socialist women to the struggles of women in Asia, Africa and Latin America. Socialist women from these countries have been drawn into the activities of ICSDW, scholarships have been established to give valuable training in community development and in other fields and individual women's organisations have raised money for specific projects. British Labour women have played their full part in this expanding field of work and an international fund exists for this purpose.

Conferences too have changed. There are regular triennial

conferences to discuss the important topics facing Labour and socialist women but additional conferences and seminars have been added to ICSDW's programme. Recent activities have included a study project in East Africa in 1968 when Kenya and Madagascar were visited; valuable contacts were made at a conference on 'The contribution of women to the development of the community' in Madagascar with women from many African countries.

Another international seminar was held in Eastbourne in 1969 which women from Asia, Africa and Latin America attended alongside the European participants. An international seminar in Israel in 1970 and one in Singapore the following year were held for the express purpose of extending ICSDW's programme to women from developing countries.

The other new area of activity has been within the United Nations and its family. ICSDW has consultative status as a non-governmental organisation with the Economic and Social Council (ECOSOC) of the UN and with UNESCO and it is also interested in the work of the ILO. This international aspect has provided a useful guide to the programme of ICSDW in developing countries and has added a new dimension to its work in which British Labour women have been fully involved.

Finally we come to the seventies and, should we need further proof of the continuing interest and involvement in international affairs and activity, they can be found both in the special contribution Labour women made to International Women's Year in 1975 and in their constant discussion of international problems at both regular meetings and periodic conferences.

Notes

1. *Annual Report, Women's Labour League 1909,* p.6, Labour Party Library.
2. *Annual Report, Women's Labour League 1911,* p.9, Labour Party Library.
3. The *League Leaflet* (International notes) April 1911, p.4, Labour Party Library.
4. *Labour Woman,* January 1915, p.169, Labour Party Library.
5. *Labour Woman* (an international issue), January 1915, Labour Party Library.
6. *Labour Woman,* August 1925, p.135, and September 1925, p.150, Labour
   Party Library.
7. *Labour Woman,* January 1927, pp.1, 9, and 14, Labour Party Library.

5 EARLY YEARS IN THE TRADE UNIONS

Dame Anne Godwin

While the Women's Labour League was developing its organisation, experimenting in social reforms and lending its support both in the struggle for franchise and the establishment of international socialist contacts, there were two other areas of public life — the trade union and consumer cooperation — where like-minded women had been working valiantly over an even longer period for the establishment of women's organisations, the free expression of their views and the solution to their problems. Indeed, in both of these fields, trade unionism and cooperation, women were, in fact, active well before the organisation of Labour women, politically, had started.

This chapter and the next seek to tell the story of the developments of women's work in these two important spheres of working-class organisation.

Throughout the nineteenth century the economic position of women workers was one of almost unrelieved poverty and deprivation. Trade union organisation had succeeded during the century in establishing standards for craft workers but except in the textile industries, women's occupations were mainly unskilled, with conditions and wages that had earned for them the ugly designation of 'sweating'. In 1890 a committee of the House of Lords defined sweating as 'earnings barely sufficient to sustain existence; hours of labour such as to make the lives of the workers periods of almost ceaseless toil, hard and unlovely to the last degree'. Against such a background, with little support from organised male workers, it is not surprising that trade unionism failed to establish itself. A number of women's organisations appeared and disappeared throughout the century. Small, local and with little or no bargaining power, they lacked both experience and advice. One woman decided to find a remedy.

Emma Paterson (Emma Ann Smith) has been described as middle class and in the sense that she never experienced acute poverty or hardship, the designation is correct. But she was a working woman all her short life, starting as assistant secretary to the Working Men's Club and Institute Union, when she was still only eighteen years of age. Four years later she became secretary to the Women's Suffrage Society and from these experiences she emerged a champion of oppressed women, an equalitarian and an ardent feminist. She enlisted the help of a group of middle-class men and women (Lady Dilke, then Mrs Mark Patterson, among them), and in 1874 the Women's Protection and Provident League was formed to promote the formation of women's societies and provide a centre for them.

When Mrs Patterson died in 1886 at the early age of 38, there were thirty affiliated societies. In the main they were small and depended too much on one dominant personality. There was Mrs Ellis, who formed a Union of Women Weavers, ran a ten-week strike, was victimised and faded out with the union; Mrs Mason who stirred the Leicester Hosiery Women's Union to life, became the first woman to serve on a Trades Council, attended the TUC in 1877 and died young, the union dying with her; and Miss Whyte, more fortunate, whose Bookbinders' Union survived until 1913. There were others, notably Miss Emily Faithfull, who not only organised women in the printing trades but established a place of employment for them, the Victoria Press, staffed entirely by women.

In 1875, Emma Paterson breached the all-male trade union citadel, the Trades Union Congress, and thereafter she attended annual congresses until her death, accompanied by a representative of her small Societies. They were received with courtesy in spite of her uncompromising attitude to equalitarian questions. At times she seemed more feminist than trade unionist, as when she opposed protective legislation on the grounds that it was degrading to women to be classified with children and, more realistically, that it would reduce their earning power. When she secured in 1884 the passing by Congress of a resolution 'that the franchise should be extended to women on the same grounds as men' it is doubtful whether she approved of the reasoning of the woman delegate who claimed that single women and widows had a right to the vote as compensation for not having a husband!

She was an advanced thinker on women's questions and bridged the years to the twentieth century when she persuaded the TUC to include women in their request for working men to be appointed as factory inspectors. Vera Chinn, appointed in 1930, was the first woman inspector with experience of working life.

When Mrs Paterson died, the League continued giving to women's organisations a firm central base. It was not great in her time but it was the creator of great things. As far as possible and consistent with her strong convictions, her policy was to conciliate and cooperate with the unions, a policy continued by her successor, Lady Dilke.

Such an approach was impossible for their ardent contemporary, Annie Besant (Annie Woods). 'Gently born', as she herself expressed it, in 1847, her life had been a battlefield from her early twenties, when she abandoned early piety for bellicose atheism and thence moved to socialism, fighting her causes 'joyously and defiantly. . .a perpetual carrying of the fiery cross'.[1] When in 1888 the match-makers in the East End of London, in their precipitous strike, turned to her for help, her response was immediate.

She had in truth been the catalyst in the situation. She was co-editing with W.T. Stead a journal called the *Link* (the *Torch*) brought into being to cast a light into dark places and to expose. The light shone on a great match-making factory where the women workers were not only scandalously paid – the weekly pay might be as much as eight shillings or as low as five shillings – but exposed to a system of fines and deductions; exposed too to the dangers of a disgusting facial disease known as 'phossy jaw'. The employers tried to coerce the women into signing a repudiation of the *Link* accusations, dismissed those who refused and so precipitated one of the most famous strikes in trade union history. The women were unorganised, unsupported and penniless. Annie Besant rallied her socialist friends – Bernard Shaw among them – to rouse public opinion, she collected funds, fed the strikers and very wisely enlisted the experienced Trade Unionists of the London Trades Council to secure a settlement entirely favourable to the women. When all was settled she established and ran a Matchmakers' Union but it proved as impermanent as other women's unions when her influence was withdrawn.

Her exit from trade unionism was as stormy as her entrance. That same year a long planned international Trade Union Conference was held. Annie Besant attended and infuriated her fellow British delegates by attacking them in an international assembly for leaving her 'a woman of the middle class' to organise the unskilled women.[2]

Lady Dilke, associated with the Women's Protection and Provident League from its inception, took over the Presidency in 1886 on the death of Emma Paterson. She was a woman of great culture, deeply religious and concerned with the social problems of the day, particularly those of working women. For seventeen years, until her death in 1904, she fostered and promoted the aims of the League (renamed the Women's Trade Union League). She carefully cultivated the goodwill of the Trades Union Congress and from 1889 onwards regularly attended the Annual meetings. The meeting for women held in association with the Congress, which she established, continues to this day. Above all she took care to expand the direct links between the League and the unions catering for women. The Textile Unions and the Shop Assistants' Union had been early associates; now she turned her attention to the new General Unions, formed since the match-makers strike, catering for unskilled workers, and open to women from their inception.

It was her husband, Sir Charles Dilke MP, described by J.J. Mallon as the genuine forerunner of the Labour Party, who first tried to establish a legal basis for wages through his Wages Boards Bills. He introduced them annually from 1900 onwards, and though all were lost they served to educate public opinion and to pave the way for further action, and eventual success.

Under Lady Dilke's guidance the League had strengthened its position inside the unions and was poised and ready for what was probably her greatest service to women, the appointment as Secretary in 1903 of Mary Macarthur. The appointment was made on the recommendation of Gertrude Tuckwell and Margaret Bondfield. Both were experienced in the work of the League and the ways of the trade unions.

Gertrude Tuckwell had been honorary secretary to the League since 1893, acting at the same time as secretary to her aunt, Lady Dilke. She was born in 1860, her father was a radical clergyman, and deeply concerned at the condition of the agricultural worker. 'I was brought up', she said, 'in an atmosphere of social reform'. In 1883 she came to London and worked as an elementary school teacher in a poor quarter of Chelsea and when her aunt died she succeeded as President of the League.

Margaret Bondfield was already a national figure, with a harsh experience of the realities of a working woman's life behind her. From a country background and a happy family life — she was born in Chard, Somerset, in 1873 — she had gone into shop work in her early teens, moving from Chard to Brighton and thence to London, under the 'living in' system. She described the system in her evidence to the Truck Committee in 1907. As a girl in her teens, she said, she had shared a room with, 'a woman of mature age who led a life of a most undesirable kind. . . There was another girl in the same room who was suffering from consumption. I was in that house for three years and could have been out any night. . .without the firm knowing anything about it.' The Shop Act of 1892 laid down a maximum of seventy-four hours as a working week for those under 18 but eighty hours, she said, were general. She joined the Shop Assistants' Union and in 1896, represented the London membership at the Annual Conference, the only woman in the assembly. In 1898 she was appointed a full-time official of the Union with the title of assistant secretary and a salary of £2 a week, and in 1899 she found herself again the only woman at a trade union assembly, the Annual Conference of the TUC. Her standing in the Union was high when she met Mary Macarthur at the Union Conference in 1902 and recognised in her the force that moves mountains.

'She was' said Gertrude Tuckwell, 'a bright light that burnt itself out too soon.' Margaret Bondfield wrote: 'she had a panting breathless life sustained with unfaltering nerve, courage and determination.' Mary Agnes Hamilton, her biographer, sums up: 'she had the gift, without which other organising qualities are nothing. . .of lighting in other minds sparks from the flame that glowed in her own.'

At the age of 22 she had left the comfort and security of a middle-class home – her father was a prosperous draper in Ayr – and was converted to trade unionism and later to socialism through membership of the Shop Assistants' Union. The Women's Trade Union League was a perfect medium for the development of her gifts: she would not have survived the straitjacket of an orthodox trade union.

The League had continued through the years the policy established by Emma Paterson, of giving help to those unions with women in membership, and of setting up independent women's societies where no organisation existed. After three years of intense activity, Mary Macarthur faced squarely the failure of this policy. She had travelled the country, fostering resistance to low wages and establishing little local societies, and had met with considerable success. She realised that the success was short-lived. There were no roots to those local organisations; no stability in unions formed in a flurry of industrial unrest. She had brought 12,000 new members into the League and measured against the size of the problem, it was nothing. Her answer was to form a central union for women, on the lines of the new general unions of unskilled workers, with central funds and local branches fully under central control. Gertrude Tuckwell agreed and in 1906 the National Federation of Women Workers was set up. After six months it had 2,000 direct members organised in 17 branches, and though thereafter exact membership figures were difficult to obtain – Mary had a habit of anticipating increases – there was no doubt as to the influence of the new organisation. Wherever there was trouble for women workers, or a question concerning them to be asked or answered, in the House of Commons or the Press, the Federation was available. 'They were no more than a stage army', wrote

J.J. Mallon, 'But they said they represented the working women of
Great Britain and they made so much noise that they came to be
believed.' To those who had seen the apathy and acquiescence that
poverty had imposed on so many women, a stage army was better
than no army and any noise was better than none.

Mary used every instrument that came to her hand. She sought her
audiences wherever they were to be found, standing on a kitchen chair
outside factory gates or lecturing fashionable ladies in a London
drawing room. Her magnetic personality brought hope to poverty-
stricken women wherever she went.

The task of organising and negotiating for low paid factory workers
was very great but the real problem lay with those women working in
isolation in their own homes. Here among the makers of baby wear and
women's wear, lace and artificial flowers, the button makers and hook
and eye carders was sweating of a wide-spread character, a very sink of
poverty. A week's work might bring in no more than four or five
shillings. John Galsworthy, taken to see for himself the horrors of the
system, broke down and wept.[3]

Mary was convinced that a minimum rate established by law was the
only answer and she found a strong ally in A.G. Gardiner, editor of the
Daily News, the liberal 'cocoa' newspaper. He ran a series of articles of
exposure and followed this up by promoting in 1906 a Sweated Trades
Exhibition, a bazaar belonging to Dante's inferno'.[4] The interest of
royalty was secured and Princess Henry of Battenburg opened the
display. There was set out the work performed, the wages received,
the pitiful household budgets, the poor work places. 30,000 people
visited the exhibition before it moved from London to the provinces.
The practical result of this assault on the sensibility of the public was
the setting up of an influential League for the Abolition of Sweating.

Mary was an active member of the Anti-Sweating League and when
J.J. Mallon joined the committee, with his wealth of knowledge, the
direction of its policy was assured. It was agreed that there must be
legislation to enforce minimum rates in sweated occupations, with
wages boards as the instrument. It needed all Mary's powerful
personality to win the Unions over to statutory wage fixing even on a
limited scale.

The 1906 General Election established the Labour Party as a
parliamentary force and the new Members pressed for and secured a
Select Committee to enquire into sweating, but its terms of reference
were narrow, and confined to home working. This was disappointing
for the experience of the Federation was that over major areas of

factory employment, sweating of women workers was rife. A Board of Trade enquiry held in 1906 produced a figure of twelve shillings per week as an average rate for women; but the figure was suspect since the cooperation of employers was voluntary and bad employers do not make voluntary returns to government departments. Even on the basis of the figures received, Sydney Webb found the conclusions unsatisfactory. There were factors such as short-time working and sickness which in his view reduced the average to 10s10½d.

Mary took full advantage of the setting up of the Select Committee and did not hesitate to go outside the terms of reference. Undoubtedly she was a woman to whom things happened. Some time previously she had spent six weeks in hospital with diphtheria, contracted in a slum house, from a woman engaged in lace-trimming baby clothes by the dozen, on a wage of one penny per garment. This incident combined with the great weight of evidence she produced made her the star witness. The Select Committee recommended the setting up of Wages Boards and in 1909 Winston Churchill, President of the Board of Trade, piloted a Bill through the House that became the first Trade Boards Act. Only four Boards were set up and the first statutory wages — 2½d to 2¾d per hour — were very low. but even so they represented substantial increases for thousands of women. Above all, the principle was established. It is in no sense derogatory to the great work of J.J. Mallon to state that credit for the establishment of the system rests squarely on the shoulders of Mary Macarthur and her unfailing supporter Gertrude Tuckwell, who together supplied the drive, the imagination and persistence to turn an idea into a fact. At the outbreak of war in 1914 there were thirteen Boards in operation and the number reached 41 by the mid-1920s.

But at the time a further great battle had to be fought. Chainmaking, notorious in the Black Country for low wages for women, was one of the four Boards first set up and, in May 1910, a rate of 2½d per hour was fixed. This meant nothing to the men. They had been organised by an able local leader, Tom Fitch, into a strong union and tolerable rates and conditions had been secured. The situation of the women was very different. They worked for the most part on small forges set up in sheds and outhouses in their own backyards, finding their own fuel and tools and earning at best 7s to 8s a week; 5s to 6s was usual.

The new rates meant big increases for women but the firms within the Employers' Association were prepared to pay; not so the many employers and middlemen who were outside the Association. They used the six months delay provided in the Act as an opportunity to pile up stocks, and persuaded many women, too ignorant to realise what they were doing, to contract out of the Act using the threat that otherwise they would get no work. Mary Macarthur decided that if employers could so frustrate the purpose of the Act, no Trade Board would be safe. Two things, she said, must be done; first, the good employers must give firm undertakings to pay the rate, which they did; second, the cheated women must strike. It was a desperate move, for the women would be penniless.

Much credit for handling the strike must go to the woman on the spot, Julia Varley. She set up an influential local committee to collect funds and embarked on some inspired publicity. She brought the women out from their back streets into the prosperous centre of Birmingham, hung with their chains and with placards bearing the words, 'Britain's disgrace, 1*d* an hour'. She said that the women who paraded were between 60 and 90 years of age. She took them to the Annual Congress of the TUC and on to the platform, silently raising their chained hands. The effect can be imagined. For all that, it was a bitter struggle and lasted ten weeks before the employers capitulated and the women returned to work, with wages doubled in some cases.

Julia Varley was a Bradford woman, born in 1871 and working as a part-timer in a mill at the age of 12, a branch secretary at the age of 16 in what was known as Ben Turner's Union, the Weavers and Textile Workers. When in 1904 she was appointed a member of the Bradford board of guardians, she decided to find out what it was like at the receiving end and went 'on the tramp', sleeping as a vagrant in casual wards in Yorkshire and Lancashire and exploring London's underworld in common lodging houses. She served two terms of imprisonment for the suffragette cause. She was secretary for a period to a small organisation in Birmingham, the Amalgamated Women Workers, affiliated to the TUC on a membership of 300 and associated with the Women's Trade Union League, and in 1912 she became a full-time official of the Workers' Union and Chief Woman Officer on its amalgamation with the Transport and General Workers' Union. She was a member of the General Council of the TUC for 12 years.

With the success of the Cradley Heath strike, the first firm basis for women's wages was achieved. It was only a first step but it was the beginning of the end of sweating in its extreme form.

The summer of 1911 was long and hot, and there was much industrial unrest. The East End of London was in a ferment. The women in the glue factories, the pickle factories and the jam factories and other unskilled factory occupations decided — almost simultaneously it would seem — that they had had enough. They erupted into the hot streets in a confusion of unorganised, unprepared strike action. It was said that at one time as many as twenty strikes were in progress. In such a situation Mary Macarthur was superb. She descended on the area with her band of helpers, and somehow brought order out of chaos. She appealed to the public, not for money but for food, and food — and money — were forthcoming. Thousands of loaves of bread and milk and other foods had to be distributed daily in the heat and dust and the stink of unwashed humanity. Somehow settlements were reached and trade union membership established. It was estimated that a minimum of £7,000 a year was won in wages, with increases from 1s to 4s a week on wages previously no more than 7s to 9s a week.

There was at that time a lady of considerable wealth and standing who was fighting her own small battle against exploitation. Susan Lawrence was asking questions about the wages of cleaners employed by the London County Council and getting no satisfaction from the replies. She was a member of the Council; as was the custom then, and since, her Tory principles were disguised, for municipal purposes, as Municipal Reform. She decided to consult Mary Macarthur on her problem and thereby took the first step that led to conversion to socialism, a prison sentence and a position in HM Government.

Arabella Susan Lawrence was born in 1871 into a wealthy legal family. She was educated at a girls' public day school and was admitted to Newnham College in 1895. She was thus one of the early band of women to take advantage of the new higher education for women, and successfully took an honours course in mathematics but Cambridge did not then, or for many years after, award degrees to women. She entered into public work almost immediately on leaving Cambridge, greatly influenced by the work of Lord Shaftesbury, and became a Manager of Church Schools, and in 1900 a member of the London School Board. She was coopted to the LCC in 1904 and elected a member in 1910. Two years later, after her meeting with Mary Macarthur, she resigned, having meanwhile won her battle for a living wage for the cleaners and thrown in her lot with Mary's team of workers.

Susan had a fine logical mind, invaluable to the Federation in the years of her service with them, and a singleness of purpose that kept her firmly in the course she had chosen. It seemed to her friends that her appearance, tall, dignified and tailor-suited, did not change much over the years, save in one respect. In her early days she wore a monocle.

J.S. Middleton described his trepidation when asked to persuade her to discard it before she plunged into East End politics but she responded willingly and she returned to the LCC in 1913 as a Labour member.[5]

The addition of Susan Lawrence to the Federation helpers greatly facilitated the setting up of an Approved Society under the National Health Insurance Act of July 1912. The policy of the Federation, fearing the effect of deductions from low wages, was a non-contributory scheme but this was politically impossible. The Act provided that the administration should be centred on existing or created Friendly Societies, on a financial basis intended to ensure that good management and proper oversight of claims would enable Societies to accumulate funds and pay additional benefits. In fact what it ensured was that Societies, whose range of members covered the better paid, secured the highest return for their members. Mary Macarthur resolved to establish an Approved Society for women, with a double purpose, first to secure for women the best that the Act offered and second, to introduce them to trade unionism in the hope that they would take up full membership. It is doubtful whether the second objective materialised, though 22,000 members were enrolled in the Society. The first was frustrated by women's high sickness claims.

These led to the setting up of a Government Committee in 1914, with Margaret Bondfield as a member to enquire into the level of claims. Mary, in a memorandum of evidence wrote 'it is my conviction that. . . this extra sickness of women is due to their great poverty. . .the low wages. . .involving insufficient and often improper food'. Five years later, in her memo attached to the report of the War Cabinet's Committee, Dr Janet Campbell wrote: 'The evidence which has been received by the Committee supports and emphasises the above findings.'

At the outbreak of war Mary Macarthur had gathered into the service of the Federation of Women Workers a team of highly talented women. Margaret Bondfield after years of service with the Shop Assistants' Union and with increasing interest in political action, had taken up work with the ILP, but she now returned to her earlier sphere and became organising secretary; Susan Lawrence took charge of the legal work; Madelaine Symons* and Isobel Sloan* assisted and there was a team of organisers in the field. Unemployment was heavy in the early period of the war, but the demand for women to replace men called up for service grew. Engineering, including munitions, was the first to expand. There had been for some years a small number of women employed in the metal trades, and in the making of cartridges, but the Amalgamated Society of Engineers (now the Amalgamated Union of

Engineering Workers) closed their doors to them and they were almost entirely unorganised. The employers' reaction to the first inflow of women was to offer rates of 2½d to 2¾d an hour, though the cost of living was already rising. The ASE took fright and entered into an agreement with the employers on substitution, known as the Shells and Fuses Agreement. No women were present at the negotiations nor was there any consultation with the Federation of Women Workers or any other group representing women when the government intervened and a Treasury Agreement was concluded, forming the basis for the Munitions of War Act of March 1915. Before the end of the war, half a million women were employed on munitions but the basic conditions and legal restrictions of their employment were settled by an exclusively male union and an exclusively male government. Lloyd George's undoubted intention was that employers should not utilise women's war work as a source of cheap labour. The unions' intention was that women should not undercut the men whose jobs they took over. Four main classes of work emerged; women on women's work; women partly on men's work; women wholly on unskilled men's work; and women wholly on men's skilled work. And the great argument on the meaning of the Treasury Agreement began.

The first priority of the Federation was to organise the war workers, and an agreement was made with the ASE which secured their cooperation though their own doors remained closed to women. Mary Macarthur became a member of the wages sub-committee of the central Munitions Labour Supply Committee and, in September 1915, the famous L2 Circular was issued, providing £1 per week time rate (at age 18) for women in controlled establishments, equal piece rates and equal rates on payment by results, and an equal time rate for skilled workers. Thereafter Susan Lawrence and Isobel Sloan spent much of their time dealing with the cases of unfair payment brought to the Federation. In March 1916 a Special Arbitration Tribunal was set up, with Susan Lawrence as a member. Gradually the Tribunal extended the scope of the 'engineering £1' to war work other than engineering and reduced hours of work from 53 per week to 48. There were thousands of 'controlled' firms covered by the Orders and although the difficulty of 'policing' them was very great, the overall effect of the Orders was to bring some sense into the chaos of women's rates of pay.

Unfortunately the Tribunal did not award equal war bonuses and this added to the confusion on the issue of substitution. As the war proceeded, new practices, new subdivisions of labour, new products blurred the issue. To whom did the substitution provisions apply? Did it apply to time rates or only to piece rates? Pressed by the Federation and the Women's Suffrage Societies, Lloyd George took refuge in the device of setting up, in September 1918, a committee – the War Cabinet Committee on Women in Industry, 'to investigate and report upon the relations which should be maintained between the wages of women and men, having regard to the interests of both as well as to the value of their work. . .' On such a reference he may have hoped to avoid an examination of charges of breach of faith. It was a forlorn hope. Sylvia Pankhurst on behalf of the East End Suffragette Federation had secured a letter from him in March 1915 stating that 'women undertaking the work of men would get the same piece rates as men. . . if women turn out the same quantity [they should] receive exactly the same pay'. The Federation of Women Workers were able to give extensive evidence of evasion.

There were two women on the Committee, Dr Janet Campbell and Mrs Sydney Webb. The Committee as a majority, in the face of evidence to the contrary – the War Office and Admiralty had manifestly disregarded the orders of the upstart Ministry of Munitions and fixed their own rates – decided that there had been no breach of agreement. Beatrice Webb would have none of this. She produced a minority report stating in trenchant language that, 'The Treasury Agreement of March 1915 embodied a pledge that the women employed on war work in substitution of men should receive the same pay as the men they replaced. . .this pledge was applicable without exception. . .to all degrees of skill and to all methods of computing wages. . .[it] has been wholly ignored by some Government Departments and only fulfilled by others, tardily and partially. . .no Government Department has carried out the pledge in its entirety. . .(including the Ministry of Munitions).' She then proceeded to examine the whole basis of women's wages left, she said, to 'the higgle of the market' and 'the principle of having no principle'.

This was not the first time Beatrice Webb had used the medium of an official minority report to expose fallacies and to recommend reforms. The majority report of the Royal Commission on the Poor Law in 1909 was completely overshadowed by her brilliant minority report; it could with truth be described as the base on which Lord Beveridge later built up his Welfare State proposals.

She was born (Beatrice Potter) in 1858 into a wealthy Victorian family of eight sisters. She was endowed with both beauty and intellect and from her long partnership with Sydney Webb came the carefully-researched documents and pamphlets which guided Labour Party policy through its formative years. Their monumental *History of Trade*

Unionism, first published in 1894, is still a major source book for trade union studies.

The Committee did not report until 1919 and Lloyd George may be presumed to have succeeded in one of his objectives, that of avoiding a showdown with his War Departments. The Federation's allegations were proved correct to the satisfaction of all fair minded people but the war ended with an established pattern, particularly in engineering, that persisted through the years, of areas of work designated women's work and carrying a woman's rate of pay.

Lloyd George's problems with those troublesome women war workers were not over. Immediately after the Armistice nearly all the 26,000 women employed at Woolwich Arsenal and in other parts of London, received one week's notice of dismissal. The women were no longer prepared to accept such treatment and they assembled in formidable thousands on the Embankment to march to the House of Commons. The *Woman Worker,* the journal of the Federation, described the action as 'spontaneous'. Was it wholly so? Was Mary Macarthur unaware? Dorothy Elliott, then a young Federation organiser at the Arsenal, says that she did know. But she was now the responsible head of a responsible organisation and it would have been her duty to warn members against such an unlawful assembly within a mile of Parliament. As it was, the demonstration had been made before Federation officials sped to the scene, the women were diverted peacefully to Kingsway Hall while Mary with a deputation went to Whitehall to interview an apprehensive Lloyd George. She emerged with an immediate date for the payment of unemployment benefit and a bonus of one month's pay.

One development of the war years was the emergence of trade union organisation among women clerks and typists. The Post Office had employed women from the 1870s, openly boasting of the financial saving to the department, but the real influx of women into offices came with the typewriter and the telephone in the 1890s. The National Union of Clerks had struggled to organise men and women since its formation in 1890 and in 1903 the Association of Women Clerks and Secretaries (then the Association of Shorthand Writers and Typists) was formed, largely propagandist and equalitarian.

It was not until the war years, with the concentration of clerks in large war establishments, that real opportunities for white-collar trade union recruitment emerged. The NUC concentrated on engineering; the AWCS on government departments. In 1918 the Association appointed its first full-time general secretary, Dorothy Evans and in

1919 an organising secretary, Christine Maguire. It was an excellent
combination, application and steadiness on the one hand, inspiration
and daring on the other. The Association's membership rose from
2,000 in 1919 to 8,500 in 1921.

It was by its nature a temporary increase, and the problem of post-
war dismissals had to be faced. How best to serve the women? The
Association decided to secure for them some part of the permanently
expanded work of government departments, notably in the Ministry
of Pensions, mainly staffed by women from its inception. Evidence was
given on these lines to the Lytton Committee, and accepted in their
1921 report, and thousands of the Association's members became civil
servants and members by agreement of the Civil Service Clerical
Association (now the Civil and Public Service Association).

Christine Maguire went to the CSCA as a full-time official to service
the expanded woman membership. W.J. Brown was the General
Secretary. There was much that was unsatisfactory in the position of
women in the service; prior to 1914 they had been recruited separately,
almost entirely confined to low grade work and segregated into self-
contained sections. Christine, more enthusiastic than tactful, challenged
the attitude of the men members of the Association. W.J. Brown, equally
tactless, spoke loudly of sex-starved females. Thus an area of conflict
grew. Both protagonists were mavericks in their own way but when the
inevitable clash came, W.J. won and Christine resigned, later to retire
to a convent, her great promise of service to women workers only half
fulfilled.

The women clerks had always had strong links with the equal pay
movement, and in 1929, Dorothy Evans, still General Secretary of the
Association, gave evidence on the issue to the Royal Commission on the
Civil Service. There were five women on the commission, three of them
Labour stalwarts – Mary Agnes Hamilton, Barbara Ayrton-Gould and
Eveline Lowe. When the Commission reported in 1931 there was
jubilation among women civil servants. Though it was split on the issue
of equal pay the Commission recommended an end to the segregation
of work into men's and women's sections, and the opening of all grades
to both sexes, 'a fair field and no favour'.* Women civil servants rightly
saw this as the breakthrough. Where men and women entered through
the same exams, did identical work and passed through the same

---

* The Foreign Office managed to get itself excluded from this recommendation
and it was not until 1946 that the Diplomatic and Consular Services were
opened to women.

promotion procedure, the logic was irresistible. Equal pay was still a long way off but from then on, the end was sure.

By the end of the war the position of women in industry had been transformed. Trade Unionism was still weak but no longer impermanent. Wages were low compared with men's but helpless exploitation was over. New areas of work had opened and old areas were expanding.

When Mary Macarthur died in January 1921 it was effectively the end of the era of organisations catering for women only, establishing their own policies and staffed by women officials. Mary had seen the limitations of this approach and had arranged to amalgamate the Federation of Women Workers with the National Union of General and Municipal Workers, forming a separate District, with Margaret Bondfield as District Secretary, Madelaine Symons as her assistant and six Federation organisers to cover the country; Miss Elliott in London, Miss Codrington in Bristol, Mrs Williamson in Sheffield, Mrs Pearson in Manchester, Miss Lees in the Eastern Counties and Miss Howarth in Birmingham. At its peak the Federation had a membership of 70,000. After two years of war dismissals there were still 30,000 women to transfer. From this period the story is mainly one of women inside predominantly male unions, their women leaders operating in a man's world.

It is doubtful whether Margaret Bondfield was happy in the new environment. She had always been strongly political and international. In 1919 she, with Mary Macarthur, attended as advisers to the British Trade Union delegates the first conference of the International Labour Organisation, and dealt with the employment of children. Mary worked on the first international maternity convention, to provide for leave of absence from work for women for a period before and after childbirth. A more detailed story of this conference is contained in 'Labour Women and Internationalism', pp.84-93.

It had been arranged that the TUC should take over the functions of the Women's Trade Union League and one of Mary Macarthur's last acts was to secure two seats for women on the General Council. Julia Varley held one seat and Margaret Bondfield the other. She would have been the first woman President of Congress but for the advent of a Labour Administration in 1924 and her resignation from her Chairmanship of the General Council to take up office as the Parliamentary Secretary of the Ministry of Labour. In this post she was so successful that in the second Labour government in 1929, Ramsay MacDonald made her the first woman cabinet minister, serving in that administration as Minister of Labour. Her great gift to the movement was her power of oratory,

greater some found than Ramsay MacDonald in his heyday. She
remained throughout her great career essentially the country girl of her
upbringing, deeply religious and idealistic.

Gertrude Tuckwell continued to work for women. The Women
Health Visitors' Association (now the Health Visitors Association) owed
much to her support and when in 1929 she was made a Companion of
Honour, their Annual Report records 'no other Association can boast
of such a President whose interest and sympathy are always theirs and
who still has enough to spare for wider objects common to mankind'.

Against a background of expanding work opportunities leaders of
working women were beginning to emerge who were no longer
dependent on middle-class assistance. Anne Loughlin became an
organiser for the Tailors and Garment Workers' Union in 1915 at the
age of 21 when she had already five years of shop floor experience, a
shop steward in her teens and a centre of union activity in Leeds.
Mechanisation was aiding the Trade Boards in the needle trades in the
final elimination of home sweating and trade unionism was speeding
the process. One of the first Boards — ready made and wholesale
bespoke tailoring — settled an hourly rate in August 1912 of 3¼d but
Leeds was well organised and secured 4d. The trades were wholly
covered by Trade Boards — Anne Loughlin served on nine — and union
agreements were put through Board machinery and given statutory
authority, thus sweeping into the net the small employers who were
always the most difficult. Four-fifths of the workers were girls and
women but Anne Loughlin was never a women's official. In 1915 she
became National Organiser of the T&GWU with a membership of
10,000, travelling the country to negotiate, to organise and settle strikes,
and to deputise for the General Secretary on national wage negotiations.
The membership was over 100,000 when in 1948 she became the first
woman General Secretary of a mixed union. Much of her work lies
outside the time span of this chapter but it must be recorded that she
became the first President of the TUC in 1943.

In general women formed a minority in mixed unions and male
interests were dominant. The experience of Mary Bell Richards in the
National Union of Boot and Shoe Operatives (now the National Union
of Leather, Footwear and Allied Trades) was not unique though her
method of handling her problems probably was.[6]

One of her fellow (male) Executive members termed her bitter, but
the union historian Alan Fox concedes that 'it is difficult to avoid the
conclusion that many male union members were not taking women's
claims and struggles very seriously. They were treated in a manner

compounded of faint contempt and lofty condescension.' This was written of the period 1911 when Mary Bell, already a member of 15 years standing, took control of the troubled Leicester Women's Branch. From 1906 the branch had been officered by women. They were not a submissive group and in 1911 there was a devastating breakaway, leaving Mary Bell with only 58 members and every office to fill. By 1916, when she became full-time President of the Branch, the membership was 2,000 and when she retired in 1939 it was over 6,000.

Mary was pugnacious and feminist. She stayed in the union not to capitulate but to fight from within. There had been long delays in securing negotiating rights for women. Mary Bell Richards (she married in 1916) held the view that if women wanted anything done they must do it themselves and the men complained that she not only regarded the Branch as hers but that she thought the Branch was the Union. She was deeply angered in the early 1920s when the Executive insisted on a 'common front' on wage cuts, when she knew that circumstances of the trade in Leicester would have enabled her to avoid them; angered, too, when the Executive, overwhelmingly male, shrugged off her plea for an equal minimum wage and opposed the opening of all departments to women. She started a women's social club 'for educational purposes, the need of combination and sex-consciousness'. After 22 years of combat on the union's Executive, she won through to a mutual wry tolerance.

There were other women who resolved to make the system work as far as possible without friction. Florence Hancock working in the General Workers' Union from Bristol in a generally low paid area, organised with her male colleagues, over a field too wide for rivalry. All her life she held the view that loyalty to the movement came first, and she placed the welfare of the workers before ideology. She was 18 when she and her fellow workers in a milk factory in Chippenham, her home town, took the desperate step of a strike against low wages and a tyrannical foreman, but she had started full-time work at the age of 12½, as a washer-up at 3s a week, and she was already seasoned.

As the unions moved into the grim 1920s her experience was that of other women organisers. It had never been easy to organise women; now new problems arose. A temporary Wage Regulation Act had frozen wartime rates of pay for one year but then they began to fall. Dorothy Elliott (Mrs Owen Jones) organising in Lancashire and London, recalls two wage cuts in one year in one of her industries. The tactic of the unions, she says, was to anticipate demands for reductions by claims for improvement. Here lay the difference from earlier experience. 'We were fighting a rear guard action but at least we were fighting.'

Dorothy (her father and mother were both teachers) was still at university at the outbreak of war, and during a Social Service Course at the LSE she worked for the Federation in the East End with Eleanor Calthrop, joining the staff of the Federation in September, 1918. In 1924 she was recalled from Lancashire to the Headquarters of the NUGMW to take over much of Margaret Bondfield's work and in due course become Chief Woman Officer.

The Central Committee for the Training and Employment of Women resumed its pre-war work but, says Dorothy, there was little they could do but offer training in domestic work. Over 400,000 had left this work during the war and showed no inclination to return. It had a bad reputation and trade unionism had failed to penetrate. Jessie Stephens, herself a domestic worker in Glasgow, tried in 1909-10, through her Scottish Domestic Workers' Federation but she admits that it never achieved more than 200 members. Getting women back to domestic work was a recurring theme of the post-war years. In 1919 Jessie was a member of a Committee on Domestic Service set up through the Women's Advisory Committee of the Ministry of Labour. In 1923 another committee was set up by the Ministry 'to enquire into the present conditions as to the supply of Female Domestic Servants'. One of the heartbreaking tasks of trade union officials, as Dorothy Elliott recalls, was to represent their members before Courts of Referees, to try to secure additional unemployment benefit. It became the practice of the courts to ask women with wholly industrial experience whether they had sought domestic work, a form of pressure which added to its unpopularity.

If the heroic age of Mary Macarthur came to an end in the depression years of the 1920s, there were still women prepared to carry on the hard and at times thankless task of trade union organising. Belle Jobson*, Aberdeen bred, helped in the task of organising agricultural workers into the Scottish Farm Servants' Union, and became President of the Scottish TUC in 1937. Alice Horan broke through male prejudice and secured male support to become a London member of the Executive Council of the NUGMW before moving to wider responsibilities in the Union. Mary Quale*, deprived by ill-health of her national position in the T&GWU and a seat on the General Council of the TUC, resumed her devoted voluntary work for women Trade Unionists in Manchester. So the story does not end and justifies the faith of Gertrude Tuckwell, who in her ninety-first year sent a message to the Annual Conference of Trade Union Women, 'Look to it that ye lose not the things that we have wrought'.

Notes

1. Annie Besant, *An Autobiography,* T. Fisher Unwin, 1893, Fawcett Library.
2. B.C. Roberts, *The Trade Union Congress 1868-1921,* Allen and Unwin, p.121.
3. Leslie Hunter and Margaret Stewart, *The Needle is Threaded,* Heinemann (Newman Mcame), p.126.
4. Quoted from Hunter and Stewart, p.136.
5. J.S. Middleton, *Memoirs* (not yet published).
6. Alan Fox, *A History of the National Union of Boot and Shoe Operatives 1874-1957,* Oxford: Basil Blackwell, pp.309, 484.

6 WOMEN AND COOPERATION

Jean Gaffin

What power did working-class married women have before they had the vote? Precious little — except that they had the power to decide where they spent their husband's wages. This was particularly important to the only retailers with a national identity: the retailing cooperative societies. They had a national federation (the United Board, later the Cooperative Union), and their own weekly newspaper, the *Cooperative News*. Those women spending the wages at their local cooperative thus had a ready made way of communicating with each other. They began to do this in 1883, when Mrs Acland became the first editor of the Women's Corner in the *Cooperative News*.

Mrs Alice Acland (1849-1935)[1] was the daughter of a Minister, and went to her father's Church school. Her husband was an Oxford don with an interest in education and social welfare activities; he inherited a baronetcy in 1919. She and her husband believed that cooperation would benefit the working class, and they travelled extensively in the north of England, meeting cooperative leaders and their wives. Mrs Acland believed that women should have outlets for activities outside their household duties. Through her friendship with the editor of the *Cooperative News*, Samuel Bamford, she came to start the Women's Corner, which she edited from 1883-6.

In her very first column,[2] Mrs Acland claimed that it was to be the means by which 'we women open our minds to each other, to make known our wants, our thoughts and our fancies to each other'. She went on to claim that men saw women's role within the cooperative movement not to help or to vote, to criticise or to act, but to buy. She complains of the low esteem in which men held women, asking why the feeblest kind of man is called an 'old woman' and why 'woman hearted' is a term of reproach. 'It is our own fault, and men have not, perhaps, been unwilling that it should be so', declared Mrs Acland, demanding 'In this matter of cooperation. . .why should women not do more than we do? Why should we not hold cooperative "mother's meetings", when we may bring our work and sit together, one of us reading some cooperative book aloud which may afterwards be discussed. . .Men are going forward; let us go too. Bravely and hopefully, not going out of our province, but working in it. making each household a truly cooperative establishment.'

This column brought an immediate and excited reaction. By April 1883 Mrs Acland could announce triumphantly in her Women's Column that the 'Woman's League for the Spread of Cooperation had begun'. One typical complaint appearing in the correspondence leading up to the formation of the Leagues was, 'It is all very nice for men to come home from their day's labour and find the house nicely in order, having nothing to do but take up a newspaper. . .but has not the day been long and tedious to us, with nothing but four walls to look at and babies to attend to?' For married women did not generally go out except to shop. The idea of meeting at their cooperative shop was in keeping with their view of themselves as homemakers: a view perhaps being reinforced by the growth of women's magazines in the 1880s.

The League (which became the Women's Cooperative Guild in 1884), was the very first separatist working-class women's organisation – the Labour Party and trade union women's sections were to follow.

Within a year there were six branches, and two members of the Woolwich branch of the Guild were elected to their Society's Education Committee. The Guild from its earliest days attracted highly educated women,[3] like Mrs Acland, who saw the Guild as a way of guiding working-class women towards enlightenment and self-esteem. But there was, too, an early response from women brought up in cooperative households, with no previous outlet for cooperative work. Miss Greenwood, Secretary of the Rochdale branch of the Guild, one of the first branches, was the daughter of a Rochdale Pioneer.

The initial attitudes and activities of the Guild were much influenced by its founder and first General Secretary, Mrs Acland. The early values were simple and moralistic: a woman's place is in the home, keeping busy, and learning to be a better household manager and a better cooperator. She gave the Guild a motto, 'study to be quiet and do your own business', arising from her desire not to arouse the antagonism provoked by the dress and manners of some contemporary advocates of women's rights.

Mrs Acland affirmed[4] 'the thing to be done is to see whether there is not special work which can be done, not only best by women, but by women only', adding that women knew little of business, so that 'if we thrust ourselves into committees of management we shall be liable to make ourselves and our kind laughing stock, and stumbling blocks too'. One of their decisions at the 1884 Edinburgh Cooperative Congress, where the League held its own meeting, was that there should be 'no platform speaking, no advertising, no going out of women's place'. (Public speaking was accepted as an important part of the League's activities the following year.)

The values and concerns of the early, mainly middle-class leadership was reflected in early branch activities and in the articles in Women's Corner. Branches organised classes on dressmaking and home nursing. Members studied cooperative principles, and loyalty to the cooperative store was paramount. Branches started clothing clubs and children's clubs. Articles looked at earthquakes, art, and the problems of young girls in 'disorderly houses'.

Despite a humble view of their role, they met prejudice from men cooperators. Some husbands objected to their wives going out when they were at home. Members of Cooperative Committees and managers of stores objected to the interference of customers in the way the shops were run. This attitude from men within the cooperative movement and within their families could not have helped the women cope with the conflict within themselves, seeing their role as the traditional one (at home), and yet becoming aware of their own potential to which Guild membership was to lead.

A thorough education in cooperative principles and the practical experience of participating in a democratically organised movement like the Guild, enabled working-class women to play a larger part in the running of the cooperative movement itself. Guild branches managed their own affairs, but joined with other Branches into Districts, and the Districts into six Sections, covering Britain. The Central Committee, which controlled Guild policy and suggested campaigns and activities, was elected at Sectional Conferences. Annual Classes for Guild officials at all levels were held, helping the women to become more effective in organisation, administration and propaganda. As Guildswomen became more confident, and their competence recognised, they began – albeit slowly – to be elected to offices within the cooperative movement, and to outside bodies like the Poor Law guardians. Yet there seemed always to be tension between the men in the movement, concerned for commercial success and high dividends, and the women, with a concern for the ethical success of cooperation.

Many of the early Guild leaders saw the cooperative movement rather like evangelicals saw the Church, and perhaps the decline in religious attachments in this period was linked to their missionary zeal about spreading the idea of cooperation. These ideas embodied virtues like thrift and self-help (no doubt influenced by Samuel Smiles whose *Thrift* was published in 1875).

Elimination of competition and the worst excesses of capitalism by partnership and by production for use was seen to be an important part of the cooperative movement. As wage earners were united in trade unions, so wage spenders were to be united too.

Many of these early leaders were attracted to the cooperative movement from a background of Christian Socialism. Christian Socialists had played an important part in the formation of the cooperative movement. They helped formulate the Industrial and Provident Act. They had put their money as well as their theories into producer cooperatives, most of which failed. Early Guild leaders were far from revolutionaries, believing that in the joint partnership of capital and labour would come emancipation for the workers. Not surprisingly, then, when the Guild became concerned with social reform, it was gradual and not revolutionary change that they campaigned for.

Mary Lawrenson was a founder member of the Guild, and its General Secretary from 1885-9. She was influenced by Ruskin and was an admirer of Christian Socialism. Vansittart Neale, a leading Christian Socialist, wrote to her when she was General Secretary of the Guild and he the Secretary of the Cooperative Union, that he would be pleased to do anything to further the Guild. He went on, 'You rightly appreciate the functions of Cooperation in my judgement in speaking of it as a "gospel", the song of peace on earth and goodwill to mankind, and it must be regarded not as a substitute for the ancient Gospel, but as the complement of it.'[5]

The Guild was later able to produce its own leaders. Miss Reddish was President of the Bolton Branch of the Guild, 1886-1901, a member of the Central Committee in 1889, and Guild Organiser from 1893-5. She had left school at 11, starting work at home winding silk on a frame, and later she worked in a cotton mill, eventually becoming a forewoman in a hosiery mill. She was a socialist, fighting for a society based on equal efforts in producing and equal participation in the results, so'that idleness should cease to revel in luxury and labour pine in want; that vice should no longer flitter in the palace and virtue droop in the hovel; that man's inhumanity to man be a thing only of the past'.[6]

An early leader with a different background again was Catherine Webb[7] (1859-1947), whose father was a coppersmith and a director of the Cooperative Wholesale Society. Her mother was interested in astronomy and polar exploration, and Catherine founded and was first Secretary of the Battersea Branch of the Guild, and chaired the Guild's first conference in 1886. She lectured for the Guild in several parts of Britain during the 1890s, was a delegate to the Cooperative Congress and later became a member of the Central Board of the Cooperative Union. She pressed for the participation of women in all cooperative committees, and argued strongly for more education of managers and employees in the principles of cooperation. In 1904 she edited *Industrial Cooperation* which became the standard text book for cooperative education for many years, and in 1927 she wrote a history of the Guild which she called *Woman with the Basket.* She was a Liberal, regarding the cooperative movement as an entity in itself with members holding different political opinions. In her later years she was involved with Morley College, as lecturer, then governor, then writer of its history.

This early leadership, made up of Christian Socialists, Liberals and Socialists, guided the Guild from a concern with women as peaceful homemakers to women as peaceful agents of social reform. Social improvement was an early goal.

There was an early insistence on self-improvement. Mrs Acland's very first Women's Corner had suggested that women bring *work* to do when they meet. Their hands should be busy even outside the home. One member was worried in case Branch meetings 'dwindle down to mere gossip',[8] and the 1889 Report talks primly about the difficulties of getting members to take an interest in serious topics, as 'They have a great distaste for what they consider "dull" and "dry". . .cooperation and all economic subjects are difficult and require thought and attention. To give women a knowledge of cooperation is one of our first objects and we must not shrink from trying to realise it.'

If some of these early leaders did not seem to want the members to enjoy themselves, the members certainly did enjoy themselves. Previously the only meetings working-class married women had attended had been mothers' meetings, attached to the church, the promoters working *for* and not *with* the women who came along.

The contrast was made by a Guild member: 'One is democratic and the other autocratic.'[9] The friendliness of branch meetings and the enjoyment of social activities comes over as very positive, whatever the changes that came in Guild policies and activities.

The major change was from a concern with household management and cooperative affairs alone, to wider concerns. The new involvement was with issues concerning women inside the home (e.g. campaigns for divorce law reform and maternity improvements), and issues affecting women outside the home (e.g. the fight for votes for women). This change is associated with the change of leadership in 1889, when Miss Margaret Llewelyn Davies became General Secretary, aided by Lilian

Harris who worked within the Guild from 1893.

Margaret Llewelyn Davies[10] (1861-1944) was christened Margaret Caroline, but took the family name of Llewelyn. Her father was Rector of Christ Church in a poor part of Marylebone, London, where she was born. He was influenced by Christian Socialists, whose leaders, like Kingsley, were close friends. He translated Plato's *Republic*. Her mother was a Unitarian, and her love of beautiful things was passed on to her daughter. Margaret was brought up in an atmosphere of advanced thought and social commitment. That her father was not promoted as his abilities deserved was thought to be due to his liberal attitudes. One of her uncles was an active worker for women's suffrage and a friend of John Stuart Mill. An aunt of her father's side was Emily Davies, founder of Girton College, Cambridge. She had six brothers, two of whom were friends of Bertrand Russell at Cambridge, and are mentioned in the first volume of Russell's autobiography.

After leaving Cambridge, Margaret Llewelyn Davies became a devotee of the cooperative movement – influenced by her father. G.D.H. Cole considered that her decision to devote her life to the cooperative movement was a turning point in cooperative history, seeing her as by far the greatest woman actively identified with the British cooperative movement, inspiring women to take the lead in cooperative progress, instead of following existing leaders. She became Secretary of the Marylebone Branch of the Guild in 1886, was on the Executive by 1887 and was elected General Secretary in 1889. In that year she moved, with her family, to the parish of Kirkby Lonsdale in Westmorland. The Guild Office was in her home until 1908, when it returned to London – this saved the Guild the expense of an office, and she was unpaid for her work. She was a strong believer in the voluntary nature of Guild participation, seeing it as more democratic, but perhaps failing to understand that payment would have enabled poorer women to stand for office. The post of General Secretary was a paid one after her retirement.

Margaret Llewelyn Davies was concerned with the internationalist aspects of the Guild, helping to found the International Women's Cooperative Guild in Basle, in 1921. She was sympathetic to the Russian Revolution (although not a communist), and was the first Chairman of the Society for Cultural Relations with the USSR, enlisting as Vice Presidents people of the calibre of H.G. Wells, Bernard Shaw, Aldous and Julian Huxley and Virginia and Leonard Woolf (who were close friends). At her death, she left £20,000. A wide range of interests are reflected in the bequests that she made. Apart from personal bequests, she left money to the International Cooperative Women's Guild, the Peace Pledge Union, War Resisters International, The Howard League for Penal Reform and the Commons Open Spaces and Footpaths Preservation Society.

A friend from her Cambridge days recalls her as a tall, gracious woman, with a deep pleasant voice and a vivid personality. She was not a natural orator, according to her niece; she prepared speeches carefully in advance but her platform success was due to her striking presence, which commanded admiration and affection. She was described as outspoken and straightforward, sometimes impatient, but with a tender respect for the hard lives and poor opportunities of working-class women which made it impossible for her to command them, or hurry them or fail them in sympathy. But she was apt to be distressed rather than stimulated by differences of opinion. Her views were more extreme than those of the majority of the Guild, but they were tempered by the habit of testing theories against the lives of her working-class women friends.

Margaret Llewelyn Davies was convinced that the worker could not be helped by the rich: they must help themselves. But she was aware of the reality of middle-class leadership of the Guild. In a revealing paragraph in her Guild History she writes of those women with time at their disposal, who are connected with the Guild as 'Editors of Women's Corner, as Organizing Secretaries and as occasional Branch Presidents or Secretaries. . .whose sympathies attracted them to a working-class organization rather than to philanthropic work'. These women stand for election on an equal basis with other members and 'must identify themselves with working-class interests, and come as interpreters of the needs and wishes of the workers. The Guild does not seek outsiders of "position" to preside over its functions or direct its councils.'[11] This ability to relate to and identify with the Guild membership was perhaps due to what her niece describes as her imaginatively constructed temperament which was complemented by the practical and organising capacities of Lilian Harris.

Lilian Harris was a lifelong friend, companion and colleague of Margaret Llewelyn Davies. She was the daughter of a wealthy Bradford banker, who came to live at Kirkby Lonsdale in 1850, building himself a large house. When the two women were given the Freedom of the Guild in 1922, Miss Davies described her first meeting with Lilian Harris, 'sitting at home in the lovely county of Westmorland, trying to occupy herself with carving and embroidery', but she had been brought out into the world to serve the Guild. Lilian Harris was cashier of the Guild in 1893, and Assistant Secretary from 1902 until 1921. The smooth running of the Guild office was undoubtedly due to her administrative abilities. She inherited £3,200 from Miss Davies.

The Social Composition of the Guild

If these well-educated middle-class ladies were the Guild's early leaders, who were the rank and file? They were. mainly, respectable working-class women, for of course, it was the respectable working-class man who was active within the cooperative movement. Prices were usually higher than other retailers, worthwhile to those able to spend a little more, for the sake of the surplus that was saved and returned as dividend. But the prices put the cooperative shops outside the reach of many, and the membership fee was hardly an encouragement for the very poor to join Societies.

That cooperation attracted the stable working class is recognised by Beatrice Potter (later Webb), who wrote 'poverty and irregular habits form a lower limit to the growth of cooperation. Fastidiousness and the indifference bred of luxury constitute a higher limit to the desire and capacity for democratic self government.'   Beatrice Potter took an early interest in the cooperative movement, but she did not seem to have been involved with the Guild. (It was at a Cooperative Congress that she 'came to a working compact' with Sydney Webb, marrying him in 1892.)

Clementina Black, of the Women's Trade Union Association, was an old friend of the Guild and spoke at their very first delegate conference. In an enquiry undertaken by the Women's Industrial Council[13] into the conditions of married working women, she distinguished four groups. Group A had inadequate income but did not earn; group B did earn, because their family income was inadequate (due perhaps to low pay, sickness, unemployment or desertion); group C did not earn, and their income was adequate; group D had an income adequate for necessities, but did earn. Where did Guild members fit into these groups? Clementina Black said that groups C and D 'covered that great body of intelligent, able and efficient mothers, examples of whom may be seen at meetings of the Women's Cooperative Guild. It is safe to say that no country in the world possesses better citizens than these. They form the very bulwark of national prosperity in the material sense of the word.'

In fact, few Guild members appeared to work. The 1890 Report mentions that about 2,000 members in the Northern Section were married women living at home, whilst 260 worked at trades. (About 25 per cent of all women were working in 1880, and this percentage hardly increased during the period we are examining.) More single than

married women worked, and most Guild members were married women.
   But the Guild members worked hard enough at home. Margaret
Llewelyn Davies quotes one member as saying, 'one of the things the
Guild teaches is system. To be able to attend branch meetings and
conferences, and do your household duties, you must have system in
your home work. You can't loiter over it. The Guild really gives a zest
to it.'[14] An example of a system used by a Yorkshire member was:

Monday	Washing. Guild at 7.
Tuesday	Sewing, ironing, Education Committee 7.30.
Wednesday	Darning and sewing.
Thursday	Cleaning rooms. A cooperative meeting.
Friday	Baking and do kitchen.
Saturday	Cleaning and get clothes ready for wash.

Another Guild member, a Poor Law guardian, wrote:

> I have a splendid constitution and the busy life suited me. Most of
> my lectures and addresses have been thought out when my hands
> have been busy in household duties, in the wash tub, when baking,
> or doing out my rooms. Somehow the work passed more quickly,
> and I have not felt the work so hard when my head has been filled
> with other things.[15]

And the Guildswomen worked hard before their marriage. Writing in
1904, Margaret Llewelyn Davies pointed out that of Presidents of the
Guild, one began work at 8, another worked full time at 10, another
began work as a 'winder' at 6½ and another was a servant by 11.
   Meanwhile, their husbands worked. In 1904, the husbands of the
members of the Central Committee of the Guild worked as engineer,
organist, carpenter, manager of cotton mill, tailor and one woman was
the widow of a gasfitter.
   The lives of the Guildswomen *were* different from the lives of the
very poor. But their lives were also very different from the lives of the
middle class, a contrast which is most beautifully described by Virginia
Woolf. Invited to the 1913 Guild Congress by Margaret Llewelyn Davies,
Virginia Woolf describes her reactions. She tries to imagine the lives of
the women speaking at the Congress, and writes:[16]

> one could not be Mrs Giles of Durham because one's body had never
> stood at the washtub; one's hands had never wrung and scrubbed

and chopped up whatever meat it may be that makes a miner's supper. . .One sat in an armchair or read a book. One saw landscapes and seascapes, perhaps Greece or Italy, where Mrs Giles must have seen slag heaps and rows upon rows of slate roofed houses. Bakers and butchers did not call for orders. They did not sign a cheque to pay the weekly bills. . .If they travelled it was on excursion day, with food in string bags and babies in their arms. They did not stroll through the house and say, that cover must go to the wash or those sheets need changing. They plunged their arms in hot water and scrubbed the clothes themselves. In consequence their bodies were thick set and muscular, their hands were large, and they had the slow emphatic gestures of people who were often stiff and fall tired in a heap on hardbacked chairs. . .The Congress dispersed; and the separate members who had stood up so valiantly and spoken out so boldly. . .went back to Yorkshire and Wales, Sussex and Devonshire, and hung their clothes in the wardrobe and plunged their hands in the wash-tub again.

And she says of the discussion:

All these questions which matter so intensely to the people here, questions of sanitation and education and wages, this demand for an extra shilling, for another year at school, for eight hours instead of nine behind a counter or in a mill leave me, in my own blood and bones untouched. If every reform they demand was granted this very instant it would not touch a hair of my comfortably off capitalist head. . .I am a benevolent spectator. . .In all that audience, among those women who worked, who bore children, who scrubbed and cooked and bargained, there was not a single woman with the vote. Let them fire off their rifles if they liked, but they would hit no target; there were only blank cartridges inside.

But a look at some of the campaigns fought by the Guild showed these cartridges were not always blank, and were always well aimed.

The Campaign to bring Cooperation to the Poor

With the zeal of missionaries, Guild members began to campaign to extend the benefits of cooperation to the poor early in 1884. Guild campaigns were always well planned and well executed. Pamphlets and papers were printed, with practical suggestions. Formulated at Central Committee level, such papers would be discussed at all levels of the

Guild: at Sectional Conferences and Branch meetings as well as at the Annual Congress. A typical pamphlet of this campaign was 'Cooperation in Poor Neighbourhoods'.[17] It argued that high prices and high dividends kept the poor away from the cooperative movement. To attract them, a People's Store was advocated. It would supply wholesome goods at cheap prices and in small quantities. The store would keep the poor out of debt by insisting on cash payments, yet enable them to save. There should be a cooked meat and coffee shop. The poor needed nourishing food, but found it difficult to obtain because of the limited amount of food they could buy, ignorance of cooking, overcrowding, bad grates, lack of cooking utensils and a reliance on the frying pan because it saved fuel and trouble. A loan department was also advocated, to tide people over temporary misfortunes, to 'lend without taking advantage of necessity' as the pamphlet said. This should undermine the habit of weekly pawning. These proposals showed the Guild accepting the fluctuating incomes of the poor, offering self-help to overcome these irregularities rather than arguing for a fundamental change in circumstances. They would be helped in a way that would enable them to gain self control and a sense of their own dignity.

The proposal was not just for a store — it would include club rooms, or a settlement, with propagandist work being carried on by resident helpers, bringing personal help. It would be a centre for cooperative activity in the area as well as attracting people from the public house.

Many cooperators were scornful. If the poor did not make use of the advantages of cooperation they were not worth helping. One Guild member[18] felt it was too big a leap to go from respectable stores to a shop to attract slum inhabitants. She wanted to help the class 'who like ourselves are industrious thrifty and self respecting', but whose small wages or uncertain employment oblige them 'to make a little money meet a great deal of needs'. Even if cheaper goods led to lower dividends for those buying the better goods at their store, 'cooperation is not to enrich individuals but for the good of the greatest number'. Guild members were themselves concerned about cheaper prices — it was often a topic for discussion by branches, and one pamphlet made the point that lower prices would enable Guild members to spend all their money within the cooperative movement.

Sunderland was the Society that proposed to the 1900 Cooperative Congress a motion on 'the desirability of having branch stores in districts where the very poor reside' and Sunderland pioneered the idea, opening its Coronation Street store in April 1902. The area was known

for its high record of death, disease and crime. The store was a new
block, with grocery department, butcher, cooked food department,
flour store, a hall to hold 100 — plus kitchen, scullery and two
bedrooms for resident workers. (Margaret Llewelyn Davies was in
charge for the first three months.)

A newspaper report described the store as standing out 'with a
certain splendour against the drab and dirty surroundings'. The project
is described as 'a mission to help the poor. . .to help themselves . .
ladies show how to keep out of debt. . .no patronage, no charity but
a centre of real neighbourliness and absolute social equality'. And the
men are pictured too, 'in their seedy garments, smoking their pipes in
the Hall on Sunday evenings, grateful for such a good exchange for
the public house'. The article ends 'from the slums, s foul as any in
England, people find their way to the Store, and into these homes the
cooperative ladies find their way. If cooperation, in other words thrift
and self-respect, can succeed here, you reflect, it can make its way
anywhere.'[19]

Trading figures showed the store making a profit, whilst winning the
trade of the poorest. In its first three months, 136 people joined the
Society, and 600 children joined the Penny Bank. At the beginning of
1904 two permanent, paid workers had been appointed to the
settlement, trade was good and a dividend of 2s was declared. By
September, the Directors of the Sunderland Society proposed to the
Quarterly Meeting that the settlement should close. It was passed by
82 votes to 25, and Coronation Street became an ordinary, trading
branch.

Why? Catherine Webb suggests the Society opposed the idea because
it took the narrow view that democracy in cooperative trading meant
that no district should have special treatment not accessible to all'.[20]
G.D.H. Cole considered the objection was not the threat of lower
dividends as much as the feeling within the Sunderland Society that
what was being tried was outside the sort of self-help they were used
to, it savoured of soup and blankets, even if the poor were paying for
the soup and blankets.[21]

The campaign went on for a little while. Funds were raised. Some
Societies opened stores in poorer areas. Entry fees to Cooperative
Societies were lowered. But as the Guild widened its range of interests,
this issue petered out.

Wider Concerns of the Guild

The 1909-10 Report of the Guild reflects a widening concern. Special enquiries were undertaken on wage-earning women's budgets, gratuities at government factories and the divorce laws. They campaigned for the provision of sickroom appliances by the cooperative movement, to get more cooperatively made products into cooperative shops, against sweated labour and against credit trading. They met with trade unions, political associations and Temperance Societies. Their fight for better wages for women cooperative employees and for the vote deserves some discussion.

At the 1904 Guild Congress, a resolution supporting full adult suffrage was passed. The Central Committee had to decide after that whether they would fight for full adult suffrage alone, or whether to support measures that did not go that far. A Manifesto was issued to branches setting out the Guild's position. The key paragraphs stress that although womanhood suffrage was their goal, the Guild left itself free to support any measure that would be a step in that direction. The Guild's arguments for votes for women were set out in the Manifesto too. One was that members controlled the family purse and were entitled to vote because family spending was directly affected by government legislation. Another argument was that the unpaid labour of cooperative women in the home was as valuable to the nation as wage earning, whilst cooperative wage-earning women needed the vote to help them in their struggle for better wages and industrial conditions. The vote, then, would help to raise the status of women in industrial and family life.

The campaign for the vote was fought with varying degrees of enthusiasm after this Manifesto until the vote was won in 1917. The Guild welcomed the formation of the Cooperative Party in 1917, Congress passing a resolution urging cooperative women to join the party, and to 'stand aside from any party whose programme does not include the replacement of capitalism by the democratic control of industry, and does not publicly state the sources from which its funds are derived'.

The ambivalence about whether to go all out for universal suffrage or compromise in the name of practical politics contrasted with the attitude of other women's organisations, but was in keeping with the Guild's preference for half a loaf rather than none. A preference which shows in some of their other campaigns, as when they fought for higher wages for women employees of the cooperative movement — but not for equal pay.

In the 1890s there had been meetings between trade unionists and cooperators to encourage trade unionists to become cooperators and vice versa. Guild members had taken part in these meetings, seeing collective action by wage spending women as the other side of an equation in which producers formed trade unions to further their interests. Concern for working conditions shows in Guild campaigns against goods produced with sweated labour; agitation for the production of leadless glaze pottery; the fight against production of poisonous matches; as well as campaigning to reform the Factory Acts. But the biggest was the campaign with Guildswomen, as consumers, fighting for women as producers.

The campaign was a long one, starting with an enquiry in 1895 into the working conditions of 2,000 women working in cooperative stores, and begun before the Amalgamated Union of Cooperative Employees had recognised that 'women required a living wage' — as the 1906 Guild Report tartly said. The Central Committee of the Guild wanted to work with the Amalgamated Union of Cooperative Employees, and in 1907 passed a resolution urging Branches to discuss with local branches of the union that a minimum wage scale should be adopted of 10s at the age of 18 and 16s per week at 21.

After discussions with the Union's Executive and the United Board's subcommittee on the minimum wage, the Guild adopted a scale rising from 5s per week at 14 to 17s at 20.

The Guild's case was put in a paper[22] published in 1908 — at a time when women's wages averaged a third of a man's wage. It argued that women had families to support, and unmarried women cared for parents. It rejected the argument that higher wages led to a loss of trading through higher prices or lower dividends: if the law did not allow profits to be made out of low wages, employers would make their profits through better organisation and more efficiency. The paper appealed to Guildswomen to accept the need for more education for girls, urging them not to allow their daughters to work for pocket money wages but to encourage them to join unions and value their work. It emphasised the fundamental reason for low pay for women, the one making the rest difficult to remedy, 'the generally supposed inferiority of women to men. Women as well as men are responsible for the view, for they have accepted it and passed it on generation after generation.'

Branches worked on, putting pressure on local unions and local Societies to adopt the minimum wage scale for women. Women membership of the union rose from 500 in 1908 to 2,700 in 1912. Societies paying the minimum wage rose from 30 in 1908 to over 200 by 1912. The Cooperative Wholesale Society adopted the scale in 1912.

This campaign showed the Guild fighting consistently for what it believed in, fighting at branch as well as national level. It showed the women putting their idealistic view of the cooperative movement to practical use. The *Manchester Guardian* called this particular victory, 'a triumph for the progressive power of democratic organisation and a vindication of women's capacity for politics'.[23]

Most members of the Guild were married women so the campaigns to improve the medical care received by working-class mothers — mothers who were 'voiceless and unseen'[24] - was enthusiastically received by members. But attention shifted to perhaps their most important campaign: the fight for financial help for mothers in the form of Maternity Benefit.

The Campaign for Maternity Benefit

The National Insurance Act of 1911 introduced health and unemployment insurance. At an early stage of the legislation, the Guild asked about the position of married women in relation to health insurance proposals, and an informal deputation saw the Attorney General, Rufus Isaacs (Lloyd George being away). In preparation for the deputation, an enquiry among Guild members was undertaken; the findings were that the great mass of wage earners could not provide adequately for childbirth. Provision was made at the cost of the women, who either saved out of the housekeeping money, just as they needed more nourishment, or took on extra work, just as they needed more rest.

The Guild welcomed maternity benefit, but wanted the (planned) 30s benefit to be used to pay the doctor or midwife — and the balance to be paid to the *woman*. Other demands were that sick benefit should be paid to wage-earning women for two weeks before and four weeks after confinement, that one third of the insurance commissioners should be women, and that there should be a national system of medical care.

The Act, as finally passed, incorporated many of the Guild's suggestions, including a voluntary scheme for non-wage-earning married women, but the proposal that the Maternity Benefit should be the property of the mother was ignored. Leading Guildswomen were appointed to the Advisory Committees set up under this Act.

When an Amending Bill to the 1911 Act was proposed, the Guild again campaigned vigorously for the Maternity Benefit to become the mother's. Once their other recommendations (on abolition of the doctor's prescribed fee and four weeks' confinement pay were conceded), they concentrated all efforts on the paying of Maternity

Benefit to the mother. Resolutions from over 300 branches went to Ministers and MPs. Lobbies of MPs took place, and when the Bill went to Standing Committee, Guild leaders explained their views. Opposition came from the five Labour men on the Committee, 'who took a definite line against the view that the benefit should be the woman's property'.[25]

Although passed in Committee, the Clause was to be opposed in the House of Commons when the Bill returned there. Within days, 7,000 signatures were collected in favour of the maternity benefit being the mother's property. Signatures were gathered from district nursing associations, midwives, Poor Law guardians and members of all political parties. The amendment making it possible for a husband's signature to be accepted only if authorised by the wife was carried. 'Much more than a remedy for a grave abuse of Maternity Benefit was won by this victory. The first public recognition of the mother's place in the home, and a new step towards some economic independence for wives', was how the Guild's 1913 Annual Report saw this victory.

There was yet another battle over the 1917 National Insurance Amendment Bill. The Guild opposed the suggestion that women leaving insurance schemes on marriage should receive a £2 Marriage Benefit and lose ordinary benefits. The Guild's alternatives suggested that an additional maternity benefit should be given for the first child. The Bill went so quickly through the Commons, the Guild had to press its point in the Lords (not that the Guild was much in love with the House of Lords).[26] Tactics included lobbying Peeresses, pleading with them to get their husbands to attend the Lords and vote. An amendment was agreed: Marriage Benefit was withdrawn. The Guild had won sick benefit for six weeks within a year of leaving employment, as well as a Maternity Benefit of 30s for the first child, born within two years of marriage.

To return to the medical care issue, the Guild fought for a scheme for national maternity care, through the Public Health Services. The ultimate success of this campaign was only partly due to Guild agitation. There was widespread concern for national efficiency (related to the poor health of recruits for the Boer and First World Wars), and concern for the falling birthrate. This campaign, with its stress on maternity care to improve the health of the citizens, was conceded for reasons more to do with national self-interest than compassion for poverty stricken mothers. But once again, the campaign was well fought, and skilfully prepared.

The Guild had set up a Citizenship subcommittee in 1912, to watch for and to initiate legislation in the interest of married working-class women. In 1913 the subcommittee took National Maternity Care as its special subject for the year. Margaret Bondfield and Margaret Llewelyn Davies, as Secretary and Chairman of the subcommittee, talked with health visitors, doctors and civil servants as well as visiting cities like Sheffield and Birmingham, to discuss their Municipal Infant Welfare schemes. A deputation saw Herbert Samuel, President of the Local Government Board, later in 1914. Proposals included compulsory notification of births; local authority Maternity Centres, set up with the help of Treasury grant, and the appointment of municipal midwives. Mr Samuel was sympathetic but pointed out that local authorities were already permitted to do much of what was demanded. A Memorandum was prepared for the Chancellor of the Exchequer. It argued for a Ministry of Health based on the public health side of the Local Government Board. It outlined the principles on which the scheme for National Maternity should be based. These included equal consideration for mother as for father; and the maternity services to be universal, not associated with Poor Law or inquisitorial methods. Working-class women should be associated with the administration for fear of 'scientific, eugenic and official views overriding individual and family rights'. The Guild argued for local maternity committees to be made compulsory (they were already permissive), with married working-class women as members, as 'members of the Guild feel strongly that "ladies" who have sat on charitable committees may be out of touch with the view of independent working women'. These committee members would not only see that schemes were implemented, but would help with non-medical work, and act as a channel of communication, allowing the voices of the mothers to be heard.

The scheme was to include a Maternity Centre to treat and advise mothers and infants, the centres to be local, small and homely. Midwives should be able to call on doctors, who in turn could call on specialists and there should be sufficient hospital accommodation in addition to the setting up of maternity homes.

In June 1914 a Local Government Board Circular was issued to Public Health Committees, and most of the Guild's suggestions were included. The offer of a grant of 50 per cent for expenses incurred on maternity and welfare work was particularly important.

Within a few days of this circular, war was declared, and the question of saving life was even more important. The Guild's 1914 Annual Report saw the Guild's scheme for the care of the mothers of the race to be their great contribution to the problems of the war. Guild branches discussed the circular, and action included pressure on their own local Public Health Authorities and enlisting the cooperation of other women's organisations, and of Labour organisations like the Independent Labour Party, which circulated the scheme to Labour Councillors. The National Union of Women's Suffrage Societies and the Women's Liberal Federation both lent an organiser to the Guild for short periods during this campaign.

A deputation from the Guild, and a wide range of supporting organisations visited Herbert Samuel, still President of the Local Government Board but also Chairman of the Government's Committee on the Prevention and Relief of Distress. He was sympathetic, but explained the scheme put forward already by his Department included supervision of midwives, health visiting, maternity centres for expectant mothers and children up to school age, and maternity hospitals. He thought that these large proposals could only be slowly introduced at local level, but promised another circular calling attention to the subject.

This was followed up by local pressures on Health Authorities, described as inaugurating a new relationship between working-class women and local authorities – it included local propaganda, press campaigns, and when Guild members attended Council meetings, it meant Guildswomen entering the Council Chamber for the first time. By 1915 there were thirty-six Special Maternity Subcommittees, and fifty Guild members belonged to them. The campaign went on as schemes were implemented but victory came only in March 1918, with the Maternity and Child Welfare Act. This made the setting up of Maternity Committees compulsory and home helps possible.

Influential during this campaign was the publication in 1915 of *Maternity: letters from Working Women,*[27] with a preface by Herbert Samuel. The book contained letters from members in response to enquiries about conditions at maternity. Reviews[28] included that of *The Times Literary Supplement:* 'A book of notable interest and of singular distinction. The whole book deserves careful study. The letters are human documents, straightforward, outspoken and quiet.' The *British Medical Journal's* review included the comment, 'A remarkable book, which the profession in general, and the obstetrician in particular, will do well to read and ponder over.'

In his Preface to the book, the Rt.Hon. Herbert Samuel praised the Guild's efforts to improve the conditions of married women, pointing out that under existing conditions a large part of Britain's possible population is wasted before birth and in infancy – a crucial point during a World War, of course. The preface relates infant mortality to ignorance, malnutrition and poverty, and says local authorities have wide powers; local councillors and electors needed to use them.

After the Preface, the Introduction to the book suggests that the letters quoted are from women above rather than below the level of their class: 'there is no doubt that the woman who is secretary of a branch of a Guild lives in better conditions than the average working women. If the conditions of their lives are as described, the overwork and poverty must be tenfold or twentyfold where wages are less and employment more precarious.' Poverty, lack of knowledge, lack of skilled advice and treatment, the heavy work of women at home and at the factory all contributed to the problem. But so did the personal relationship between husband and wife, for both in law and popular morality the wife is the inferior in the family, 'the life and duty of working [class] women is still regarded by man as care of the household, the satisfaction of man's desires and the bearing of children. . .inevitable that mothers are overlooked, they have been hidden behind the curtain which falls after marriage, the curtain which women are now themselves raising.'

No wonder the book had an impact, with its vivid descriptions of the sufferings of working-class mothers. One woman wrote:

When I had my second baby I had to work all through again as my husband was short of work and ill. . .so there was another poorly baby. . .I had to go out to work again at the month end, and put the baby out to nurse. I had to get up at four in the morning, and get my baby out of bed, wash and dress it, and leave home by five, and stand all day until half past five and then walk home again with my baby. I had to do this with three of them.

The personal meaning of the infant mortality figures comes over in a particularly moving letter from a woman whose husband was out of work for 8 of the 9 months of her first pregnancy, so she worked on the railway, for 17s per week, walking nearly six miles night and morning, or paying 5d for the train fare.

By the time my second child was born my husband's wages had increased to £1 1s for 72 hours. By that time hard work and worry and insufficient food had told on my once robust constitution with the result that I nearly lost my life through want of nourishment, and I did after 9 months of suffering lose my child. No one but mothers who have gone through the ordeal of pregnancy half starved, to finally bring a child into the world to live a living death for nine months can understand what it means. . .I had to work at laundry work from morning to night, nurse a sick husband and take care of my child, 3½ years old. . .I had to provide for my coming confinement which meant I had to do without common necessaries to provide doctors fees. . .I had to depend on my neighbours for what help they could give during labour and the lying-in period. . . but from the second day I had to have my other child with me, undress him and see to all his wants, and was often left six hours without a bite of food, the fire out, and no light, the time January and snow had lain on the ground two weeks. . .Is it possible under such circumstances for women to take care of themselves during pregnancy, confinement and afterwards?

But the victory won with the passing of the 1918 Maternity and Child Welfare Act was not to last. The economic climate meant tactics had to change from arguing for improvements to defending what had been achieved. This is reflected in the 1921 Report, which recognised that 'the political campaign to cut down expenditure on the public health services so essential to the national life has made it impossible to work for new developments, and has rendered it necessary to concentrate on the defence of what had already been gained'. In the following year, cuts are reported. With the government pledged to such economies, and local authorities preoccupied with housing difficulties, the Guild's leadership decided to concentrate on housing, rather than continue the fight on better maternity care.[28]

Despite these setbacks, this was a successful campaign. When the Guild first took up the issue of National Care of Maternity, the Central Education Committee of the Cooperative Union would not allow the word 'maternity' to appear on a syllabus of classes.[29] The Guild pressed for reforms just when the government was worried about the health of army recruits and about the falling birth-rate, and they won the sympathy and respect of Herbert Samuel at the Local Government Board. The members were united in their commitment to the improvements being fought for — a unity of a different kind than that shown when the Guild took its courageous and controversial stand on reform of the divorce law.

Divorce Law Reform and the Fight for Self-Government

When a Royal Commission on Divorce Law Reform was set up in 1909, Margaret Llewelyn Davies and Mrs Barton (then Assistant General Secretary) were asked, as officials of a working-class women's

organisation, to give evidence. The Guild's evidence was the only
contribution from a working-class women's organisation, and so
attracted much newspaper attention. The evidence was based on
answers to a circular sent round to branches. It asked members for
their views on whether the grounds for divorce should be the same as
for men, and whether divorce proceedings should be cheaper. Replies
were received from 429 branches, representing over 22,000 women.
Of this number 414 branches favoured equality before the law,
including 25 branches actually opposed to divorce; 361 branches
favoured cheaper divorce. (The circular also asked for views about
women serving on juries, and only 320 branches were in favour of this.)

Agreement on the basic issues of divorce law reform was combined
with a commitment to family stability. The 1911 Sectional Conference
Resolution in favour of divorce law reform states, 'this conference
believes that such a law would prevent widespread suffering and
degradation, would stimulate to better behaviour, would result in
happier home life and higher standards of morality, and would
strengthen what is best in married life'.

Working Women and Divorce (1911),[30] a book based on the evidence
sent in by branches, showed the inadequacy of the existing law, and the
hardship caused by the expense of divorce proceedings, and by the
unequal treatment of men and women.

An additional questionnaire was sent to 124 Guild members,
discussing the more radical notion of divorce by 'mutual consent' or
'serious incompatibility', as well as inclusion of other grounds, like
cruelty. One hundred members wanted to include cruelty, 82 approved
of mutual consent and 75 approved of the idea of serious
incompatibility. When the Report of the Royal Commission on Divorce
was published in 1912, the Minority Report included an attack on the
Guild's evidence.

The Majority Report recommended that the grounds for divorce
should be adultery, bigamy, cruelty, desertion after four years,
drunkenness, commuted death sentence and that the grounds should
be the same for men and women. Special courts to bring divorce within
the financial means of the poor were recommended, as was restriction
of press reporting. Resolutions supporting the Majority Report were
passed by the Labour Party and the Women's Labour League. The
Guild welcomed the Majority Report, and passed a resolution
advocating mutual consent after two years separation as additional
grounds for divorce. This was an advanced position — it took until 1969
before mutual consent became grounds for divorce — and it was not

surprising that their stand on an issue that appeared to undermine the position of men in the family, and had significance for catholics, was challenged.

Manchester and Salford Catholic Federation wrote to the Guild objecting to their stand on divorce law reform, as grants to the Guild came from Cooperative Societies and the Cooperative Union, which had catholic members who disapproved of divorce. Margaret Llewelyn Davies replied sharply that 'the Committee wish me to say that they consider the reform of the Divorce Law one of the most important moral and social reforms which affect cooperative women, and therefore cannot alter their action in regard to it'. The United Board also wrote to the Guild, asking them to consider giving up their work on divorce law reform, because otherwise it was bound to lead to disruption in the movement.

Margaret Llewelyn Davies and the President, Mrs Gasson, wrote a detailed reply. They made it clear that although there was a minority within the Guild opposed to divorce, this minority never tried to dominate the Guild. They considered that an outside body like the Catholic Federation had no right to dictate the Guild's action on a vital social and moral reform. Dealing with the Guild's relationship with the rest of the cooperative movement, the letter states that the Guild always acted independently not in the name of the cooperative movement: 'even in our strictly cooperative campaigns, on behalf of anti-credit, extension of cooperation to the poor, minimum wage, it has seemed often as if the official movement preferred us to work apart'. The letter ended defiantly: 'The knowledge that fruitful ideas and far-reaching reforms may spring out of anything so prosaic as shopkeeping only increases the respect for loyal buying which is the ABC of Guild work.'

War had been declared. The Guild's grant from the Cooperative Union was £400 and they received £150 from the CWS. When the Central Board of the Cooperative Union discussed the Guild's grant in 1914, two members of the Manchester and Salford Catholic Federation attended to put their case.

One, Mr McCreary, was a member of the Education Committee of the Longridge Society. Describing himself as an earnest and sincere cooperator he contended that he had always understood that cooperation had nothing to do with religion, that divorce was a religious question for catholics, and that his society would collapse if catholics withdraw support — they made up about 80 per cent of the membership. There was a long debate, during which one man declared that the present controversy should be a lesson to the Guild that 'they must satisfy themselves with the cooperative movement alone`; even clearer was the man who said, 'if the Board had to pay the piper, they should be able to call the tune'.

This hostility was countered by Mrs Gasson, a member of the Central Board and former Guild President, who argued that the matter was not a religious one, that she had never seen a question more enthusiastically discussed, and she hoped it would be many years before the United Board took upon itself to dictate to the Women's Guild with regard to policy.

The Resolution carried at the end of the debate gave grants to the Irish and Scottish Women's Guilds, but said that 'the application of the English Women's Guild for a grant of £400 be agreed to on condition they cease their agitation in favour of the alteration of the divorce law and that in future the Women's Guilds be requested not to take up any work disapproved of by the Board'.

At its first Congress following this debate, the Guild passed a resolution reaffirming its independence declaring it could not accept these conditions, 'believing that the future progress of the Guild and of the cooperative movement depends on Guild policy being democratically controlled as in the past by the members themselves'.

Because of the war, public action in support of the reforms in divorce law could not be undertaken. But the dispute between the Guild and the Cooperative Union was a bitter one. Both sides published articles and pamphlets. Only 30 of the Guild's 611 branches opposed the Central Committee's stand over self-government, and over £400 was collected by May 1915. It came mainly from branches but sympathetic individuals and organisations contributed too. Both sides of the dispute manoeuvred to ensure resolutions were on the agenda for the next Cooperative Congress. There were eighteen resolutions favourable to the Guild. The Salford Catholic Federation got two resolutions endorsing the Central Board's decision onto the agenda. The Central Board's own Resolution was passed. It asked Congress to endorse the action already taken, and 'confirmed its right to withhold grants from any organisation which, in its opinion, is pursuing a policy detrimental to the best interests of the Cooperative Movement'.

Before the vote, the debate was long: fifteen pages of the Congress Report! Arguments centred on the extent of catholic interference within the cooperative movement and the issue of free speech. The majority view was put by a printer, who begged Congress:

for heaven's sake, to let the movement be one that did not make men or women worshipping at their own altars feel that their conscience was being outraged by an alien question being introduced into the movement. This was a business question, too. It had to do with the selling of tea and sugar and treacle and the rest of it. With every respect to the Women's Guild, there was nothing in it to make it of so much value as the disruption of the movement.

One of the few women who talked in the debate, Mrs Wimhurst from Woolwich, said wryly that she noticed that when men talked about religion they became curiously intolerant.

The Guild taught its members not only to be cooperators but to be citizens as well. Social reform consisted of things that merged together; it could not be chopped up into sections. . .Far deeper than the question of divorce, they were engaged in a world war for freedom of speech and action; and yet in the cooperative movement, where they ought to be working together they were fighting with one another. . .the question of divorce was secondary, but freedom of speech in the movement was vital.

The war created problems for the Guild: towns were dark, halls were taken over by the military, women worked at every kind of job, members had relatives killed or wounded. Membership declined and some branches closed. Subscriptions to Central Funds were raised from 2d to 4d voluntarily at first but then by rule, in 1916. Nearly £200 was collected from a special appeal. The Guild had to economise, but the leadership and membership together were determined that the Guild would not suffer from the withdrawal of the grant. The Guild reapplied for a grant in 1917, and was offered the same conditions. The Guild refused it. But Margaret Llewelyn Davies, whilst refusing the grant on those terms, in her letter requesting the money explained that 130 Liberal women were being trained as speakers and the Guild wanted to train speakers and arrange classes on the vote and how to use it. The proposal was rejected.

Meanwhile, the Cooperative Union had set up a Survey Committee to which Margaret Llewelyn Davies had given evidence. The Survey Committee's proposals were that the Guild should recognise the ultimate authority of the Cooperative Union and that the Union should appoint representatives on the Guild's Central Committee. The Guild was totally opposed to this. They were an organisation supported by women, yet the Cooperative Union, where men held most official positions, wanted to influence them! The Survey Committee's report was never implemented, but its appearance during the Guild's fight for self-government showed how threatened the Cooperative Union felt by the reaction of some of its members to the Guild's independent stand.

Yet within a year the split was healed. The Central Board asked for a meeting with the Guild. Renewal of the grant was recommended, on the basis of work undertaken by the Guild the previous year. If the grant was withheld in future, the Central Board would give reasons for doing so. Regular meetings between the Cooperative Union's Central Board and the Guild's Central Committee were held, and one result was that the Guild was asked to send a delegate to the Cooperative Congress.

This episode cost the Guild £1,600 in lost grants, but it gained in self-confidence — it had taken on the Goliath of the Cooperative Union, and won. At the same time, the granting of political suffrage to women and their role during the war, as well as the rise of the Cooperative Party had improved the status of women as potential supporters in a wider sphere than simply buying. By 1922 the Cooperative Union had recognised the status of the Guild when Margaret Llewelyn Davies became the first woman Chairman of the Cooperative Congress (and the last until Eva Dodds was elected President for the 1975 Edinburgh Cooperative Congress).

After the War

It has been difficult to give an adequate picture of the range of Guild concerns: from loyalty to the local store to the white slave traffic. And after the war, a growing emphasis on peace and international issues. The Guild remained a progressive force, for example, they were the first women's organisation to pass a resolution in favour of legalising abortion at their 1934 Congress.

After the war the Guild faced problems. Due partly to its very success, many of the most effective members were drawn more and more into public work. The Guild was represented on central bodies such as the consultative committees of the Ministry of Health, and twelve Guildswomen were among the first women Magistrates appointed. Competition from other women's organisations was growing. In 1922 Margaret Llewelyn Davies resigned, after thirty-two years as General Secretary, and Lilian Harris retired after twenty years as Assistant General Secretary. There was a debate about the voluntary nature of service to the Guild, but after their retirement, Guild officers were to be paid. Miss A. Honora Enfield became the new General Secretary, and Mrs Eleanor Barton the Assistant General Secretary. Although elected by the membership, the Central Committee made it very clear, through a circular to branches, who they thought the best candidate was. And she won.

Alice Honora Enfield[31] (1882-1935), the daughter of a banker, was educated at Somerville College, Oxford, taking a degree examination before degrees were awarded to women. She taught for several years in a secondary school, and worked on the administration of the National Health Insurance Acts. She saw the cooperative movement as the surest road to social peace, and became private secretary to Margaret Davies in 1917, then General Secretary in 1922. Her particular value to the Guild was her skill in guiding the campaign for improved state insurance benefits for women. She became Secretary of the International Cooperative Women's Guild in 1922, and gave up the English Guild post in 1925 to concentrate on the International Guild. She was an active pacifist, and was associated with the National Peace Council.

Mrs Eleanor Barton[32] (1872-1960) was born in Manchester, but little is known about her early life. She settled in Sheffield after her marriage in 1894, and joined the Guild in 1901. She took on a range of Guild positions, becoming Treasurer in 1913 and President a year later. In 1919 she lectured in America on maternity and child welfare. She was Secretary of the Guild from 1925 to 1937. Her husband was a Labour Party activist, a Sheffield City Councillor, and author of a book called *World History for the Workers*. In 1921 and 1923 she was a Parliamentary candidate in Kings Norton, Birmingham, coming second in the poll both times. She was a pacifist, and she served on many government and cooperative bodies. She was the first woman Director of the Cooperative Newspaper Publishing Society.

The Guild recognised their debt to Misses Davies and Harris by awarding them the Freedom of the Guild. At the ceremony, Margaret Llewelyn Davies talked about her relationship with the Guild membership. For progress, the rank and file had to have confidence in their elected leaders, but also the leaders had to have confidence in the rank and file; it was this mutual confidence that enabled the Guild to accomplish so much.

She had more than the confidence of the rank and file — the letters she received from Guild members and from branches all over England are preserved in the Harris Papers.[33] The regret and shock that was felt on her retirement and the affection and admiration she inspired, come over very clearly.

Margaret Llewelyn Davies' Presidential Address to the 1922 Cooperative Congress was impressive. She examined the national and international economic situation. She described the characteristics of cooperation, seeing the abolition of profit and the introduction of democratic control as nothing less than a revolution, but a revolution not grasped by the public, nor by many cooperators. She regretted that there were no women yet on the board of the CWS or in Parliament, declaring, 'the ways of loosening the hold, both in men's and women's minds, of a man's prescriptive right to an administrative post and of giving women adequate representation must be found before our machine will become fully democratic'.

But the former President, introducing her, seemed not to recognise the equality of the contribution women could make to the movement. 'I think', he ventured, 'that the entry of women into national and international affairs will bring with it that spirit of sweet reasonableness which is so necessary and which will tend to remove all questions of strife among nations.' He concluded by saying that Miss Davies was a lady of first rate intellectual power, but that she might feel the stress of Congress proceedings, and appealed to the delegates to 'remember in all our proceedings we have a lady in the Chair'.

Some Conclusions

The early success of the Guild lay in the way it changed the lives of working-class women too old to have benefited from later developments in public education. The Guild enabled women to contribute to public life, to the Labour movement and to the cooperative movement in a way difficult to envisage had they not taken advantage of the early educational and training activities of the Guild. Hall and Watkins[34] wrote in 1937 that 'the devoted service of many fine women to the Guild and its work stand out as one of the brightest features in cooperative records, and testifies to the great influence which the Guild exerted upon members of the Cooperative movement'.

Bonner[35] compares the Guild to the Fabian Society in its campaigns, in the way that the Guild always made sure of its ground by study and discussion, and then shaped opinion through widespread and intensive campaigning. The Guild's influence for progress within the cooperative movement, and in legislation affecting women at home as well as at work, justifies this praise and the conclusions of G.D.H. Cole[36] who wrote:

In comparison with the activities of other sections of the growing
Women's Movement, the doings of the Women's Cooperative Guild
were always unspectacular and even sedate. There was something
unhurried and certain of itself, idealistic in a quiet way, but always
practical, expecting a great deal in terms of intellectual response.
The Guild knew the conditions it had to deal with; its leaders
understood how small a chance the working-class housewife had
been allowed of looking beyond the concerns of hearth and home. It
seized on these very things, in which its members had special
knowledge and experience, to serve as the foundation of its work.
That was the secret of its outstanding success.

The period we have looked at is one of increasing representation of
women on cooperative bodies, and later, on outside bodies, as
Appendix IX shows (see p.207).

The Guild was reformist, but its achievements were of more practical
value to working-class women than the unrealised and more radical
objectives of other groups. Their optimistic assumptions about the
potential for social change of the cooperative movement were misplaced.
They might well be surprised at existing inequalities of wealth and
power, at the inequalities of access to the social services and how slowly
the status of women has been to improve. But perhaps the best way to
assess the importance of the Guild is not by looking at the judgement
of historians or at statistics but by looking at the effect of the Guild
on just one of its ordinary members.

Guild members told their stories in a book, published in 1931,
called *Life as We Have Known It*. [37] One chapter is the story of Mrs
Layton, born in Bethnal Green, who started work at the age of 10, and
went into service at 13. She talks of her marriage and the poverty her
husband's ill-health caused. Her second child died from lack of
nourishment. Later, she became a midwife, achieving retrospective
qualified status.

The first Cooperative Society she joined failed and she lost £12,
but she said that she gained more than £12 of knowledge, and 'my life
brightened so much that everything seemed changed'. She later joined
another society, and became President of her new Guild branch. She
lectured to other branches, and won a Cooperative Union essay prize.
Soon she became a member of her Society's Management Committee,
and went on national deputations in connection with the Guild's
Maternity Benefit Campaign. Particularly satisfying to her was going
in a deputation to the Prince of Wales Fund's Executive, when they

decided not to give relief to unmarried women. She argued that she represented 30,000 married women, and that the Guild would not be resentful if relief went to the unmarried; the committee changed its policy before she left the room.

She became Vice President of the Guild, and read a paper at an International Cooperative Women's Guild Conference in Europe. Money for such activities was found by turning her old coat, blacking her hat, repairing her own shoes and running an allotment.

Mrs Layton joined the Cooperative Building Society and supervised the building of her own house, which she put in her own name. She writes:

Sometimes my husband rather resented the teachings of the Guild. The fact that I was determined to assert my right to have the house in my name was a charge against the Guild. The Guild, he said, was making women think too much of themselves. I did not quite agree with him there, although I did and still do think the Guild has been the means of making its members think more of themselves than ever they did before. The Guild's training altered the whole course of my life. When I look back and think what my life might have been without its training and influence I shudder. . .It is impossible for me to say how much I owe to the Guild. It gave me education and recreation. The lectures I heard gave me so much food for thought I seldom felt dull, and I always had something to talk to my husband about other than the little occurrences of daily life. . . From a shy nervous woman, the Guild made me a fighter.

Notes

1. J. Bellamy and J. Saville (eds.), *Dictionary of Labour Biography,* vol.I, London: Macmillan, 1972, p.5.
2. *Cooperative News,* 6 January 1883.
3. G.D.H. Cole, *A Century of Cooperation,* Manchester, Cooperative Union Ltd., 1944, pp.215-26.
4. *Cooperative News,* 10 February 1883.
5. M. Llewelyn Davies, *The Women's Cooperative Guild, 1883-1904,* Kirkby Lonsdale, Westmorland: Cooperative Women's Guild, 1904, p.18. See also P.N. Backstrom, *Christian Socialism and Cooperation in Victorian England,* London: Croom Helm, 1974.
6. M. Llewelyn Davies, *The Women's Cooperative Guild, 1883-1904,* p.31
7. J. Bellamy and J. Saville (eds.), *Dictionary of Labour Biography,* vol.II, London: Macmillan, 1974, p.396.
8. *Cooperative News,* 22 December 1883.

9. M. Llewelyn Davies, *The Women's Cooperative Guild, 1883-1904.* p.38.
10. J. Bellamy and J. Saville (eds.), *Dictionary of Labour Biography,* vol.I, pp.96-9. Dr K. Davies and Miss M.O. Davies (nieces of M. Llewelyn Davies). Typescripts lent by University of Hull, Department of Economic and Social History.
11. M. Llewelyn Davies, *The Women's Cooperative Guild. 1883-1904.* p.150.
12. B. Potter *The Cooperative Movement in Britain,* London: Swan Sonnenschein & Co.. 1891, p.226.
13. C. Black (ed.), *Married Women's Work,* London: G. Bell and Sons Ltd., 1915, p.1.
14. M. Llewelyn Davies, *The Women's Cooperative Guild, 1883-1904,* p.151.
15. M. Llewelyn Davies (ed.), *Life as We Have Known It,* London: Hogarth Press, 1931, pp.133-4.
16. M. Llewelyn Davies (ed.), *Life as We Have Known It,* pp.xxi-xxiii.
17. M. Llewelyn Davies, *Cooperation in Poor Neighbourhoods,* Kirkby Lonsdale. Westmorland: Women's Cooperative Guild, 1899, pp.4-7.
18. Quoted in material left by Lilian Harris to the London School of Economics, comprising papers. photographs and manuscripts relating to the Women's Cooperative Guild. LSE Miscellaneous Collection, 268 M 363.
19. *Daily News,* February 1903. Cutting in LSE, Misc. Collection, 268 M 363.
20. C. Webb, *The Woman with the Basket,* Manchester: Cooperative Wholesale Society's Printing Works, 1927, p.94.
21. G.D.H. Cole, *A Century of Cooperation,* p.223.
22. Women's Cooperative Guild, *A Cooperative Standard for Women Workers.* paper presented to Annual Congress, June 1908.
23. Quoted by Dr K. Davies in typescript lent by Hull University.
24. C. Webb, *The Woman with the Basket,* p.11.
25. *Annual Report,* Women's Cooperative Guild, 1913-14, p.23.
26. *Annual Report,* Women's Cooperative Guild. 1917-18, p.8.
27. Women's Cooperative Guild, *Maternity, Letters from Working Women,* London, G. Bell and Sons, 1915.
28. *Annual Report,* Women's Cooperative Guild, 1915-16, pp.1-10.
29. E. Barton, *The National Care of Motherhood,* London: Cooperative Women's Guild, 1918, p.6.
30. *Working Women and Divorce,* An account of evidence given on behalf of Women's Cooperative Guild before the Royal Commission on Divorce, London: David Nutt, 1911
31. J. Bellamy and J. Saville (eds.), *Dictionary of Labour Biography,* vol.I, pp.112-13.
32. J. Bellamy and J. Saville (eds.), *Dictionary of Labour Biography,* vol.I, pp.38-40.
33. LSE, Misc. Collection, 268 M 363.
34. F. Hall and W.P. Watkins, *Cooperation,* Manchester: The Cooperative Union Ltd., 1937, p.180.
35. A. Bonner, *British Cooperation,* revised by B.Rose, Manchester: Cooperative Union Ltd., 1970, p.126.
36. G.D.H. Cole, *A Century of Cooperation,* p.226.
37. M. Llewelyn Davies (ed.), *Life as We Have Known It,* pp.1-55.

PART II   THE MOVEMENT TODAY

7 WOMEN IN THE LABOUR PARTY TODAY

Oonagh McDonald MP

Earlier chapters have already recorded the story of the beginnings of the women's movement in the spheres of Labour politics, trade unionism and consumer cooperation. They have described how the organisations started, their triumphs and disappointments and the steady determination which was never daunted by failure and did not allow complacency to rob success of its full potential.

In politics we have already seen how Labour women's political organisation began life in 1906 in the Women's Labour League and how, in 1918, under the new Labour Party constitution, the League became the Women's Section of the Labour Party, with Dr Marion Phillips as their first Chief Woman Officer.

Throughout most of its history, apart from the rather dead period of the fifties, when political parties lost their post-war impetus, the women's organisation of the Labour Party has always been deeply involved with the problems of the community. In 1939, a Glasgow woman's letter to *Labour Woman* described the women's section as the 'married women's trade union'.[1] Her description may not be entirely accurate, but she certainly caught the spirit of the women's movement in the Party.

Labour women fought for women's rights, and for their homes and families. We now take for granted the benefits for which the women's sections, the 'married women's trade union', struggled in the past. They pressed for free school milk, a school meals' service and, with their work to eradicate the dangers of maternal and infant mortality, helped to pave the way for the introduction of the National Health Service after World War II. School milk and school meals were the fruits of their most successful campaign of the 1930s — the nutrition campaign. This campaign was based on the pioneering work of Sir John Boyd Orr, whose book *Food, Health and Income: Report of a Survey on the Adequacy of Diet in Relation to Income* was published in 1936. His research helped to show the important and hitherto unrecognised connection between diet and health. A poor diet led, not only to rickets and scurvy, common amongst poor children, but also to other diseases, and to listlessness and apathy. The new knowledge was disseminated in the press, especially by Ritchie-Calder, a Fabian and

144

now a Life Peer, who was a reporter with the *Daily Herald* from 1930-41. On this basis the women were able to force an ignorant public and an unwilling Tory Government to acknowledge the extent of malnutrition and near-starvation amongst the poor and its effects on their mental and physical health.

The campaign was successful because it was unremitting and well-organised. It involved the ordinary members of women's sections who disclosed details of their house-keeping budgets and provided the concrete evidence required by the leaders of the women's organisation, who were members of the Standing Joint Committee of Industrial Women's Organisations. This Committee comprised representatives from the trade unions, the Cooperative Women's Guild, and the Labour Party and they, led by Labour's Chief Woman Officer, Mary Sutherland, were able to show that many families could not afford both to pay the rent and buy adequate food. They were able to lobby MPs and send deputations to ministers, their demands being backed by vivid case histories of hardship.

In 1933, the *Lancet* published a subsistence diet,[2] worked out by the British Medical Association and costed at 5s 8d per man per week. Labour women were able to show that the cost of the recommended diet was far higher than the BMA realised. Members of the women's sections sent in many examples of actual budgets showing that the cost of the subsistence diet was often more than £2 2s 6d for a man, his wife and three children aged between six and fourteen years. Set against the full unemployment benefit for a married man of £1 11s 3d per week, it was obvious that many families could not afford a basic subsistence diet. It was far beyond the means of most working-class families, especially the unemployed. And disturbing reports from medical officers of health and from school teachers bore out their claims.

These showed that, in 1931, 50,000 children were suffering from malnutrition and many more were undernourished. Even worse, the attempts to improve some of the conditions of working-class people sometimes led to greater hardship. For instance, in 1933, the medical officer of health for Stockton-on-Tees published a report which showed how, by moving half a slum tenement population from the centre of the town to a new housing estate on the outskirts, the death rate on the new estate was considerably higher than among the other half of the slum tenement population left in their slum dwellings: that in fact, in 1923-9, the death rate per thousand was 22.91, while in 1928-32 the death rate on the new estate had risen to 33.55 per thousand. But in the slum tenements the death rate had remained static. He attributed this surprising disparity to a considerable reduction in real incomes on the housing estate owing to increased rents, higher food prices in the shops on the estate than in markets in the town and increased travelling expenses, all of which had combined to make an adequate diet impossible.

The nutrition campaign was also designed to educate Labour women, and, in turn, the public, about the importance of an adequate and balanced diet. The publicity given in *Labour Woman* to the subsistence diet,[3] and the necessity of milk for children served that function as well. Members of the women's sections were urged to press for the full provisions of the School Meals Act, and for the provision of school milk. By 1931, 157 local education authorities out of a total of 317 provided school meals for 320,000 children. Some local authorities, Kent and Walsall for example, refused to feed necessitous children. Slowly however throughout the thirties more and more local authorities provided milk for school children, but mostly parents had to pay for it. Tribute must be paid here to Dr Edith Summerskill*, who brought all her medical knowledge and experience to the support of this nutrition campaign.

In 1938, a headmaster writing in *Labour Woman*[4] explained that many families could not afford to pay 2½d a week for school milk for each child. The children were often proud and pretended that they did not like milk, but the real reason for refusing it was poverty. The headmaster paid for milk for 200 children out of his own pocket. He was not alone. Many teachers paid for both milk and boots for their pupils.

The women's sections responded to continuing brutal poverty by waging another cost of living campaign, drawing upon their own bitter experience. A member from Cambridgeshire described the burden of increased costs of cooking on primus stoves, the regular means at that time of providing hot meals for whole families in many country areas. Lancashire women suffered terribly from low wages, frequently no more than £1 a week. The record of all this poverty and hardship helped to prepare the way for the 'safety net' of National Insurance, the ending of the hated Means Test, and for better facilities for school children. This is not to suggest that the Labour women's organisation should receive the sole credit for the introduction of all these benefits. There were, of course, many other factors all of which helped to bring about the Education Act of 1944 and the National Insurance Act of 1946.

The real contribution of Labour women's efforts was to turn issues such as an adequate diet, the price of basic food, maternal and infant mortality and pit head baths into front rank political issues. Apart from their efforts, the 'central' issues of the economy and international relations would have dominated political discussion and political action in the 1930s and it is hard to see how the problems which the women forced into the political arena would otherwise have emerged as such.

It is difficult to imagine men making the provision of school milk, family allowances or maternal mortality a central political issue. Not that men did not take part in such campaigns, but political interests arise out of the role one plays in society and one's status in it. Working-class women had a dual role involving work outside the home, at lower rates of pay, with the constant risk of unemployment, and the responsibility of caring for children. Their political campaigning naturally reflected these interests. In a period of high unemployment their demands for proper pay and conditions of work met with considerable hostility and resentment.

Demands for better provision for their children sometimes met with opposition even in the Labour movement. For example, the trade union movement was at first unwilling to support the campaign for family allowances, because, understandably enough at the time, they felt that employers would resist demands for higher wages on the grounds that employees were receiving the allowances. Family allowances were already being paid in France, Norway, Sweden and New Zealand,[5] as *Labour Woman* reported. Eventually, the trade union movement was persuaded to support family allowances, and their fears that this would affect collective bargaining and the rate for the job, were shown to be unfounded. The Family Allowances Act was passed in 1945 by the wartime Coalition Government, and first operated by the Labour Government in 1946.

In 1937, the Standing Joint Committee of Working Women's Organisations had presented a 'Children's Charter' to the National Labour Women's Conference at Norwich. The Report called for the provision of cash allowances for children up to two years, better maternity and child welfare services, day nurseries, education up to 16, child guidance clinics and protection for the rights of the child. This battle for children's rights was a continuation of the work of the Women's Labour League in the early years of this century. The earlier reports on 'Protecting the Nation's Mothers' and the report to the 1936 Swansea Conference on 'Nutrition and Food Supplies' and the ensuing discussions had done invaluable work of political education. The 1937 Report carried into practical politics the fight for first-class conditions of nutrition and education for all children up to the age of sixteen. That was their achievement. Since then the fact that such issues are part of politics has been taken for granted.

Throughout its history the women's organisation has also fought for women's rights. In 1935, the Standing Joint Committee gave evidence to the Royal Commission on the use which was being made of the Anomalies Regulations to deny unemployment benefit to thousands of women who should never have been brought under the Regulations.[6] Married women industrial workers were contributors to the Unemployment Insurance Fund, and yet were denied benefit when they were entitled to it. As a result of the Committee's evidence the Commission recommended that there should be no discrimination against married women as such.

The women's organisation also pressed for proper compensation for war injuries and, in 1941, they succeeded in ensuring that compensation was not restricted to members of the civil defence organisation and gainfully employed persons alone. The right to compensation was extended to the whole adult population. The initial legislation of 1940 had provided no compensation at all for housewives injured, say, during an air raid, as though women were somehow non-persons, of no value to anyone, including their families. Even then, typically, the rate of compensation for a woman's injury was only two-thirds of a man's.

The passing of the British Nationality Act in 1948 marked the end of a successful campaign to allow a British woman to retain British nationality on marriage to an alien, but also made it impossible for an alien woman to automatically acquire British nationality by marrying a British husband. This condition that alien women should establish their claim to British nationality was necessitated by certain abuses taking place at that time.

These were successful campaigns for women's rights. But there were failures, too. In 1947 the Labour Government felt unable to introduce equal pay in the public services under government and local authority control, because the country could not afford it. In a spirit of cooperation with the new Labour Government in a difficult post-war situation, the women's movement accepted the judgement then, but took the matter up again later.

The battle for women's rights continued to a greater or lesser extent throughout the fifties and was revived with some vigour in the sixties. Pressure for equal pay and equal rights and opportunities mounted during the sixties particularly, as indicated in repeated resolutions at National Labour Women's conferences calling for equal pay and for better training facilities and better general conditions of work for women. These resolutions emphasised women's dual role as workers and as mothers and housewives. The campaign led to the Labour Government's Equal Pay Act of 1970, which made the introduction of equal pay for equal work mandatory by the end of 1975. It was appropriate that Barbara Castle, as Secretary of State for Employment and Productivity, had the privilege of piloting this legislation through Parliament.

This campaign for equal opportunities and equal conditions for the sexes led to the appointment of a study group by the National Executive Committee of the Labour Party in November 1967. The Study Group investigated the extent of discrimination against women in Britain and recommended policies to enable women to achieve equal rights. In 1968, the National Conference of Labour Women considered a report entitled 'Discrimination Against Women', which was partly based on information contained in women's sections' replies to questionnaires. The discussion which followed the Report at the National Conference was of a very high standard and was no doubt helpful to members of the Study Group. An interim report, *Towards Equality: Women in Social Security,* was produced in March 1969 and, finally, a Green Paper on *Discrimination Against Women*[7] was published in 1972, when Labour was in opposition.

It described clearly and coolly the wide ranging discrimination women experience in every aspect of their lives; in marriage, in taxation, in work, in social security. The Green Paper was widely published and well received by the media just because it carefully documented the extent of discrimination and perhaps also because of its essentially practical nature. It was, after all, published at the end of a decade in which, increasingly, the status of women was the theme of many discussions and when the women's liberation movement, which started in America, was having some impact here in Britain, bringing to public attention the question of women's role in the family, in work and in the community, which had lain dormant in the immediate post-war period.

Women's liberation helped to stimulate women to think about equality, and the Green Paper provided an essentially practical approach to the whole question of women's rights and their place in society. The Green Paper was also seen by the Labour women's organisation as the necessary counterpart to the Equal Pay legislation of 1970. It had an extremely important impact on the Labour Party itself. It roused the Party to deeper understanding of the disadvantages women suffer in our society, and once again it brought an issue, which some people have liked to think of as marginal, to the centre of political controversy.

However, to set up a Study Group and to produce an opposition Green Paper, even one which is well received, are only the first steps in bringing about the recommended legislative changes. The National Labour Women's Advisory Committee had to work, first to persuade the Party that the recommendations for ending discrimination should become the policy of the Party and especially that the commitment to end discrimination against women should be included in the Manifesto for the elections of 1974. They were successful. The Manifesto contained Labour's 'Charter for Women'.[8]

The success of the campaign was demonstrated by the fact that the government took up the issue so speedily on assuming office. The Government's White Paper, *Equality for Women*, was published in the summer of 1974.

But the efforts of the National Labour Women's Advisory Committee did not end there. Nothing less than an even balance of the sexes in political life was their strategy so they had important suggestions to make about the White Paper — that for instance it seemed to rule out 'reverse discrimination', which, if correct, would make it impossible to provide additional training facilities for women to enable them to compete on equal terms in employment. The National Committee stressed the necessity for day care facilities, if women are ever to achieve job equality. It would also be necessary to introduce supporting legislation to end unfair treatment for women in such areas as taxation, and matrimonial and family law.

The Sex Discrimination Bill was introduced in March 1975. It goes beyond the White Paper, as a result of consultation with women's organisations, trade unions and other bodies, in two important respects. The Bill extends the definition of discrimination to include practices which are discriminatory in their effects, even though inadvertently so. It also permits positive action by employers and training bodies by way of single sex training to end the domination of certain kinds of employment by either men or women. In other words, the Bill allows 'reverse discrimination'. In addition, the Social Security Pensions Bill was introduced in February 1975, and, amongst its other provisions, the Bill ensures a fair state pension scheme for women. Both these measures are now on the Statute Book. These were important steps forward, but the Committee is now giving attention to other related items which require separate legislation and action. Getting equal rights and equal opportunities for women is hard work. It means careful research, constant pressure and exposition on the part of the women's organisation. Women will only end discrimination against themselves if they work unremittingly towards that aim; and that state of affairs is not easily achieved.

The women's organisation of the Labour Party was, naturally enough, sufficiently committed to the campaign for women's rights to work patiently for the appropriate legislation. The importance of their work in highlighting the problem of discrimination against women, and of their recommendations for legislation has been acknowledged by the Home Secretary.

It is unlikely that the Labour Party, had it not been for Labour women's efforts, would ever have worked so hard for women's rights. Not that the party without the women's organisation would not be concerned about the subject, but because the issue would continually be forced into the background by more immediate problems.

The women's organisation must continue to exist in order to fight for women's rights. Up to the present time it has acted as a pressure group seeking to influence the direction of government policy and to help in forming Labour's policy by propaganda, by lobbying MPs, and sending deputations to ministers. It is only recently, though, that the women's organisation, through the National Committee has come to play a more definite role in policy-making.

The National Labour Women's Advisory Committee, and the National Conference of Labour Women have recently played a larger part in the process of policy-making within the Labour Party, especially on topics of great concern to women. Although, of course, the women's organisation is only one among a number of influences on policy-making within the party.

The decisions taken at the National Conference of Labour Women are not binding on the party. Nevertheless the Conference portrays the views of the women members, not only on their rights and needs as women, but also over the entire field of policy and on the actions of Labour Government. Those decisions are always seen by the National Executive Committee.

In the same way the National Labour Women's Advisory Committee, consisting of two women representatives from each region, functions in an advisory capacity, expressing the views of the women's organisation throughout Britain. The Committee's decisions, while not binding on the party, can be channelled through the various committees or subcommittees of the party or direct to the National Executive Committee. The Chief Woman Officer can attend all the Committees of the party including the NEC. In this way the channels of communication are kept open and the women's organisation can bring some influence to bear on the development of policy.

One member of the National Advisory Committee describes the process this way: 'The Committee, although an advisory committee is, I feel, increasingly having an influence on policy-making.' Another member of the Committee traces the growing influence of the women's organisation to the revival of the women's movement in the early 1960s after the quiet period of the fifties. 'The women's organisation began to be more outward-looking and forged stronger links with other women's organisations. Women outside the Labour Party wanted to know what Labour women were thinking on social issues and, as a result, women generally began to study the social problems of the 1960s which were crying out for attention.'

The role of the women's organisation has not been confined to campaigning on issues which concern women, their families and their homes. The women's movement has had an important part to play in preparing women for a more active political role in the party, in local government and in service on public bodies. Some members of the National Advisory Committee feel that the party has consistently failed to recognise the importance of the women's organisation in this respect. Perhaps the party as a whole has failed to realise that political maturity comes only through involvement in some kind of struggle.

Probably the best organised and most successful campaign so far undertaken by the National Advisory Committee was that started in 1967. It began with consideration of the place of women in the organisation of the party, that is on the NEC, in regional constituency organisation, the National Labour Women's Conference, party candidatures, local and national, and discrimination against women of every type and kind.

In the face of growing criticisms in some sections of the movement of the existence of a 'separate' women's organisation, it seized the opportunity of the National Executive's 'Simpson Enquiry' to establish a more influential role for the women's organisation. Opposed to the recommendation that the reserved seats for women on the NEC should be abolished, it took up the challenge and fought back against this threat to women's position in the centre of power within the party. The battle was fought largely within the NEC and included deputations from the National Labour Women's Advisory Committee to the NEC and the Parliamentary leadership. In 1971 a statement from the National Labour Women's Advisory Committee on *Women and the*

Labour Party was presented to the NEC and was widely debated throughout the party. This was the first indication that the National Labour Women's Advisory Committee were determined to see something like parity between men and women in the party before being prepared to concede any of the reserved places for women at any level. A dialogue between the National Labour Women's Advisory Committee and the NEC has continued ever since. In 1974 in response to a recommendation that the party should adopt a strategy for moving towards parity, the NEC asked for a report on the obstacles to women in politics and public life to be prepared. This report provided a basis for action and for a more determined effort to promote women candidates.

From its inception the women's organisation has been active in education and training. But, because of changing conditions and needs, the kind of training has been constantly adapted to meet new circumstances. In the thirties, as in the early days of the movement, the majority of women had only received elementary education. They needed the basic training which they received in Section meetings and through the pages of *Labour Woman* under the firm guiding hand of Mary Sutherland, Chief Woman Officer. Many of the articles in *Labour Woman* described vividly the work done by Labour controlled local authorities — for the mentally ill, for young delinquents or in providing home help services and maternity and child welfare schemes.

With this kind of information to hand women were able to work for the party more effectively in both local and national elections. Week by week, in Section meetings, this kind of political education continued, and all the while thousands of Labour women were quietly, but very effectively, becoming politicised.

Labour Woman ceased publication in 1971 but training and political education has been continued by weekend schools and conferences, and through the questionnaires and discussion papers circulated by the National Committee.

The campaign to encourage and train more women for public life, in local government and in service on public bodies, continued there, just as in Parliament, but we find far too few of them. Some people are apt to think that the position must have improved over recent years, but when we look at the records, we find that this is not the case.

In 1934, for example, 25 per cent of the sixty-nine newly elected Labour councillors in London were women; and three metropolitan London boroughs with Labour majorities had women mayors. *Labour Woman* reported that many woman members had been coopted on to the committees through which London's schools, hospitals, public institutions and services were administered. In 1937, there were twenty-one women on the Labour benches in County Hall. In 1939, the first woman chairman of the London County Council was elected, Mrs E.M. Lowe, JP. She was an extremely good business manager and her election was a fitting event to mark the fiftieth anniversary of the election of three women to the London County Council, who were actually unseated on the grounds of sex in 1889. Mrs Lowe was first elected by West Bermondsey in 1922 and after the Labour victory of 1934, she was made chairman of the Education Committee, and in 1937, chairman of the Establishment Committee.

The success of women on the London County Council could well have been partly due to the influence of Herbert Morrison. Bernard Donoghue and G.W. Jones, in their book, *Herbert Morrison: Portrait of a Politician* note that

> Morrison was keen to use the talents of women. In addition to Dr Rickards he appointed as chairman Mrs E.M. Lowe to education and Miss Agnes Dawson to General Purposes. He loved to appoint women to positions which they had never held before, like Mrs Helen Bentwich to the Fire Brigade Committee, much to the consternation of the fire officers who felt such a committee was not suitable for a female; and Lady Nathan to the Metropolitan Water Board, 'to stir up that lot'.

But perhaps his appointments were as much due to the considerable influence of Freda Corbet and Ruth Dalton, as to Morrison's broadmindedness.

In 1946, a landslide Labour victory in local government elections, following Labour's Parliamentary success in 1945, brought many women councillors into office. In the London County Council elections, Labour won 1,038 seats in 28 Boroughs, out of a total of 1,357 seats. 255 Labour women were returned, and there were five Labour women mayors in London and at least seven elsewhere including Bradford, Huddersfield, Rotherham, Wakefield and Newport.

This gives an impression of some of the best years of Labour women's representation as local councillors. The years mentioned here were good years for Labour in local government elections, and in such years a larger number of Labour women than usual are likely to be returned; but we can see how little progress has been made over the years towards equal representation of men and women on local councils, when we compare one of the best recent years for the election of women councillors in Bristol, five in 1964, with six Labour women councillors and one woman alderman, in 1937.

The picture outlined above of the extent of Labour women's representation in local government is necessarily impressionistic. But, as with Parliament, the number of women representing the party in this way is very small. As far as local government goes the last official figures of female representation were published in the Maud Report in 1967,[9] and these indicate that only 12 per cent of Council members (of all parties) were women. Since the reorganisation of local government, Transport House has monitored Labour women's representation in the 1973 and 1974 local government elections with the following results:

In the 1973 elections, in the Metropolitan and Non-Metropolitan Boroughs, of 6,085 successful Labour candidates only 786 were women or 12.9 per cent.

In 1974, in the Greater London Boroughs 203 Labour women were elected out of a total of 1,090 successful Labour candidates or 18.6 per cent. In Scotland the same year, the percentage of successful Labour women to men was 6 per cent in the regions and 8.8 per cent in the districts.[10]

Women are not merely regarded as second-class citizens but are often completely overlooked. The numbers of Labour women serving on public bodies are not available, but, as the following examples show, it must be small. The Post Office does not have a single woman on its governing body. Neither does the Electricity Council, nor the National Bus Company, nor the Civil Aviation Authority. Even a government-appointed organisation like the Design Council, with its wide influence on consumer and domestic goods, has only three women compared with twenty-five men. The Arts Council of Great Britain has only three women compared with seventeen men. The influential Research Councils concerned with Agriculture, Medicine, Natural Environment and Science are composed entirely of men. The House of Lords, now largely a government-appointed body, has only 50 women out of a total membership of 1,105.[11] Some of these bodies work in private, but they have a great impact on the lives of ordinary men and women and should therefore be more representative of the community as a whole. In May 1975 a Labour MP, Ms Maureen Colquhoun, presented a private member's Bill entitled 'Balance of the Sexes', to ensure equal representation on public bodies, but it failed to get a Second Reading.

The contribution of Labour women to local government has often been out of all proportion to their comparatively small numbers. Some have given long and arduous service. For example, Mrs Jessie Smith was elected to the West Riding County Council in 1937 and was a member of the Education Committee, taking a special interest in child welfare and special category children, until that council disappeared as a result of local government reorganisation in 1974. She became chairman of the West Riding County Council Finance Committee in 1958, an unusual position for a woman, and made good use of it by presenting more budgets than any other person. She has been chairman of Yorkshire Council of Further Education since 1975, and is currently a vice-chairman of its Planning Committee.

She was a member of Leeds Regional Hospital Board, and held the chairmanship of Huddersfield Hospital Management Committee until its disappearance in 1974, and is now a member of Kirklees Area Health Authority. Jessie Smith has since become a member of Kirklees Metropolitan Council, work which she finds challenging and exciting since there are a large number of immigrants in the new combined area. For more than forty years she has been engaged in work for the Labour Party, at constituency and regional level. She was also a member of the Yorkshire and Humberside Economic Planning Council, and is a Vice-Chairman of Yorkshire Arts Council. The picture here is of an intelligent, hard-working woman, well respected in her local community, and one who is both flexible and always ready to take an interest in new social and political problems.

Jessie Smith was widowed in 1957 and has no family. But other Labour women have not let the responsibilities of family life deter them from serving the party in local government. Mrs Millie Miller now MP for Redbridge, Ilford North, was elected as a local councillor in the Metropolitan Borough of Stoke Newington and served on it until 1959 with one break of three years. When she was first elected, she was pregnant, and her daughter was born when she was already a councillor. However, when necessary, she was able to make *ad hoc* arrangements for caring for her daughter – the Hall porter in the Town Hall kept an eye on her pram whilst Millie Miller attended meetings! Later, she became Mayor and reluctantly agreed to being called 'Mr Mayor' because the title referred to the office and not the person. Ten years later, as Mayor of Camden, she was experienced enough to reject this and at her inauguration said 'Call me Madam'. Millie Miller's service in local government has also been long, varied and demanding: for example, she later became a member of Camden Council and then Mayor from 1967-8. In 1971, she was leader of the Labour Group when Labour won back Camden from the Tories. During that period Labour fought a long and bitter battle on the Housing Finance Act, and many others on property speculators. As an MP she now brings much practical experience to that role. These are just two examples, one from the regions and one from London of the many outstanding women in local government. Such women have a contribution to make to the Labour Party and more should be encouraged to serve the party in this way.

Many women have benefited from the political education programmes of the women's sections and councils, and from the practical experience gained from being officers in the women's movement. Probably no-one has done more in the field of political education for women than Grace Colman, who sat in Parliament for Tynemouth 1945-50. All through the years of the Second World War, and before, she was tireless in lecturing to women's gatherings and had a quite unique aptitude for putting intricate subjects into such simple language that everyone understood.

Nor should we forget the splendid work both of organisation and of political education done by Dame Sara Barker, Mrs Constance Kay and Miss Betty Lockwood who held successively the joint post of Chief Woman Officer and Assistant National Agent and directed the work of the women's organisation in the politically vital 1960s and early 1970s.

Sara Barker came to Head Office in 1952 from regional work in Yorkshire to serve as Assistant National Agent. In 1960 she added the duties of Chief Woman Officer to the work she was already doing in the Organisation Department. In 1963 she was appointed National Agent of the party — the first woman ever to hold that post and the only one, so far. In 1968 she even became the Acting General Secretary of the Labour Party for several months. Hers was certainly the most distinguished career that any woman to date has achieved in the work of political organisation in Britain and her name is remembered — with deep affection and the highest regard.

Constance Kay succeeded Sara Barker as Chief Woman Officer in February 1963 devoting herself almost entirely to the work of women's organisation. Her steady work in building up the women's activities of the party, especially in the realm of local and regional conferences, did much to enable Labour women to play a full part in the election campaign of 1966.

Betty Lockwood became the Chief Woman Officer and Assistant

National Agent of the Labour Party in September 1967. It was while she was guiding and encouraging the work of Labour women that the party first started to investigate the extent of present day discrimination against women. Then they publicised the facts in a Green Paper and campaigned for equal opportunities for women. This resulted in the Sex Discrimination Act, 1975, and the setting up of the Equal Opportunities Commission, of which Betty is now the full-time Chairman. Not only Labour women, but all women who are interested to play a part in public life owe much to Betty Lockwood's leadership.

From the Sections, women have gone on to serve the party as ward secretaries, constituency secretaries, party officers, local councillors and Parliamentary candidates. But they are still under-represented in the power structure of the party at grass-roots level. There are still not enough women in such positions in the party. Their weak position within the party reflects their weak position in society generally.

The statement by the National Labour Women's Advisory Committee on 'Women and the Labour Party' of 1971, points out that 'although no analysis exists it appears that in the majority of constituencies, on the General Committee and the Executive Committee, there are more men than women. . .We note with concern that although there is a more open attitude to sex roles among some young people, this does not seem very obvious in politics. The imbalance in the power position of men and women can be clearly discerned in Labour youth organisation. The 1971 Young Socialists Conference had only 25 per cent girls as delegates, and there are no girls at all out of a total membership of eleven on the National Committee of Young Socialists. On the National Organisation of Labour Students, there are three girls out of a membership of twenty-two.'

All the indications are that women still have a long way to go. Women still occupy a weak power position within the party. They have gained some ground in service on public bodies, and in local government. But the goal of equal representation is a long way off.

The reasons for the failure to achieve that goal are to be found, first of all in the way in which girls are brought up. They are not encouraged to see themselves as leaders and as accepting responsibility. In the words of a recent government report: 'The general impression is that boys are trained to be achieving, independent, competitive and self-sufficient, whereas girls are trained to be comforting, dependent, cooperative and group-orientated.'[12] It is not just that parents tend to encourage their daughters to stay at home and to be dependent, whereas their sons are taught to be outgoing and independent. Parental attitudes are echoed in school text books, in the choice of subjects open to girls in schools, in comics and on television.

The impact of the media, particularly television, is a new factor. So many aspects of television productions, films, advertising, presentation of news, reinforce the belief that women are, and should be, comforting, dependent, lacking in ambition, absorbed in caring for the home and family, confined, in other words, to the traditional feminine role. Labour women of the 1930s and 1940s did not have to contend with such a powerful counterblast to their efforts to free themselves, though they had other problems to face of a different order.

This early training is not the only obstacle to women's greater involvement in politics. If it were, it might be more easily countered. It becomes a much more serious obstacle, because for a crucial period of their adult life, roughly between the ages of 18 and 36, women are usually confined to the home and immersed in caring for young children. Their political development is not normally a continuing process. And if women have been taught that politics is not really their concern, because it is an unfeminine pursuit, and if they are limited to the home, then their opportunities for meeting people are less than men's, they are less likely to receive political information, and they are not involved in the conflict situations of working conditions which would politicise them. Furthermore, they continue to shoulder the main responsibility of caring for the home and the children. The constant emotional and physical demands of looking after the young make it difficult for women to participate in political life during this important period between the ages of 18 and 35. Many women do not therefore gain the necessary experience to enable them to enter public life when they are free to do so.

In this context, the women's organisation has an important role. It provides political education. It gives women confidence and experience. The women's organisation can draw women into the political arena by first involving them in discussions and campaigns which relate to their own interests of home and children. The women's organisation can also examine the difficulties which prevent women from entering public life, and, in explaining these to the women themselves and to the party as a whole, open up the way to overcome the difficulties. For this reason, Transport House produced the document, *Obstacles to Women in Public Life* in 1974 on the basis of information from the women's organisation and women candidates. This was used to encourage the party to make a more definite attempt to encourage women to enter public life.

If Labour women are to achieve the goal of equal representation in public life, then they must not be so limited to the home in the important years of early adulthood. It is obvious that the chief obstacle is the lack of adequate and flexible child care facilities. It is the unequal burden of child care, which, more than anything else, causes and maintains the structure of inequality. Without child care provision, the attempts to establish women on an equal footing with men in public life will only have a limited success. In this struggle, Labour women should look to the women of the past, for inspiration, to the women of 1930s with their strength and energy in spite of the heavy burdens of ill-health and poverty. They must realise, too, that it is a battle which women must fight for themselves, and this again underlines the need for the women's organisation. No one else will do it for them.

Notes

1. *Labour Woman,* May 1939, p.12, Labour Party Library.
2. *Labour Woman,* April 1933, p.53, Labour Party Library.
3. Hector Munro in *Labour Woman,* April 1933, p.58, Labour Party Library.
4. Eddie Williams, letter to *Labour Woman,* February 1938, p.25, Labour Party Library.
5. *Labour Woman,* December 1958, p.168, Labour Party Library.
6. *Report of Standing Committee of Working Women's Organisations,* 1935, p.1, Labour Party Library.
7. *Discrimination Against Women,* Opposition Green Paper, The Labour Party, Labour Party Library.
8. *Election Manifesto,* Labour Party, 1974, p.27.
9. Royal Commission on Local Government in England, *Report* (Radcliffe-Maud), 1969, HMSO.
10. *Report to Labour Women's Conference,* 1976, pp.21-2, Labour Party Library.
11. M. Colquhoun, MP, Statement on Balance of Sexes Bill, *Hansard,* 16 May 1975, pp.930-60.
12. *Women and Work; Sex Differences in Society,* Paper No.10, Department of Employment and Manpower, HMSO, p.25.

8 WOMEN IN TRADE UNIONS TODAY

Margaret McCarthy

There are a number of traditional beliefs about women in trade unions. Women are difficult to organise. They play no real part in trade union activity and are happy, however large their numbers, to be organised and represented by men. They dislike all forms of militancy and are not prepared to take strike action in support of their grievances, however justified. As a consequence of this apathy, the problems and aspirations of women at work go largely unremarked and unresolved by the trade union movement as a whole.

Is this an accurate picture of women trade unionists today? This chapter attempts to make a rough survey of some of the facts in an effort to understand what is happening today and indicate the extent to which these beliefs give a true picture of what is in fact happening.

Let us look at the current figures of membership for women trade unionists, both as a proportion of organised labour as a whole and as a proportion of the working female population. Let us try to see which unions organise large numbers of women and, if this membership is growing, suggest some likely reasons. We can then discuss the participation of women in the activities and government of their unions, both voluntary and full time. Finally, let us examine some of the aims which women trade unionists have been pursuing over the last ten years, and try to find out how successful they have been in prosecuting them.

This examination must, of course, be a cursory one. Each of these subjects either is, or deserves to be, the subject of careful and prolonged research. But it will be enough to give some idea of the progress which women have made. This should show us whether the hopes and ideals of the pioneer Labour women are any nearer to realisation than they were in the early days of the trade union movement.

However, before we look at these subjects in detail, something should be said about the problems which confront women generally at work and, in particular, the constraints which prevent them from playing a more active part in the trade union movement. It is, of course a truism to say that the majority of working women are, and have always been, expected to do at least two jobs, running a home and bringing up children, caring for elderly relations and all the other home-based activities, which are seen by society as woman's primary function, with any paid employment, or activity outside the home, as a secondary 'spare-time' occupation, which can be dropped at any moment. To build in a third activity — active participation in a trade union — requires both the sympathetic understanding and encouragement of a partner, and a degree of organisation, not only of the woman herself, but of everybody else in her life.

Membership

There can be no doubt that, in the past, war has provided the greatest opportunity of advancement for women in employment and, consequently, for the rise in the number of women trade unionists. In 1920, when the effects of the war were still visible, there were 1,343,000 women trade unionists; by 1933 this figure had slumped to 731,000, but had risen again by 1944 to 1,668,000. In the 1930s women's employment was very limited, and with only a few exceptions confined largely to low-paid jobs in textiles and clothing, domestic employment and 'ladylike' jobs for middle-class girls in nursing, teaching and increasingly in shops and offices. Apart from textiles and clothing, which have usually been well-organised in factory situations, although not in the sweat shops and home employment areas, most women working in the 1930s were either in non-organisable jobs or in 'professions' where, for men and women alike, trade unionism was looked on as an organisation for working men which was not applicable to 'middle-class' occupations.

From 1939 to 1945, opportunities were opened up in manufacturing industry, the industrial and executive grades of the Civil Service and in some of the professions where the shortage of manpower meant that women were forced into jobs where they had never previously been accepted. In the case of the Civil Service, this was made much easier because of the findings of the Royal Commission on the Civil Service which are discussed in more detail in another chapter of this book. These recommendations meant a 'fair field' for women, and the war made it possible for them to maximise their opportunities. This spread of opportunity is reflected not only in the rise of trade union membership, but also in its location. By 1944 the TUC was able to report a rise of 21 per cent in women's membership of which the largest increase occurred in the unions organising in the engineering industry.

There is of course nothing remarkable about this picture either in 1920 or in 1944. Had membership figures dropped during the 1950s in the way in which they did in the 1930s there would be little about which to comment now. However, a new economic concept — full employment — became a dominant feature in the post-war era. The need to maintain full employment became and has remained the primary target of successive governments since 1945. Because of this there has been a continuing need to find an alternative labour force which, on the whole, tends to do the less skilled and lower paid jobs as the economy expands. Together with the immigrant labour force, women have provided this alternative labour force over the last twenty years. In consequence the number of women at work has risen until today 38 per cent of the total labour force is female. This has meant that, unlike the 1930s, women have remained in potentially organisable sectors of the economy.

It is therefore not surprising to find that there has been a growth in the number of women joining trade unions over the last fifteen years. In 1958 the *Ministry of Labour Gazette* recorded the total number of women workers as 7,778,000 of which 23.79 per cent — 1,850,000 — were in trade unions. In 1973 there were 3,046,000 women trade unionists in a work force of 8,983,000, i.e. 33.9 per cent — a rise of slightly over 10 per cent in trade union density. If we look at comparable figures for male workers we see that in 1953 there were 7,789,000 trade unionists in a work force of 14,001,000 — 53.67 per cent. In 1973 there were 8,461,000 trade unionists in a work force of 14,255,000 — i.e. 59.35 per cent, a rise of slightly less than 6 per cent. (These figures are for all workers in units of organised labour, and therefore include some unions not affiliated to the TUC.) In 1974 the TUC reported that of its 10,001,401 members, 2,603,306 were women — over 25 per cent.

It is interesting to look at which unions have benefited from this growth in women's membership. The table shows major unions in the TUC with significant women membership.

When we examine the figures further we see that the largest part of growth in membership has occurred in the public sector both in the white collar and manual sectors. I have included for this purpose, as a public sector union, the G&MWU. This union organises in both the public and private sectors, but by far the larger part of its women's membership is in the public sector. In fact, taking all the unions who organise in the public sector, and adding together their women's membership, it can be seen that about 50 per cent of women in affiliated unions work in the public sector.

Most of the remaining membership is organised in unions which very

Union	Total membership	Women membership
NUPE	470,172	294,640
COHSE	121,150	80,722
NALGO	518,117	200,503
NUT	250,404	186,146
CPSA	215,702	147,549
G&MWU	863,464	269,263
USDAW	326,463	184,248
NUTGW	116,913	101,190
TGWU	1,785,496	266,348
AUEW (Eng.Sec.)	1,018,343	154,169
ASTMS	264,900	45,100
APEX	127,308	68,678

Source: TUC Statistical Statement, 1974

much represent the traditional pattern of women's employment. In the figures for the two largest unions – USDAW and the NUTGW – there is a significant membership, proportionately to male membership. In the textile, knitwear, tobacco and pottery industries, the number of women members greatly exceeds the number of men although they are a very small proportion of the TUC women's membership as a whole.

The last group of women trade unionists we should look at is in the engineering industry, largely organised by the T&GWU, the AUEW and the G&MWU with the growing presence of the ASTMS and APEX. The total women's membership of these unions seems large – just under 600,000. But as a percentage of the total membership of the unions of just under 3,000,000 it is much lower than either the percentage of women members of the TUC as a whole, or the percentage of women trade unionists in the population of working women.

Looking at the pattern of membership which has emerged, we can examine the belief that women are particularly difficult to organise and do not see trade unions as the answer to their problems. At first glance it would seem that this is not as true as it was. The rising figures of women's membership do indicate an increasing interest in the need to organise. However, a closer examination of the spread of membership shows that the most significant rises in membership occurred in the public sector, and it is generally accepted that the public sector is much easier to organise than the private sector. The term public sector is used to mean that sector of the economy in which the government is either the direct employer, the indirect employer – as in the case of local authority and health services – or has a considerable influence on the wages and conditions of workers, as in the nationalised industries.

Employers in this sector do not discourage — and in most cases
positively encourage — trade union membership. Facilities are given for
recruitment, meetings and for communication so that members can be
signed on and contacted much more easily than in the private sector
where, often, determined trade unionists have to struggle hard even to
obtain recognition. For signs of a really flourishing and determined
advance in trade union membership the private sector is a much better
guide.

The one really hopeful sign in this sector is the growth of the white
collar unions, ASTMS and APEX. From 1964 until 1970 ASTMS grew
by 296 per cent, APEX by 58 per cent. (During this same period the
white collar sectors of the AUEW G&MWU and TGWU grew by 900
per cent, 110 per cent and 47 per cent respectively, although the
number of members is insignificant as compared with the ASTMS and
APEX.)[1] Women make up about 46 per cent of the white collar labour
force and this proportion is growing. Although this growth must be
regarded as encouraging, it should be noted that in 1970 (for which we
have the last reliable figures) trade union density among women in the
white collar sector was significantly lower than that of men: 32.4 per
cent as against 42.9 per cent.[2]

The TUC Women's Advisory Committee is very conscious of this
problem of recruitment in the private sector. In 1972, USDAW moved
a resolution at the TUC Women's Conference calling for a 'national
campaign to be mounted by the TUC using all aspects of the mass
media to secure the extension of trade union organisation among all
women workers'. During that debate several speakers made it clear that
they found recruitment difficult and felt that only concentrated action
by the General Council would be effective.

> We say categorically it is now time for the women members in the
> TUC to receive some attention from the General Council. It is up
> to the General Council to make efforts now to get all women
> workers into the Trade Union movement. The need is urgent. . .
> loosen the purse strings of the General Council and show the women
> of this country that they have nothing to be afraid of if they will
> only organise themselves within the trade unions.

A delegate of the UPW said

> I come from the public sector. . .our organisation problems are much
> less serious than those of other unions. I do not think that we, who

come from the much more privileged sections of the women's working population, ought to overlook the problems which face trade unions like the T&GWU, the AUEW and USDAW. The thing which is absolutely appalling to my trade union is the very low women's membership which exists generally.

In the reply from the General Council, reported to the 1973 Women's Conference, the TUC acknowledged these difficulties:

During the year General Council Committees have considered a number of issues relating to trade union organisation which are of particular importance to women. The largest proportion of women are employed in the non-manual field (and they represent the majority of workers in the occupations concerned). While they are increasingly joining unions this is one of the areas where lack of organisation in the private sector contributes substantially to the overall density of trade union organisation among women. The TUC Non-Manual Workers' Advisory Committee considered this matter but took the view that unions preferred to deal with their own organisational problems. . .

This evidence seems to show that there is no great push from women workers to join a trade union, although they will 'sign on' if efforts are made on their behalf.

Participation

But once women — for whatever reason — have joined a trade union, how far do they take an active part in the policy formulation and government of unions? Here the evidence is more scanty, but the general impression is that women do tend to be much more passive in their trade union activities and their attendance at branches and conference is low. In 1972 it was reported to the Women's Conference that relatively few women had taken part in the TUC educational schools and courses: of a total of 370 students attending the summer school in 1971 only 23 were women. In the Congress year 1970-71 a total of 475 full time and voluntary officers attended courses in the TUC training college. Of these 23 were women. A sample survey of students attending regional linked weekends, weekend schools, day schools and evening classes and day release classes showed that approximately 12 per cent attending the first four sets of courses were women; but that on the day release courses which were for shop stewards, under 5 per cent of those attending were women.

It is still more difficult to obtain reliable figures for attendance at branch meetings. These are usually poorly attended by either sex, but many active women trade unionists complain that the attendance of women is abnormally low. A trade union official organising in engineering recently remarked: 'we had more than 500 women in the branch but none of them was willing to take an active part'. The usual reason advanced for this low level of activity is that the times of branch meetings are particularly inconvenient for women, and this is doubtless true. However, it is, in principle, possible for most branches of most unions to meet at a time convenient for the membership since the majority of union rule books only specify that the branch should meet once a month.

As difficult to obtain are the figures for the number of women holding shop stewards' positions, although these are the most significant indication of the growing participation of women in trade union affairs. However, there seems general agreement that the number of women stewards is growing and with the bargaining unit increasingly becoming the work place, this growth inevitably means that women are having a greater influence on the policy of their unions and the conditions in which they work.

A further index of participation is the number of women who attend the TUC Annual Congress. Delegates to the TUC are nominated through their branches and elected by the membership in various ways. Such delegates' jobs are usually well contested, and are a good indication of the participation of members' level of activity since delegates are voted for largely by people whose only contact is through branch meetings and conferences.

There were 1,027 delegates at the 1974 Congress of whom 60 were women. (This figure represents a slightly rising trend which began in 1972.) Of these 44 came from the eight unions which have over 100,000 women members: USDAW, GMWU, T&GWU, AUEW, NUT & GW, NUPE, CPSA, NUT and NALGO. The total number of delegates for these unions was 381. The 44 women delegates represented a membership of 1,803,956; the 337 men represented a membership of 3,915,687. (The AUEW had no women at all on its delegation.) Of these 44 delegates, 8 came from the Tailor and Garment Workers' whose rules have prescribed, since 1905, that half the delegates – at present 46 – should be women. NALGO, whose women's membership is almost double that of its men, sent 5 women out of a total of 25 delegates. The NUT whose women's membership is almost three times that of its male membership sent 5 women in a delegation of 27. Smaller unions did no better. The ASTMS, whose female membership grew faster than any other union in the previous year, sent a delegation with no women. COHSE, with twice the number of women members, sent none — as did the Tobacco Workers, Ceramic Workers and the Inland Revenue Staff Federation.[3]

When one attempts to look at the full-time officers employed in unions the same low degree of representation is repeated. This, of course, is not unexpected since in most unions recruitment to full-time officers' posts is usually made from activists inside the union. A sample of unions (in the public and private sector) representing over 50 per cent of the total TUC membership reveals a total of 30 full-time women organisers. These are not evenly distributed throughout the unions. The Tailor and Garment Workers for example, have an unusually large number — 10. The General and Municipal Workers have 9, including a national officer with special responsibility for women's membership. (It should be remembered, however, that the National Federation of Women's Workers founded by Mary Macarthur was absorbed into the G&MWU in 1919 and consequently this union has had a long tradition and experience of women officers.) The T&GWU has one woman officer — a post which can only be held by a woman. There is one woman General Secretary — but she represents a very small union, Jute and Flax Workers, with a membership of 4,000. This, of course, makes the achievement of Anne Godwin and Anne Loughlin, both of whom became General Secretaries of powerful unions even more remarkable.

Some unions are increasingly aware of the need for female participation and are making particular efforts to recruit women as full-time officers, and as members of their National Executives. NUPE, for example, which we have already noticed as one of the unions with the fastest growing women's membership, has no women officers and no women on its Executive. It is proposing rule changes in order to provide five protected seats for women on the Executive Committee. The Sex Discrimination Act recognises the need for this positive discrimination and allows trade unions specifically to set aside seats on elective bodies for persons of one sex 'where in the opinion of the organisation the provision is in the circumstances needed to secure a reasonable lower limit to the number of members of that sex serving on the body' (Sex Discrimination Act, 1975, Part V, para.49). ASTMS is also taking a positive line in recruiting women officers. Nevertheless, bearing in mind the earlier achievements of women, this remains the most unsatisfactory part of the picture.

These figures do not, however, represent the total participation of women in the affairs of the TUC. The TUC has a Women's Advisory Committee which runs, each year, a separate Women's Conference. This is not intended to be solely for women and is described as the Annual Conference of representatives of trade unions catering for women workers. Although it is, in principle, possible for men to attend, in practice the overwhelming majority of the delegates are women. The Conference is, of course, only advisory, but its decisions are referred to the General Council. It is also limited in what it may discuss to motions which 'must deal only with subjects specifically relating to the organisation of women and young persons'.

This Conference is the main forum of women trade unionists to debate their specific problems and air their particular grievances. Some of these are very long standing and as one goes through the reports of the conferences, the same issues are raised again and again: the need to provide facilities for working women; the need for equal opportunities in education and training; the problems of health and safety of women workers and, above all, the question of equal pay. The debates give a very clear picture of how women see themselves in a work-place situation and how 'second-class' they often feel in relation to their male colleagues.

But, in spite of the fact that this is the only forum for women trade unionists, it is not universally popular. One of the recurrent themes which runs through the debates is the need to abolish the Conference altogether. Some delegates feel very strongly that its presence precludes them from taking a full share in the TUC itself, and that its existence means that their problems are not taken seriously by the trade union movement as a whole. 'The Women's Conference is a sideline, it is irrelevant, it is not in the main stream of union action because it does not involve the majority of union members.' 'We have allowed ourselves to be treated as second-class trade unionists and kept as a race apart.'

Other delegates feel equally strongly that the Women's Conference should be preserved, because it is able to devote much more time to the airing of particular problems and because it is an excellent training ground for nervous newcomers. 'The fact is, until women are active in their trade union, until they are on their Executives and go to the TUC we need to have some sort of body which can press for women's rights.' 'Women can come to this Conference and get confidence for themselves by speaking to their own kind.'

It should be clear from the figures and speeches quoted above, that there is little evidence of participation by women. They have been slow to seize what opportunity has been available to them. But attending branch meetings and conferences is not the only way in which trade union members participate in the affairs of their union. All these activities are important for the healthy life of a union, but it can be argued that the most important form of participation is the disciplined response of members when the union feels it necessary to call for industrial action through majority decisions. Women have generally been thought to be 'unmilitant' and unwilling to participate in this form of union activity. A trade union official says: 'Women are generally less willing than men to take industrial action. Women usually prefer to use all other means before stopping work.' Yet there are clear signs that this is no longer true. The public sector, which as we have seen is dominated by women, has shown a surprising militancy in the last few years. Strikes by nurses and ancillary workers in the health service, the work-to-rules by local government officers and inland revenue staff, and the teachers' stoppages underline the fact that these women-dominated occupations can no longer be regarded as 'docile' and 'non-militant'. Interestingly, the trade union official quoted earlier goes on to say: 'But once women have begun a strike it is often more difficult to persuade them to go back than it is men. Women usually want to see something to show for their strike. Men often go back on a promise, but women usually want a copper bottomed promise or something better.' If past experience is any guide, moreover, participation in this form of activity will lead fairly quickly to participation in the other areas of activity which we have discussed.

Aims

Some trade unionists — men and women — say that 'the problems facing women at work are *workers'* problems and should be brought into the main body of the Trade Union movement'. This, in a broad sense, is true, but there can be no doubt that working women and women trade unionists do have aims which are peculiar to them. Some of these have been outlined earlier in this chapter.

The first and most obvious example is the problem of equal pay. The call for equal pay was first made in 1888 and was finally answered by the end of 1975. It has been one of the major topics of discussion at every Women's Conference and, due to the determination of leading women trade unionists, not least Anne Godwin and Florence Hancock, who were delegates to Washington when the International Labour Conference adopted Convention 100 agreeing the principle of Equal

Pay. On pp.33-34 there is a fuller report of this event. In the end, the crucial move towards the provision of equal pay legislation was made by a woman, Barbara Castle, whose personal association with the trade union movement was no stronger than being a fellow member of the Labour movement. Perhaps the length of time it has taken to deal with such an obvious injustice is the clearest example of the lack of power and drive which women have had in the movement.

But to grant the principle of equal pay is not sufficient to produce equality in the work-place situation. It is still possible to secure equal pay and yet to be in the lowest paid section of a particular work force. As a special report issued by the Women's Advisory Committee in 1970 says, 'The proportion of women workers who will secure the full benefits of the Equal Pay Act will be minimal unless positive action is taken now to eliminate the traditional inequalities in the education and training opportunities available to girls and women compared with similar opportunities available to boys and men.' The Advisory Committee have done much work in the interval and the Sex Discrimination Act will do much to alter this. It is unfortunate, however, that the onus of proof in this Act rests with the complainant, unlike the Employment Protection Act, in which the onus lies with the employers. So far the results of cases brought under the Sex Discrimination Act have been somewhat disappointing.

Yet this is not a recent recognition by the TUC of this problem. In 1963 it published a six point Charter of Trade Union Aims for Women. These were:

Equal pay
Opportunities for promotion
Apprenticeship schemes
Improved opportunities for training
Retraining facilities
Special care for the health and welfare of women workers

If one examines this Charter closely one sees that — with the exception of the first clause — very little has been achieved in its implementation. A special report 'The Twelve Point Charter', to the TUC Women's Conference in 1973 acknowledges this fact, although it emphasises that this issue had been raised on many occasions with successive governments. The point has been recently re-emphasised by the Department of Employment and Productivity in a paper *'Women and Work — A Review'*, which says 'Many women now have the opportunity consistent with their maternal responsibilities, of working continuously for twenty or thirty years. . .but women's share of more serious and skilled jobs in almost all sectors of employment including the professions is small.'[4]

Further help towards fulfilling the Charter has resulted from the Employment Protection Act 1975, which provides for maternity leave of up to 29 weeks, 6 weeks of which will be on full pay, with reinstatement guaranteed, and from the Social Security Pensions Act 1975, which equalises the pension rights of the sexes.

But if the Charter had been implemented during 1976, it would be no means meet the aims or solve the problems of women workers. Opportunities can be created, discrimination removed and training provided, but unless facilities are provided to help women with their traditional responsibilities in the home, none of this will count for much. This situation has given rise to continued and increasing demand for better family planning services, more nursery places, better maternity leave and flexible working hours. In these areas progress has been much slower. The progress of family planning facilities has been uneven. The same is true of nursery places. On flexible working hours — which many people regard as one of the most useful aids for working women — the TUC is extremely cautious. In a circular sent to affiliated unions on the subject in 1973, it remarked that 'employers did not usually introduce change only for the benefit of workers, and trade union representatives needed to assess very carefully the relative advantages and disadvantages for their members'.

If we survey the aspirations of women workers and their achievements, certainly over the last twenty years, the results are not very encouraging. But perhaps we should take comfort from the changing aims of women themselves. Looking back to the reports and resolutions of the 1944 Women's Conference it is clear that women's aims and expectations have changed very considerably since the Second World War. There is the same concern about equal pay, nursery education, and further education and training schemes; but it is clear that the Women's Advisory Council saw that peacetime conditions would bring a return of the low status, poorly paid jobs which had been their expectation in the 1930s. They issued a long memorandum on the status of domestic workers: 'those employed in this very important industry should no longer be looked upon as inferior beings, but should be recognised as workers performing an important social service.' In the context of conditions and expectations of the 1930s this was an important and courageous memorandum; viewed in the light of what has actually happened since 1945, it seems totally anachronistic. We have travelled a long way when women discuss the need for maternity leave, flexible hours and equal promotion prospects. The wider aspirations and rising aims of women trade unionists show more clearly than any statistical indices, the greater confidence and self-assurance of women trade unionists in the 1970s.

The Future

If the future were *always* to resemble the past then the prospects for women trade unionists would seem not to be particularly encouraging. In spite of rising membership figures, women do not seem to be participating in the affairs of their unions to any great extent. They still appear to be content to be represented by men however large their numbers. And their demands, if the realisation of their aims is any yardstick, still seem to go largely unremarked in the trade union movement as a whole.

But there are signs that the times are changing. The position of women in the work force is now recognised as significant. Indeed, it would be very difficult not to recognise this significance since they form a third of the working population, and are the majority in the service industries such as the distributive trades, nursing, teaching, catering and laundries. Because of this numerical significance, and because of the Sex Discrimination Act and Equal Opportunities Commission, government departments and agencies are being compelled to think much more seriously about the role of women in industry and about the measures which will need to be implemented so that women may play a fully productive part in the working life of the country. The Department of Employment Paper *'Women at Work – a Survey'* gives a penetrating analysis of these problems, and concludes that the most important change needed is a change in attitudes both of employers and society generally towards the traditional role of women. It disposes of the idea that there are certain tasks which can only be fulfilled by one sex:

> The review finds little evidence to support the idea that men and women could not carry out most jobs regarded as the province of the other sex with success. If jobs, careers and training opportunities were open to men and women on an equal basis, there would be no reason in terms of inborn ability why they should not aspire to almost any job, be found suitable for it and do it successfully. . . generalisations about women's work performance often overlook the fact that much of the difference probably arises because women,

more than men, are in low-status and low-paid jobs where work performance is generally lower regardless of the sex of the occupant.

Clearly, the single most important force making for such a change in attitude must be the trade union movement itself. There are signs that the movement does recognise this fact. The attempts of unions, like NUPE, to encourage more active participation through positive discrimination; the fact that, for the first time, two women members of the AUEW have won through some of the elected rounds for officials' jobs; the consideration, given in debate at the 1974 TUC Congress, to the importance of women's participation, may seem small beginnings to the solution of a large problem. But they are progress. However, it must be remembered that trade unions are democratic institutions which can, finally, only respond to the pressure of those individuals or groups who make up the movement as a whole. If there is to be a major breakthrough in attitude, it will only happen because of an increased, and increasingly active women's membership, strong enough to insist that such changes are brought about.

Notes

1. R. Lumley. *White Collar Unionism in Britain,* Methuen, 1972, pp.22 and 800.
2. G.S. Bain and R. Price, 'Union Growth and Employment Trends in the UK 1964-70', *British Journal of Industrial Relations,* November 1972, pp.568-9, Table I.
3. *Report of the Women's Conference,* TUC, 1974-5.
4. *Women and Work, a Review,* Department of Employment Manpower Survey, Paper No.11, HMSO, 1975.

9 WOMEN IN PARLIAMENT AND GOVERNMENT

Maeve Denby

The preceding chapters have shown how, since the beginning of the century, women have associated themselves with reform, radical policies and the rights of minorities. It is no coincidence that so many of them were socialists, and attached to the Labour Party. Those same beliefs which led them to fight for reform, and, as far as some of them were concerned, for the political rights of women, relate to overall principles about rights in general which are central to the philosophy of the Labour Party. So women with social consciences have often found it natural to work both for and through the Labour movement.

It would seem reasonable to expect that in working within a movement which is so concerned with equality, women would, gradually at least, become equal to men in terms of representation within the movement. Even in 1977, women have still not achieved complete equality of opportunity with men in all fields, and they were certainly a long way from it at the beginning of the century. But even if women have not yet become equal to men in terms of representation at a high level in many fields we would expect their representation at all levels within the Labour movement to set a good example. Unfortunately this is not altogether so. The previous chapter looked at women within the trade unions, which is one branch of the Labour movement in which women have not yet achieved equality; another is in Parliament and Government, which this chapter considers. Women are, and always have been, grossly underrepresented both as MPs and as candidates. Even though the Labour Party has fought successfully for the rights of a variety of groups, it has failed to consider effectively the status of women within the party. This represents one of those anomalies which are not in fact uncommon: that of an organisation which in fighting certain ills in society fails to come to terms with not altogether dissimilar ills affecting itself.

It is perhaps because of the special difficulties that women can face when entering public life, and because of the fewness of their numbers, that many women MPs have seemed so colourful. In the 'flapper' election of 1929 − the first election in which all women were able to vote − 69 women candidates stood, of whom 30 were Labour. Fourteen women were returned, of whom nine were Labour. Five of these were new members: Dr Ethel Bentham who was to die only two years later, and be replaced in the House by Mrs Leah Manning*; Dr Marion Phillips, Mrs Mary Agnes Hamilton, Miss Edith Picton-Turbervill* and Lady Cynthia Mosley*. Miss Susan Lawrence, Miss Ellen Wilkinson and Miss Margaret Bondfield were back again, as was Miss Jennie Lee, who was still only 24. They were to be joined before long, as the result of a by-election, by the first Labour peeress to sit in the Commons, Lucy Noel-Buxton*.

At about this time Ellen Wilkinson published a small book[1] describing her contemporaries in the House. She herself is summarised in the foreword by Oliver Baldwin: 'Ellen Wilkinson is small, very small, and redheaded. She is impetuous. . .she is a good judge of women, but not so good of men; the reason being that she never looks at the latter long enough to be sure her first impressions are correct. . .she would make a bad wife but a good mother.' Baldwin, aware perhaps of the dubiousness of this last comment, goes on to explain that he will not attempt to justify it, since Ellen Wilkinson herself makes many unsupported sweeping assertions. Like many women MPs, Ellen Wilkinson was to write a lot, and before she died in 1947, of asthma, her works included *Why Fascism?*, and *The Town that was Murdered*, describing her Jarrow constituency of 1935.

Perhaps the most brilliant woman in Parliament at that time, at least academically, was Susan Lawrence. She had won an exhibition in pure mathematics at University College, London, and had gone on from there to Newnham College, Cambridge. In 1930 Ellen Wilkinson was Parliamentary Private Secretary to Susan Lawrence, and described her thus:

> [She] is the real bluestocking of our age. Not the old-maidish horror of the silly anti-suffragette cartoons, but 'bluestocking' as the eighteenth century and Dr. Johnson knew them, women of wit as well as learning. . .Tall, cold, severe, plainly dressed, at first when she rose to speak the House prepared for the worst. Then they glimpsed the real Susan, the woman of delicate humour, of a merciless wit, of a logic they had believed was only masculine, of a mind which drank in facts as some men drink whisky.[2]

It was not, however, Susan Lawrence who became the choice of Ramsay MacDonald as the first woman Cabinet Minister but Margaret Bondfield, although Susan was shortly to become the Parliamentary Secretary to the Minister of Health. Margaret Bondfield had served in the trade union

movement for many years and in 1923-24 had been Parliamentary
Secretary to the Ministry of Labour. She was given the post of Minister
of Labour and as MacDonald was to say: She is a double first — the
first woman who has been admitted to the Privy Council, so that she
is now the Right Honourable Margaret Bondfield; she is also the first
woman to have taken a seat in the Cabinet.'[3] The Post-Mistress General
in G.B. Shaw's *The Apple Cart* is supposed to have been partly based
on her. Small and plump, she was the daughter of a lacemaker and was
a shop assistant at the age of fourteen. She joined the Shop Assistants'
Union, and gradually worked her way up until she became the Chief
Woman Officer of the Women's Section of the NUGMW, and in 1923
had been elected the Chairman of the General Council on the TUC.
There was no doubt about her administrative ability, and
congratulations on her appointment came from many parts of the
world as she was to testify later in her book *A Life's Work*. Mary
Hamilton — 'There are some women who are greedy of life, who gather
experiences into gulps. But [she] seems to cut thin slices of living with
her razor-edged mind, to take samples of everything, and see which
suits her essential fastidiousness'[4] — was appointed with Mrs Swanwick
to represent Britain at the Assembly of the League of Nations at Geneva
in 1929, and later she became Attlee's PPS when he was Chancellor of
the Duchy of Lancaster, and then Post-Master General.

This government was then a notable one for women, despite the
grave difficulties it had to face, and the subsequent severe criticisms
that Margaret Bondfield was to suffer as Minister of Labour at a time
of very high unemployment. The number of women MPs had increased
to fourteen, all women had been enfranchised in time for the 1929
election, and the first woman Cabinet Minister had been appointed.
But this improvement in the fortunes of Labour women was not to last.
In the General Election of 1931 all of the nine Labour women lost
their seats, and Margaret Bondfield, Susan Lawrence and Mary Hamilton
were never to return, although Margaret Bondfield was the prospective
candidate for Reading at the outbreak of the Second World War. In the
1931 election there were 36 Labour women candidates, and 62 women
candidates altogether. The big swing against Labour resulted in
thirteen Conservative women being returned to the House, one Liberal
and one Independent (the powerful Miss Eleanor Rathbone), but no
Labour women. Only three of those in the House between 1929 and
1931 were to return — Ellen Wilkinson, in 1935, and Lucy Noel-Buxton
and Jennie Lee, who had to wait for as long as fourteen years.

This blow against Labour women was not reversed until 1945. The intervention of the war resulted in a ten-year gap between elections, and in the General Election of 1935 only Ellen Wilkinson returned as the one Labour woman in Parliament. Indeed, in that Parliament there were only nine women altogether, the other eight consisting of one Liberal, one Independent. and six Conservative. Ellen Wilkinson did not allow her unique position to deter her. She was to lead the Jarrow march of 1936; to fight for the re-establishment of industry in her constituency — a fight she at least to some extent won when in 1937 Oliver Stanley announced plans for a new steel plant in Jarrow; she was to introduce a private bill to give greater protection to hire-purchase customers in 1938. She did get into trouble with her constituency party when she wrote press articles saying that Herbert Morrison would make a better leader than Clement Attlee — trouble that she survived however. She was eventually joined, as a result of by-elections, by three more Labour women: Mrs Agnes Hardie and Mrs Jennie Adamson, who were seen as representatives of the working-class housewife, and Dr Edith Summerskill, a physician.

War broke out. and Churchill formed his all-party coalition government, appointing Ellen Wilkinson to the post of Parliamentary Secretary to the Ministry of Pensions. He is said to have remarked to his friends: 'I have formed the most broad-based Government that Britain has ever known. It extends from Lord Lyold of Dolobran to Miss Ellen Wilkinson.'[5] In October she was transferred at Herbert Morrison's request to his Ministry of Home Security as an extra-Parliamentary Secretary with special responsibility for the provision of air raid shelters, and she stayed there until the end of the war. She was responsible for organising the voluntary army of fire-watchers, and spent much time visiting air raid shelters. She also, in 1942, took over the responsibilities of a colleague who was transferred to another post. Ellen Wilkinson did not spare herself, and this may have contributed to a decline in her health. After a car accident in 1942 and a glider accident the following year, she was permanently crippled, which however did not prevent her from being elected Chairman of the Labour Party in 1944. Meanwhile Jennie Adamson was appointed PPS to the Minister of Pensions, with special responsibility for the pension claims affecting women and children.

It was during the war years that women MPs frequently acted as a group across party lines. For instance, in February 1940 all the women backbenchers went to the Financial Secretary of the Treasury to demand that women be given a more responsible role in the war effort. This led to the formation of a committee consisting of these women, which met regularly and issued reports on the use of woman-power, and campaigned for the greater equality of opportunity for women in a number of spheres. In 1941 a debate was held in the House of Commons on the subject of woman-power in a wide variety of fields, and in another similar debate the following year Edith Summerskill said: 'I am beginning to feel that the war is being prosecuted by both sexes and directed by one.' Edith Summerskill visited Australia and New Zealand in 1944, as the first woman to be included in a Commonwealth parliamentary delegation. And in 1945, with the Conservative MP Miss Florence Horsbrugh, Ellen Wilkinson was made a Privy Councillor, sixteen years after Margaret Bondfield, and a few months after the first woman to sit in the House, Lady Astor, had celebrated 25 years as an MP.

So the war came to an end — a war in which women had played their part in the House of Commons as well as elsewhere. Would their status now be recognised at all levels and by other women, and so lead to equality in numerical terms in political life? Certainly the 1945 General Election showed a marked improvement in the number of women candidates. There were 87, of whom 41 were Labour. It was at this time that G.B. Shaw came up with his idea of a 'coupled vote': each elector would have to vote for both a man and a woman. This extreme solution however was unlikely ever to find favour. In the event, the massive swing to Labour resulted in twenty-four women being elected, of whom twenty-one were Labour. Lucy Noel-Buxton, Jennie Lee and Leah Manning were back. Miss Alice Bacon and Miss Margaret Herbison*, both miners' daughters and school teachers, were in at their first attempt, as was Barbara Castle, who was the youngest woman member, and a journalist. Mrs Barbara Ayrton Gould was a veteran, having fought eight elections. Mrs Lucy Middleton had been much associated with the peace movement, and had been adviser to the Hindu minorities at the Round Table Conference in the 1920s; she was also a teacher and married to a former Secretary of the Labour Party. Of the remaining newcomers, two were to become particularly noteworthy — Mrs Bessie Braddock and Mrs Jean Mann. Despite the quality of many of those women now in Parliament, a total of twenty-four was a poor showing for an age when women were recognised as having been as important in many ways as men during the war, and when as a result attitudes to them were in the process of profound change.

The Cabinet, having been once invaded by a woman, was to suffer this fate again, in the person of Ellen Wilkinson, who was appointed

Minister of Education by Attlee. Edith Summerskill had a difficult
and unpopular job as Parliamentary Secretary to the Ministry of Food
under Sir Ben Smith, for rationing was increased. Jennie Adamson
became Parliamentary Secretary to the Ministry of Pensions, although
she left Parliament in 1946 to become Deputy Chairman of the
Assistance Board. Barbara Castle, at the start of an exceptional political
career, was chosen by Sir Stafford Cripps, President of the Board of
Trade, as one of his two PPSs, with special responsibility for clothes
rationing, and, with Jennie Lee who was appointed to the Central
Advisory Committee on Housing, was chosen by the Parliamentary
Labour Party to enquire into conditions of old age pensioners. Amongst
other Committee appointments, Lucy Middleton went to the Estimates
Committee of the House, and was Chairman of a party committee on
war-damaged areas.

The Labour Government had a difficult and often unpopular time
ahead. It was a time of austerity. Rationing in main foodstuffs was
still in force in 1950. Although food subsidies were reduced by Cripps,
they still, in 1950 had an upper limit of £410 million. It could be
argued that one reason why Britain was able to survive the economic
crisis of that time, after six years of war, was because of the feeling of
public solidarity, originally engendered by the war, and maintained by
the introduction of the welfare state, used to promote justice and
greater equality of economic sacrifice. Certainly the women Labour
MPs of that time, with their male colleagues, were instrumental in
ushering in an era of truly reformist policies. In a minor key, it is
interesting to note how a couple of issues which came up have also
been of recent concern: when Princess Elizabeth became engaged to
Prince Philip, twelve women were amongst those who voted against
the proposed allowances for the royal couple in view of the difficulties
the public were having to face; at the same time, Bessie Braddock was
campaigning against the provision of pay beds in hospitals. Meanwhile
Lucy Middleton was fighting successfully for the War Damage
Commission to consider claims for compensation from those who had
missed the closing date. It was during the fuel crisis of 1946-7 that the
House was to lose Ellen Wilkinson, who died after a gruelling time of
trying to implement the 1944 Education Act. Her death was a loss to
the Labour Party in general and to the women's cause in particular.

It was also during this administration that a new record was set for
women. In December 1946, Mrs Florence Paton became the first
woman to be appointed to the Speaker's Panel of Chairman of
Committees, and in this capacity she conducted Bills through Standing

Committee upstairs. In May 1948 she first presided over the House
sitting as a committee, from the Clerk's Table, during a debate on
Scottish aviation estimates. Punch, which also carried a cartoon of the
event, commented: '[She] added a spot more history to this history-
making Parliament. . .She did it modestly and competently with just
the right combination of firmness and gentleness, and she amply
justified (in the view of some shrewd judges of chairmanship) her
inclusion in the Speaker's Panel of Chairman.'

It was in the early days of this Parliament that women MPs brought
pressure on the Prime Minister, Clement Attlee, to appoint at least one
woman on the Parliamentary Committee that was to tour India to
report on constitutional reform. As a result of this action Mrs Muriel
Nichol, MP, was appointed a member of that Committee, which
reported strongly in favour of Indian independence. Meanwhile on the
Conservative side, Lady Davidson was the first woman to be elected to
the Party's 1922 Committee.

So this was another administration during which women had made
an important contribution to the work of the House of Commons;
again the number of women candidates in the subsequent election
went up, and again the number of those returned remained well down.
The General Election of 1950, in which there was a 3 per cent swing
from Labour to Conservative, had a total of 126 women candidates,
of whom 42 were Labour. Only 14 of these 42 were returned, with a
Labour Government and a much reduced majority. The governing party
had to face the strains which resulted from a much stronger opposition
leading to many all-night sittings. There were five new Labour women
including Mrs Eirene White. Seven had lost their seats. However, the
third woman to achieve full ministerial status was appointed. Edith
Summerskill became Minister of National Insurance, and she in turn
appointed Mrs Dorothy Rees to be her PPS. Margaret Herbison became
Joint Under-Secretary for Scotland.

The government was not to last. The outbreak of the Korean War in
1950 brought about another economic crisis, and Ministers no longer
had the impetus of 1945; Aneurin Bevan and Harold Wilson resigned
following disagreements in the Cabinet. The General Election came as
early as 1951, with another 1 per cent swing away from Labour. A
Conservative Government was in power. Of the total number of 77
women candidates, 41 were Labour, and only 11 of these were returned.
Mrs Caroline Ganley*, Lucy Middleton and Dorothy Rees all lost by
narrow majorities. Winston Churchill, as Prime Minister, followed
Labour's example and appointed a woman as Minister of Education

(Florence Horsbrugh), although she was not given a post in the Cabinet until September 1953, and Miss Pat Hornsby-Smith became Parliamentary Secretary to the Ministry of Health.

All the Labour women were active in various ways during this administration. They were joined, as a result of by-elections, by Mrs Harriet Slater* and Mrs Lena Jeger, who succeeded to her husband's constituency. But clearly, as members of the Opposition, they could not have the same effect as previously, and this was still the case after the General Election of 1955, when Harold Macmillan was Prime Minister, even though there had been forty-three Labour women candidates, with fourteen of them returned. The one new Labour woman was Mrs Joyce Butler, Leader of the Labour Group on the Wood Green Borough Council. Similarly, in 1959, although there were thirty-one Labour women candidates. only thirteen were returned. One of these was new to the House — Mrs Judith Hart, who had fought two previous elections and had a young family. This number was depleted when in 1961 Edith Summerskill accepted a life peerage and moved to an active life in the House of Lords.

The 1960s were to see the revival of the Labour Party's fortunes and one might have expected the fortunes of women in politics to improve too. In fact the number of women Labour candidates in 1964 and 1966 was only thirty-two and thirty respectively, although the proportion of Labour women returned was higher. These new women who reached Parliament in these two elections were an interesting group. In 1964 Lena Jeger returned, and with her came five new members: Mrs Margaret McKay, Mrs Renee Short, Mrs Anne Kerr, Dr Shirley Summerskill and Mrs Shirley Williams. 1966 saw the arrival of Miss Joan Lestor and Mrs Gwynneth Dunwoody. There were now nineteen Labour women members.

The 1960s were to see a dramatic increase in the chances of women achieving office, once elected. There is no doubt that this was largely due to the policy of one man: Harold Wilson. His views on the equality of women are well known, and on winning the General Election of 1964 he promptly put them into practice. Given the struggle that women had to face to get into Parliament in the first place and then to achieve office up to the 1960s, the change under Harold Wilson was striking. Indeed, the election of a woman to the Leadership of the Conservative Party might well not have happened when it did, had not both Parliament and the country become used to seeing women in high office under Wilson, who in practice has been the most sympathetic Prime Minister of this century as far as the women's cause in politics is concerned.

No fewer than seven women were given appointments, and Barbara Castle became the fourth woman to reach Cabinet rank when she was appointed Minister of Overseas Development — a new Ministry. In 1966 she was transferred to the post of Minister of Transport, which no one could regard as a woman's Ministry', and in 1968 she became Secretary of State for Employment and Productivity, surely a Department which could not have expected to have a woman leading it. It was appropriate that Barbara Castle should have broken new ground in this way. She combines femininity with the toughness of approach and aggressive style which are associated with the best male politicians. Meanwhile Margaret Herbison became Minister of Pensions and National Insurance and Alice Bacon became Minister of State at the Home Office. Eirene White, after having served as Parliamentary Secretary to the Colonial Office, became one of the four Ministers of State at the Foreign Office, traditionally regarded as a male preserve. Jennie Lee was appointed Parliamentary Secretary to the Ministry of Works and Public Buildings with special responsibility for the Arts, and Mrs Judith Hart, after being Under-Secretary of State for Scotland, was appointed to the post of Minister of State at the Commonwealth Relations Office. In 1968 she became the second woman member of the Cabinet as Paymaster General. Shirley Williams, considered by many as one of the most able women politicians today, became Parliamentary Secretary to the Ministry of Labour in 1966, after serving as PPS to the Minister of Health. She was appointed as Minister of State at the Home Office in 1969. Her intellect and sincerity are the qualities to strike first, and she is an interesting example of the way in which some women can command respect on the same terms as men — namely without bothering particularly about their appearance as far as grooming is concerned — for Shirley Williams often looks untidy and in a hurry, without this detracting from her presence, or the respect that people have for her. It was during the 1964-6 administration that women were appointed as Whips for the first time. Harriet Slater became a Lord Commissioner for the Treasury and Lady Phillips was appointed Baroness in Waiting in the House of Lords.

It was not long since the first woman had presented her writ of summons as a life peer, and been allowed to sit in the Lords. This was Lady Reading (Baroness Swanborough), who had arrived there only after a lengthy and sometimes intense struggle on the part of MPs, the Lords themselves, and others. Between 1924 and 1929 Lord Astor tried unsuccessfully five times to introduce a Parliamentary (Qualification of

Peeresses) Bill, to enable peeresses to sit in the Lords in their own right.
But it was not until 1958 that a Conservative Government pushed
through legislation which included the right of women to take a seat in
the Lords as life peers. The first were Stella, Marchioness of Reading,
Dame Katherine Elliot, Mrs Barbara Wootton, and Baroness Ravensdale.
Despite this advance it was not until 1963 that women hereditary peers
were allowed to take a seat in the Lords. The Labour women members
of the Upper House have included those who were made life women
peers after long service to the Labour movement, such as Jennie Lee,
Edith Summerskill, Alice Bacon and Eirene White.

It would be interesting to try and assess what impact women peers
have made on the Upper House in the years since their introduction.
Lord Shepherd, the former Leader in the Lords from 1964-76 and an
hereditary peer, who has been a member throughout the time that
women have been in the Lords, says: 'The House of Lords has definitely
been enriched by the presence of women peers among us'. He spoke of
the excellent work being done by women on both sides of the Upper
House; by Lady Serota, formerly a Minister and now the Ombudsman
for local government matters; by Lady Birk, a junior Minister in the
Department of the Environment; by Lady Tweedsmuir who held office
in the last Conservative administration and is now Deputy Chairman of
Committees in the Lords; and by Lady Llewelyn Davies who has the
distinction of being the first ever Chief Government Whip in the Lords —
to mention only a few of those who are giving most useful service.

He spoke of other women peers working in other fields as, for
instance, Lady Gaitskell's work on Committee 111 of the United
Nations — the Emerging Nations Committee — and Lady White, who
presides over a Committee of the Environment Ministry, dealing with
the recycling of waste products. He spoke, too, of the eagle eye Lady
Summerskill keeps on all government committees and commissions
to see that women get equal consideration for such appointments.
Speaking about discrimination against women he recalled the first
Anti-Discrimination Bill started as a Private Member's Bill in the
Commons and which came to nothing. Then Lady Seear, a Liberal,
took up the matter and launched a Private Member's Bill in the Lords.
A Select Committee was appointed by the Lords to investigate the
facts (to which the Labour Party Study Group, among others, gave
evidence). All this, he thought, undoubtedly eased the way for Roy
Jenkins as Home Secretary to produce, first, the White Paper on
Discrimination and then the Labour Government's Anti-Discrimination
Bill which is now an Act. 'We are not conscious of *women* peers today',

Lord Shepherd added, 'they are colleagues in the work of the House and very good colleagues indeed.'

Since women took a major step forward in terms of governmental responsibilities during the 1960s, there can now be no question but that women in Parliament, as a whole, are taken as seriously as their male colleagues. But this success has not been matched by any marked increase in the number of women MPs in the last three general elections. In 1970, out of twenty-nine Labour women candidates, only ten were elected, and although in the two 1974 elections there were in February forty candidates, and in October fifty, this last being the highest number ever of Labour women to stand, only thirteen and eighteen respectively were returned. Of the nineteen at present in the Commons (an additional woman, Dr Oonagh Macdonald, having been returned for Labour in a 1976 by-election), eight have what may be considered marginal constituencies, which could well fall as a result of a slight swing to the Conservatives. When this Government was formed in 1974, one third to a half of Labour women in the House were included in the administration in posts varying from Assistant Whip to Cabinet Minister. Since then, however, Joan Lestor, who was Under-Secretary at the Foreign Office has resigned and Judith Hart has given up her post as Minister for Overseas Development while Barbara Castle, who for many years has served in Labour governments, lost her Cabinet post when James Callaghan became Prime Minister. At the present time Miss Margaret Jackson is Parliamentary Secretary at the Department of Education and Science, Dr Shirley Summerskill is Parliamentary Secretary at the Home Office, while Mrs Shirley Williams holds Cabinet rank as the Minister for Education. Both Miss Betty Boothroyd and Mrs Gwynneth Dunwoody have been appointed Members of the European Parliament. These six represent a third of the total number of Labour women MPs, a proportion in government which is similar to the proportion of Labour men in office.

It is therefore no longer the case that once women have got into Parliament they are at a disadvantage in relation to men. Neither can it be said that women tend to become Ministers in Departments traditionally regarded as involving 'women's' subjects, or no more so than they have become Ministers in other Departments. However, no Labour woman to date has been appointed to one of the 'big three' Ministries as Secretary of State — the Home Office, the Exchequer and the Foreign and Commonwealth Office — although, for a while, before giving way to Roy Jenkins, Shirley Williams was chief spokesman on Home Affairs in Opposition.

186 Women in Parliament and Government

The final breakthrough has not come in the Labour Party, but in the election of Mrs Margaret Thatcher to the Leadership of the Opposition. It remains to be seen whether she will become this country's first woman Prime Minister, but her achievement is notable nonetheless.

Meanwhile, however, women still lag far behind the men in numerical terms, both as MPs and as candidates. The Labour Party, in comparison with the other parties, does only a little better, despite having the kind of philosophical base which would appear to make it natural for women to be as numerous as Labour MPs and candidates as men. After the First World War, the number of women MPs crept up; for some years now, however, the number seems to have settled down to between twenty-five and thirty from all parties, with minor fluctuations from time to time. Since 1945 the position shows no real sign of improving, despite the gradually changing status of women in our society. While the number of Labour women MPs has been fairly consistently higher than that of the other two main parties, the difference is not great, and even in the record election of October 1974, the number of Labour women candidates represented only 8 per cent of the total number of Labour candidates.

This is particularly saddening when one remembers the fight that the early women socialists waged on various fronts to improve both the general lot of women and their position within our political institutions. Despite all their ideals and efforts, and despite the work put in by those women already mentioned, women, while comprising over 50 per cent of the population, still have fewer than 5 per cent of the places in Parliament. One wonders what, for instance, the Pankhursts would have said had they known that over half a century after their activities were at their height the most readily measurable index of how women are faring in the political world gives a negative answer.

Concern about the small number of women MPs does not just mean concern for women's political status. It can also be said that Parliament is more likely to be sensitive to the reactions and needs of the country as a whole if it is, as far as possible, the total society in microcosm, comprised of people of many ages and background and of both sexes. In fact it fails on all these counts, but on none so blatantly as the count of sexual numerical equality, and it may be that this distorts the emphasis of Parliament's activities relative to the concerns of our society.

The lack of women candidates and MPs is a measure of something going on elsewhere, outside political activity. It is a measure of the fact that women still do not become as involved in activities outside the home as men do, even when they have the relevant qualifications. Whether it is a measure of women's own reluctance to come forward for quite other reasons, is less clear. In any case, these two factors are likely to be related to each other. But so long as women do not participate in public life to the same extent as men, or indeed in other activities which are legislatively or economically important to our country, and so long as the role of housewife is regarded as essentially inferior to the role of breadwinner in general and public servant in particular, women's lack of representation in such institutions as Parliament helps to maintain the vicious circle in which women are regarded as second class citizens.

If the Labour Party is to help in ensuring that there are more women candidates and MPs, one of its prime tasks is to eliminate any prejudice which may exist within its organisation. Many people believe that such prejudice does exist, and is instrumental in preventing more women being chosen at selection conferences. However, such evidence as there is does not suggest that by and large this is true. When a woman does decide to try for selection to a constituency, it does not appear that overall the constituency parties are going to stand in her way. What might be the case however is that women do not find it so easy to be selected for safer seats. For instance, in October 1974, 52 per cent of the Labour men candidates were returned, but only 36 per cent of the women. This is a statistically significant difference. Similarly, Ranney[6] came to the conclusion, after examining Labour candidates and constituencies between the years 1955 and 1965, that 'women. . .were given less desirable constituencies than men'. Pamela Brookes[7] came to the same conclusion. This tendency, if it does not change, could mean that if the number of women candidates were to increase, the number of women MPs might do so only very much more slowly. If one looks at the relationship between the number of women candidates and those elected since 1929, this gloomy picture is confirmed. Does this tendency exist because Labour parties in safe or more hopeful constituencies find it harder for some reason to accept the idea of a woman MP? Or is it just that women, for reasons to do with lack of confidence, or less persistence, do not go for the safer seats? Either way, the Labour Party has a job to do.

One of the major aspects of the problem is that relatively few women, compared with men, present themselves for possible selection. One of the measures of this is the number of women on Party Lists A and B. There are virtually no women on List A (the list of those with trade union backing) and of those on List B, many do not appear to do more than get onto the list. It is as though all their political ambitions end there. In common with male MPs. the bias in terms of background of both women MPs and candidates. is towards the middle class. Indeed. it would not be surprising if there were an even greater bias in this way amongst the women than the men, given the greater difficulty women have in envisaging a parliamentary career for themselves. This will tend to mean that those women who do choose such a career need, on average, even more confidence than their male counterparts and this confidence is more likely to be found in middle-class women than their less advantaged peers. This bias is further emphasised by the lack of women who are sponsored by trade unions.

Quite apart from the internal organisation of the Labour Party, it is clear that the lack of women MPs in general reflects the position of women in society as a whole. The problems facing women who want to enter public life — that is, those problems unrelated to the Labour Party's organisation — have been much discussed elsewhere, and in particular are summarised in Betty Lockwood's report to the Organisation Committee of the National Executive Committee. They include the fact that women are more likely to be late starters in political life than men, unless they reject the role of mother; they are more likely to be financially dependent on their husbands than vice versa; the House of Commons' hours are particularly difficult for those women who, like most men, want to combine the roles of parent and MP, and so on. Women only got the vote after the First World War, despite all the efforts of the suffragettes: it is as though, so long as women fought for votes without at the same time substantially trying to change their roles in society as a whole, they were in effect fighting a losing battle; but as soon as major international events made it economically necessary for women to change their roles to some extent during the war, and to take on work normally regarded as men's work, then it was possible for women to take a step forward in peacetime. The status of women is still gradually changing in the direction of greater freedom and equality as indeed it was to some extent before the First World War, but one is forced to consider, at the rate things are going, whether another cataclysmic event is necessary for women to be able to take another step forward in terms of representation in Parliament.

While it is beyond the scope of this chapter to assess properly the contributions of women MPs individually and overall to politics, it does not appear to be the case that women are less competent as parliamentary performers than men. In fact the structure of the Chamber in the House of Commons with its club atmosphere and many microphones, is not such that a male voice is more suitable, and there is no evidence that women are less effective than men at committee level either nationally or locally. There are exceptions — Jean Mann[8] points out that in her time some women found it difficult to speak in the House:

> having got over their maiden speech, which is always an ordeal, some [women] sit for years without opening their mouths. On one occasion a gentle Lady Member electrified the House by rising to catch Mr Speaker's eye. Now, at last, we were going to have her contribution, and, as on such occasions the silence could be heard. She was called on immediately whilst we waited with bated breath. 'I was only asking for candles', she said and sat down. 'Candles' is the appropriate Parliamentary request for lights.

If one goes through Hansard to look for the contributions from the present women members however, this story does not seem to be typical.

So women have time and again shown themselves as capable as men of serving in Parliament as backbenchers and in government, and as far as the latter is concerned they have by no means always been given the easiest posts. It is time that we were able to take it for granted that there are equal numbers of men and women in the House of Commons. The Labour Party has a possible two-fold approach to the problem. It can consider the promotion of women within its own ranks, and how to overcome whatever the factors are that keep women from the better seats. On the other hand it can consider ways in which more women everywhere, and not just middle-class ones, will consider politics as a possible career. This second is the harder task. Both are necessary; but not until it is faced can we consider ourselves to have lived up to the promise of the early women socialists.

Notes

1. Eleen Wilkinson MP, *Peeps at Politicians,* London: P. Allan & Co., 1931.
2. Ibid., p.25.
3. Margaret Bondfield, *A Life's Work.* London: Hutchinson, 1945, p.279.
4. Ellen Wilkinson, *Peeps at Politicians,* p.64.

5. Hugh Dalton, *The Fateful Years,* London: Frederick Muller, 1957, p.320.
6. Austin Ranney, *Pathways to Parliament,* London: Macmillan, 1965, p.195.
7. Pamela Brookes, *Women at Westminster,* London: Peter Davies, 1967, p.243.
8. Jean Mann, *Women in Parliament,* London: Odhams, 1962, pp.35 and 36.

BIBLIOGRAPHY

Note: The books listed below have been arranged according to the chapters to which they are mostly relevant. Some overlapping is unavoidable but, where this occurs, the title is only given in the earliest chapter.

Chapter 1

Besterman, Theodore, *Mrs Annie Besant: A Modern Prophet,* Kegan Paul.

Brookes, Pamela, *Women at Westminster,* Peter Davies.

Ford, Isabella O., *Women and Socialism,* Independent Labour Party.

MacDonald, J.R., *Margaret Ethel MacDonald,* Allen and Unwin.

Kamm, Josephine, *Rapiers and Battleaxes,* Allen and Unwin.

Pelling, Henry, *The Origins of the Labour Party.* Macmillan.

Thompson Laurence, *The Enthusiasts. A Biography of John and Katharine Bruce Glasier,* Gollancz.

Williams, Francis, *Fifty Years' March.* Odhams Press.

Wilson, Francesca, *Rebel Daughter of a Country House. Life of Eglantyne Jebb,* Allen and Unwin.

Chapter 2

Carter, G.R., Glasier, Katharine Bruce and Smillie, Robert, *Baths at the Pithead and the Works,* Women's Labour League.

Glasier, Katharine Bruce, *Miners' Baths,* Labour Party.

Glasier, Katharine Bruce, *Socialism for Children,* Independent Labour Party.

Ferguson, S.M. and Fitzgerald, E., *Studies in the Social Services,* HMSO and Longmans.

Herbert, Lucy, *Mrs Ramsay MacDonald,* Women Publishers Ltd.

McMillan, Margaret, *The Child and the State,* National Labour Press.

McMillan, Margaret, *The Life of Rachel McMillan,* Dent.

McMillan, Margaret, *Infant Mortality,* Independent Labour Party.

Mansbridge, Albert, *Margaret McMillan, Prophet and Pioneer,* Dent.

Women's Labour League, *In Loving Memory of Mary Middleton,* Women's Labour League.

Van Dereyken, Willem, *The Pre-School Child,* Penguin.

Chapter 3

Fulford, Roger, *Votes for Women, the Story of a Struggle,* Faber, 1957.
Labour Party, *National Executive Minutes,* Transport House Records.
Pankhurst, C., *Christabel Pankhurst Unshackled,* Hutchinsons, 1959.
Pankhurst, S., *The Suffragette Movement,* Longmans.
Rover, Constance, *Women's Suffrage and Party Politics 1866-1914,*
    Kegan Paul, 1967.
Women's Labour League, *London Executive Minutes,* Transport House
    Records.

Chapter 4

Labour Woman magazine from vol.I, No.1, Labour Party.
Labour Women's Conference Reports, Labour Party.
Labour and Socialist International, 14/23/1/2i.
Labour and Socialist International, 14/23/1/1i.
Labour and Socialist International, Proposed International Advisory
    Committee of Women – note on draft Constitution – August 1926.
Labour and Socialist International, 15/8/2, Third Women's
    International Conference.
Labour and Socialist International, 17/8/2/2, *Bulletin* of the LSI.

Chapter 5

Besant, Annie, *An Autobiography,* T. Fisher Unwin.
Fox, Alan, *History of the National Union of Boot and Shoe Operatives,*
    1874-1957, Basil Blackwell, Oxford.
Goldman, Harold, *Emma Paterson: She led Women into a Man's World,*
    Lawrence and Wishart.
Hamilton, Mary Agnes, *Women at Work,* Labour Book Service, 1941.
Hamilton, Mary Agnes, *Mary Macarthur, a Biographical Sketch,* Parsons.
Muggeridge, Kitty and Adam, Ruth, *Beatrice Webb. A Biography,*
    Secker and Warburg.
Roberts, B.C., *The Trade Union Congress 1868-1921,* TUC.
Stewart, Margaret and Hunter, Leslie, *The Needle is Threaded, the*
    History of an Industry, Heinemann.
    Report of the War Cabinet on Women in Industry, HMSO.
    Report of Royal Commission on the Civil Service 1929-31,
    HMSO.
    TUC Reports, TUC.
    Sixty Years of Trade Unionism, 1929, TUC.
    Seventy Years of Trade Unionism, TUC.

Webb, Sidney and Beatrice, *History of Trade Unionism*, Longman,
Green & Co., 1894.

Chapter 6

Davies, Margaret Llewelyn (editor), *Life as We Have Known It*, Hogarth
Press.
Davies, Margaret Llewelyn, *The Woman's Cooperative Guild*, Women's
Cooperative Guild.
Davies, Margaret Llewelyn (editor), *Maternity: Letters from Working
Women*. Preface by Sir Herbert Samuel, G. Bell, 1915.
Enfield, Honora, *Cooperation, its Problems and Possibilities*, Longmans,
1927.
Harris, Lilian, *The Position of Employees in the Cooperative
Movement*, Fabian Society.
Webb, Beatrice (Potter), *The Cooperative Movement in Great Britain*,
Swan Sonnenschein, 1891.
Webb, Catherine, *The Woman with the Basket: The Story of the
Women's Cooperative Guild*, Women's Cooperative Guild.
Webb, Catherine, *Industrial Cooperation*, Cooperative Union.

Chapter 7

Discrimination Against Women, Labour Party.
Boyd-Orr, Sir John, *Food, Health and Income*.
Donoughue, Bernard and Jones, G.W., *Herbert Morrison, Portrait of a
Politician*, Weidenfeld and Nicolson.

Chapter 8

Lumley, R., *White Collar Unionism in Britain*, Methuen.
Bain, G.S. and Price, R., 'Union Growth and Employment Trends in
the United Kingdom, 1964-70', *British Journal of Industrial
Relations*, November 1972.

Chapter 9

Wilkinson, Ellen, *Peeps at Politicians*, P. Allan & Co.
Bondfield, Margaret, *A Life's Work*, Hutchinson & Co.
Dalton, Hugh, *The Fateful Years*, Frederick Muller.
Ranney, Austin, *Pathways to Parliament*, Macmillan.
Mann, Jean, *Women in Parliament*, Odhams.
Wilkinson, Ellen, *The Town that was Murdered*, Gollancz.

APPENDIX I: Women Candidates in General Elections Since 1918

Year	Con. Candidates	Con. MPs	Lab. Candidates	Lab. MPs	Lib. Candidates	Lib. MPs	Others Candidates	Others MPs	Total Number of Women Candidates	Total Elected
1918	1	—	4	—	4	—	8	1a	17	1
1922	5	1	10	—	16	1	2	—	33	2
1923	7	3	14	3	12	2	1	—	34	8
1924	12	3	22	1	6	—	1	—	41	4
1929	10	3	30	9	25	1	4	1	69	14
1931	17	13	36	—	5	1	4	1	62	15
1935	19	6	33	1	11	1	2	1	67	9
1945	14, 1 Ind.Con.	1	41	21 (21LP)	20	1	11	1	87	24
1950	28	6	42	14	45	1	11	—	126	21
1951	25	6	41	11	11	—	—	—	77	17
1955	33	10	43	14	14	—	2	—	92	24
1959	28	12	36	13	16	—	1	—	81	25
1964	23	11	33	18	25	—	8	—	89	29
1966	21	7	30	19	20	—	9	—	80	26
1970	26	15	29	10	23	—	21	1	99	26
1974 Feb.	33	9	40	13	40	—	30	1	143	23
1974 Oct.	30	7	50	18	49	—	32	2	161	27

a One successful – Countess Markievicz – Irish Nationalist who did not take her seat. Viscountess Astor (Con.) elected in 1919 in a by-election was the first woman to sit in the House of Commons.

APPENDIX II: Labour Women Members of Parliament

First entered Parliament	Name	Constituency
1923	Miss Margaret Bondfield	Northampton
	Miss Dorothy Jewson	Norwich
	Miss Susan Lawrence	East Ham North
1924	Miss Ellen Wilkinson	Middlesbro' East
1929 (by-election)	Mrs Ruth Dalton	Bishop Auckland
(by-election)	Miss Jennie Lee	Lanark North
1929	Dr Ethel Bentham	Islington North
	Mrs Mary A. Hamilton	Blackburn
	Lady Cynthia Mosley	Stoke-on-Trent
	Dr Marion Phillips	Sunderland
	Miss Edith Picton Turbervill	The Wrekin
1930 (by-election)	Lady Noel-Buxton	North Norfolk
1931 (by-election)	Mrs Leah Manning	Islington North
1937 (by-election)	Mrs Agnes Hardie	Springburn
1938 (by-election)	Dr Edith Summerskill	Fulham West
(by-election)	Mrs Jennie L. Adamson	Dartford
1945	Miss Alice Bacon	Leeds North East
	Mrs Elizabeth M. Braddock	Liverpool Exchange
	Mrs Barbara A. Castle	Blackburn
	Miss Grace M. Colman	Tynemouth
	Mrs Freda Corbet	Camberwell North West
	Mrs Caroline S. Ganley	Battersea South
	Mrs Barbara Ayrton Gould	Hendon North
	Miss Margaret Herbison	Lanark North
	Mrs Jean Mann	Coatbridge
	Mrs Lucy Middleton	Plymouth Sutton
	Mrs Muriel Wallhead Nichol	Bradford North
	Mrs Florence Paton	Rushcliffe
	Mrs Mabel Ridealgh	Ilford North
	Mrs Clare McNab Shaw	Kilmarnock

First entered Parliament	Name	Constituency
1945 *(contd.)*	Mrs Edith A. Wills	Birmingham Duddesdon
1948 (by-election)	Mrs Alice Cullen	Glasgow Gorbals
1950	Miss Elaine Burton	Coventry South
	Mrs D. Rees	Barry
	Mrs Eirene White	East Flint
1953 (by-election)	Mrs Harriet Slater	Stoke-on-Trent
(by-election)	Mrs L Jeger	Holborn and St Pancras South
1955	Mrs Joyce S. Butler	Wood Green
1957 (by-election)	Lady Megan Lloyd George	Carmarthen
	Mrs Judith C.M. Hart	Lanark
1964	Mrs Anne Kerr	Rochester and Chatham
	Mrs Margaret McKay	Wandsworth Clapham
	Mrs Renee Short	Wolverhampton North East
	Dr Shirley Summerskill	Halifax
	Mrs Shirley Williams	Hitchin
1966	Mrs Gwynneth P. Dunwoody	Exeter
	Miss Joan Lestor	Eton and Slough
1969 (by-election)	Mrs Doris Fisher	Birmingham Ladywood
1970	–	–
1973 (by-election)	Miss Betty Boothroyd	West Bromwich
1974 (February)	Mrs Maureen Colquhoun	Northampton North
	Miss Jo Richardson	Barking
	Mrs Audrey Wise	Coventry South West
1974 (October)	Miss Margaret Jackson	Lincoln
	Miss Joan Maynard	Sheffield Brightside
	Mrs Helene Hayman	Welwyn and Hatfield
	Mrs Millie Miller	Ilford North
	Mrs Winifred A. Taylor	Bolton West
1976 (by-election)	Dr Oonagh McDonald	Thurrock

APPENDIX III: Names of Women Labour Peers and Year First Entered House of Lords

Year	Name
1958	Baroness Wootton of Abinger
1961	Baroness Summerskill of Ken Wood
1962	Baronesss Burton of Coventry
1963	Baroness Gaitskell of Egremont
1964	Baroness Phillips of Fulham
1965	Baroness Plummer[a]
1966	Baroness Stocks of Royal Borough of Kensington and Chelsea[b]
1967	Baroness Serota of Hampstead
1967	Baroness Llewelyn-Davies of Hastoe
1967	Baroness Birk of Regents Park
1970	Rt. Hon. Baroness Lee of Asheridge
1970	Rt. Hon. Baroness Bacon of Leeds and Normanton
1970	Baroness White of Rhymney
1974	Baroness Fisher of Rednal
1974	Baroness Stedman of Longthorpe
1974	Baroness Falkender of Much Haddom in the County of Northampton
1974	Baroness Delacourt-Smith of Alteryn in the County of Gwent
1975	Baroness Stewart of Alvechurch in the County of Greater London, Fulham

[a] Died June, 1972.
[b] Left Labour Party in June, 1974 – died July 1975.

197

APPENDIX IV: Names of Labour Women Ministers and Office Holders in the House of Commons and House of Lords

Name	Date	Position held
(a) Cabinet Ministers		
Rt. Hon. Miss Margaret Bondfield	1929-31	Minister of Labour
Rt. Hon. Miss Ellen Wilkinson	1945-7	Minister of Education
Rt. Hon. Mrs Barbara Castle	1964-6	Minister of Overseas Development
	1966-8	Minister of Transport
	1968-70	First Secretary of State and Secretary of State for Employment and Productivity
	Feb.1974-6	Secretary of State for Social Services
Rt. Hon. Mrs Judith Hart	1968-9	Paymaster General
Rt. Hon. Mrs Shirley Williams	Feb. 1974	Secretary of State for Prices and Consumer Protection
	1976	Paymaster General
(b) Other Ministers and Office Holders		
Rt. Hon. Miss Margaret Bondfield	1924	Parliamentary Secretary, Ministry of Labour
Miss Susan Lawrence	1929-31	Parliamentary Secretary, Ministry of Health
Rt. Hon. Miss Ellen Wilkinson	May-Oct.1940	Parliamentary Secretary. Ministry of Pensions
	Oct.1940-45	Parliamentary Secretary, Ministry of Home Security
Mrs Jennie L. Adamson	1945-6	Parliamentary Secretary, Ministry of Pensions
Rt. Hon. Dr Edith Summerskill	1945-50	Parliamentary Secretary, Ministry of Food
	1950-51	Minister of National Insurance

APPENDIX IV *(contd.)*

Name	Date	Position held
Rt. Hon. Miss Margaret Herbison	1950-51	Joint Under-Secretary of State for Scotland
	1964-7	Minister of Pensions and National Insurance (changed name to Ministry of Social Security in 1966)
Rt. Hon. Miss Alice Bacon	1964-7	Minister of State at Home Office
	1967-70	Minister of State, Department of Education and Science
Mrs Eirene White	1964-6	Parliamentary Secretary. Colonial Office
	1966-7	Minister of State, Foreign Office
	1967-70	Minister of State, Welsh Office
Rt. Hon. Miss Jennie Lee	1964-5	Parliamentary Secretary, Ministry of Public Buildings and Works
	1965-7	Parliamentary Secretary, Ministry of Education (with special responsibility for Arts)
	1967-70	Minister of State, Department of Education and Science
Rt. Hon. Mrs Judith Hart	1964-6	Under-Secretary of State at Scottish Office
	1966-7	Minister of State, Commonwealth Affairs
	1967-8	Minister of Social Security
	1969-70	Minister for Overseas Development
	1974-5	Minister of Overseas Development
Mrs Harriet Slater	1964-6	Assistant Government Whip

APPENDIX IV *(contd.)*

Name	Date	Position held
Rt. Hon. Mrs Shirley Williams	1966-7	Parliamentary Secretary to Minister of Labour
	1967-9	Minister of State, Department of Education and Science
	1969-70	Minister of State at Home Office
Mrs Gwynneth P. Dunwoody	1967-70	Parliamentary Secretary to the Board of Trade
	1975-	Member of British Labour Delegation to European Assembly
Miss Joan Lestor	1969-70	Parliamentary Under-Secretary of State, Department of Education and Science
	1974-5	Parliamentary Under-Secretary of State, Foreign and Commonwealth Office (in charge of African affairs)
	1975-6	Parliamentary Under-Secretary of State, Department of Education and Science
Dr Shirley Summerskill	1974-	Parliamentary Under-Secretary of State, Home Office (with responsibility for Sex Discrimination)
Miss Betty Boothroyd	1974-6	Assistant Government Whip
	1975-	Member of British Labour Delegation to European Assembly
Miss Margaret Jackson	1975-6	Assistant Government Whip
	1976-	Parliamentary Under-Secretary, Department of Education and Science

APPENDIX IV *(contd.)*

Name	Date	Position held
Mrs Florence Paton		First woman appointed to Speakers' Panel of Chairmen of House of Commons and the first woman to have presided over the whole House of Commons
Baroness Wootton	1965	Deputy Chairman of Committees
Baroness Phillips	1965	Baroness-in-Waiting
Baroness Serota	1968	Baroness-in-Waiting
	1969	Minister of State, Department of Health and Social Security
	1969	Baroness-in-Waiting
Baroness Llewelyn-Davies	1974-	Captain of the Honourable Corps of Gentlemen-at-Arms (Chief Whip – House of Lords)
Baroness Birk	1974-	Lord-in-Waiting, attached to the Department of the Environment (Under-Secretary of State)
Baroness Fisher	1975-	Appointed a member of British Labour Delegation to European Assembly
Baroness Stedman	1975-	Baroness-in-Waiting

APPENDIX V: Names of Women Chairmen

Year	Chairman
(a) The Labour Party	
1929-30	Miss Susan Lawrence
1935-6	Mrs Jennie L. Adamson
1939-40	Mrs Barbara Ayrton Gould
1944-5	Miss Ellen Wilkinson
1950-51	Miss Alice Bacon
1954-5	Dr Edith Summerskill
1956-7	Miss Margaret Herbison
1958-9	Mrs Barbara Castle
1967-8	Miss Jennie Lee
1968-9	Mrs Eirene White
(b) Trades Union Congress	
1923-4[a]	Miss Margaret Bondfield
1942-3	Miss Anne Loughlin
1947-8	Miss Florence Hancock
1961-2	Miss Anne Godwin
1974-5	Mrs Marie Patterson
(c) Cooperative Movement	
(i) Cooperative Wholesale Society Board	
1922-36	Mrs M.E. Cottrell
1959-75	Mrs Eva Dodds
(ii) Cooperative Congress	
1922-3	Miss Margaret Llewelyn Davies
1973-4	Mrs Eva Dodds

[a] Resigned on becoming a member of government in January 1924.

APPENDIX VI: Women in Administration of the Labour Party

Year	Name
(a) Chief Woman Officers	
1918-32	Dr Marion Phillips
1932-60 (December)	Miss Mary E. Sutherland
(b) Assistant National Agent	
1952-62	Miss Sara Barker
(c) Chief Woman Officers and Assistant National Agents	
1961-2	Miss Sara Barker
1962-7	Mrs Constance Kay
1967-75	Miss Betty Lockwood
1975-	Mrs Joyce Gould
(d) National Agent	
1962-8 (November)	Miss Sara Barker
(e) Acting General Secretary	
1968 (April) - 1968 (November)	Miss Sara Barker

APPENDIX VII: Women on the National Executive Committee

Name	Year
Mrs F. Harrison Bell	1918-25
Dr Ethel Bentham	1918-19
	1920-26
	1928-31
Miss A. Susan Lawrence	1918-40
Mrs Ethel Snowden	1918-22
Miss Mary Macarthur	1920-21
Miss Madeleine J. Symons	1922-23
Mrs Agnes Dollan	1920-28
	1936-8
Miss Mary Carlin	1924-6
	1931-7
Mrs Barbara Ayrton Gould	1926-7
	1929-50
Miss Minnie Pallister	1926-7
Mrs J.L. Adamson	1927-47
Lady Mabel Smith	1930-31
	1932-6
Mrs Leah Manning	1931-2
Miss Ellen Wilkinson	1937-47
Miss Eleanor Stewart	1938-44
Miss Alice Bacon	1940-70
Dr Edith Summerskill	1944-57
Mrs Elizabeth Braddock	1947-8
	1957-68
Miss Eirene Jones (later Mrs White)	1947-8
	1948-53
	1957-72
Miss Margaret Herbison	1948-59
	1960-67
Mrs Barbara Castle	
(on Women's Panel)	1950-51
(on Constituency Panel)	1951-75
Miss Alice Horan	1952-7

Name	Year
Mrs Jean Mann	1953-7
Miss Jennie Lee	1958-70
Mrs Lena Jeger	1959-60
	1967-75
Miss Joan Lestor (on Constituency Panel)	1966-75
Mrs Judith Hart	1968-75
Mrs Renee Short	1970-75
Mrs Shirley Williams	1970-75
Miss Joan Maynard	1972-5

Miss Margaret Bondfield was already a member of the General Council when, in 1921, the decision that two seats on the Council should be reserved for women became operative. From that date these reserved seats have been held as follows:

Miss Margaret Bondfield	1921-4
	1925-9
Miss Julia Varley	1921-5
	1926-35
Miss Mary Quaile	1924-6
Miss Anne Loughlin	1929-53
Miss Florence Hancock	1935-58
Miss Anne Godwin	1949-63
Miss Ellen McCullough	1958-63
Miss Winifred Baddeley	1963-8
Mrs Marie Patterson	1963-75
Miss Audrey M. Prime	1968-75

APPENDIX IX: Guild Representation and Growth

Guild Representation and Growth

	1891-92	1899-1900	1909-10	1919-20	1929-30[b]
Number of Branches	98	273	521	783	1395
Membership	4-5,000	12,809	25,942	44,500	66,566
Members of Co-op Education Committees	73	163	317	662	864
Members of Co-op Management Committees	6	21	51	220	344
Members of Central Co-op Board	—	1	1	3	4
Cooperative Union Education Committee	—	1	2	3	1
CWS Delegates	—	32	88	380	omitted
Congress Delegates	—	8	23	68	omitted
Poor Law Guardians	—	36	48	200	247
Local Authorities	—	—	1	26	81
Maternity Committees[a]	—	—	—	290	336

Notes: [a] not formed until 1918
[b] there is a great increase in other kinds of service this year, e.g. 10 Aldermen, 83 JPs.

Source: Annual Reports of the Guild.

In 1973 the Guild was 90 years old. Women formed 80 per cent of the membership of the cooperative movement. In 1972, membership was 24,935, in 853 branches. Twelve Guildswomen were aldermen and 80 JPs.

It is worth noting the growth of the cooperative movement itself in this period.

Growth of the Cooperative Movement

	1881	1914	1922
Number of Societies	981	1,385	1,321
Members	547,000	3,000,000	4,500,000
Trade	£15m	£87m	£167m

Source: A. Bonner, *British Cooperation,* rev. by B. Rose.

BIOGRAPHICAL NOTES

Adamson, Mrs Jennie, Member of Parliament Dartford Division, 1938-45 and Bexley, 1945-6; Parl'ty Secretary Ministry of Pensions, 1945-6; in 1946 became Vice-Chairman, National Assistance Board; Member National Executive Labour Party, 1927-47.

Andrews, Mrs Elizabeth, organised the work of Labour women in Wales for many years; her great interests were nursery schools and miners' baths; she was one of three women who gave evidence to the Coal Commission of the demand that pit head baths be provided without delay.

Ayrton-Gould, Mrs Barbara, Member National Executive of Labour Party; Member of Parliament for Hendon North, 1945-50; Vice-Chairman, British Council, 1948-50.

Bell, Mrs Harrison, maiden name was Harrison; married J.N. Bell and attached his surname to hers; afterwards always known as 'Harrison Bell'; was ardent Cooperative member and propagandist especially in N.E.; Member of National Executive Committee of Labour Party, 1918-25; first Chairman National Joint Committee of Working Women's Organisations; Director of Cooperative Society; served on Executive of Labour and Socialist International.

Blatny, Fanni, of Sudetenland, was the Grand Old Lady of European refugees in London during the Second World War. She had been active in the Socialist International for many years before she came to London.

Blume, Isabelle, a well-known, Belgian political figure; sought asylum in Britain when Belgium was invaded by Nazis; was a member of the Shadow group of Belgian Ministers formed in London during World War II, under the leadership of Camille Huysmans.

De Brouckère, Lucia, was the daughter of the veteran Belgian Socialist politician Louis de Brouckère with whom she fled to London when the Nazis invaded Belgium.

Carlin, Miss Mary, was an officer of the Transport and General Workers' Union organising the Transport Women's Guilds for the Union. From 1924-6 she served on the National Committee of the Labour Party and again from 1931-7.

Carlisle, Lady, 1908, President of Women's Liberal Association; personally sympathetic to Women's Suffrage but when asked to

support Cooperative Women's letter to Premier Asquith found it
not possible to commit her organisation.

Cawthorne, Mrs, country born, but married Hull dock worker; wrote
to Labour Representation Committee asking for facilities for women
to understand trade unionism and Labour politics; served on first
National Committee of Women's Labour League.

Ciolkosz, Lidia, wife of Adam Ciolkosz, well-known Polish Social
Democratic leader in London, came here with her husband when the
Communists invaded Poland. Since then they have striven to keep
Social Democracy alive in Polish circles against great odds.

Crout, Mabel (now Dame), devoted fifty of her more than eighty years
to the work of Local Government in Woolwich; for forty years was
a devoted official of the Woolwich Labour Party, which owes much
to her skill and valiant service.

Dawson, Miss Agnes, ardent feminist and great humanitarian; Chairman
of General Purposes Committee of London County Council; in the
days when women teachers had to resign posts on marriage she
fought for their freedom to continue their work, so making it
possible for Herbert Morrison to introduce this reform; worked for
more satisfactory education for children handicapped either
physically or mentally.

Despard, Mrs Charlotte, was an ardent socialist and suffragette; in 1918
she unsuccessfully fought Battersea North as a Labour Candidate.

Dollan, Mrs Agnes, was a well-known Labour speaker in Glasgow and
on Clydeside; she was the first Labour woman to contest a seat on
the Glasgow City Council; she served on the National Executive
Committee of the Labour Party 1920-28 and 1936-38.

Drake, Barbara, niece of Beatrice Webb; a great fighter for women's
rights; cooperated with Mary Macarthur and Susan Lawrence during
First World War in the struggle to get and maintain equal pay for
women who undertook men's work, when they were called to the
Forces; in 1925 coopted on London County Council Education
Committee and later made an Alderman which she remained until
1946; fought hard for school milk; great advocate of comprehensive
education.

Dunwoody, Mrs Gwynneth, Member of Parliament for Exeter 1966-70;
Parliamentary Secretary to Board of Trade 1967-70: she is now
Member of Parliament for Crewe; daughter of Morgan Phillips, a
former General Secretary of the Labour Party.

Elkin, Mrs W., for many years Hon. Secretary of the Middleton-
MacDonald Baby Hospital in Kensington, until it was integrated into

the National Health Service; she was a well-known social worker, taking special interest in Jewish Girls' Clubs.

Freundlich, Emmy, was a well-known leader of the Cooperative Movement in Austria. Freundlich was President of the International Cooperative Women's Guild. She sought refuge in London when the Nazis invaded Austria.

Ganley, Mrs Caroline, gave a lifetime of service to the Cooperative Movement and to the Cooperative Women's Guild; Member of Parliament for Battersea South 1945-50; Member of Battersea Borough Council; member of Price Regulation Committee London area.

Gore-Booth, Ms Eva, sister of Countess Marcievicz (who was elected to Parliament 1918, but refused as Sinn Feiner to take her seat), Eva Gore-Booth was a member of the Manchester and Salford Association of Machine, Electric and other Women Workers. As their representative she attended Labour Party Conferences.

Gossling, Mrs Nance, early member of Women's Labour League she worked for Baby Clinic and Baby Hospital until they were taken over by the Borough Council of Kensington and the National Health Service, respectively, helping to raise money by regular sewing parties and other means, wife of Arch Gossling, one-time Labour and Trade Union Member of Parliament.

Gotthelf, Herta, was editor of the German Social Democratic Women's magazine before coming to London when Hitler seized power in Germany; when the war ended she returned to West Germany and was soon to become Chief Woman Officer of the SPD.

Hawkins, Mrs, Foundation member of Women's Labour League seconding resolution which brought it into being at Leicester in 1906.

Herbison, The Rt. Hon. Margaret, a teacher; Member National Executive Committee Labour Party 1948-59; Under-Secretary of State, Scottish Office 1950-51; Minister of Pensions and National Insurance 1964-7; Chairman of Labour Party 1956-7; Member Women's Consultative Committee.

Hope, Miss Mabel, one of the earliest women delegates to Conferences of the Labour Party representing Post Office Workers. She was also a member of the Women's Labour League and a supporter of women's enfranchisement.

Horan, Miss Alice, 1896-1971; born in London; followed her father's trade of tailor; joined National Federation of Women Workers; became member of General Council of National Union of General

and Municipal Workers 1916; was Lancashire Organiser for her
Union 1926 and Chief Woman Organiser in 1946.

Jewson, Miss Dorothy (in later life Mrs Campbell Stephens), was one of
the first three Labour women Members of Parliament; elected in
1923 for Norwich; member of ILP National Administrative Council;
frequently represented ILP on national and international women's
committees.

Jobson, Ms Belle, member of Scottish Farm Workers' Organisation and
Chairman of Scottish Trades Union Congress.

Kerr. Mrs Anne, Member of Parliament for Rochester and Chatham
1964-70; sat on the London County Council for Putney; fought
hard and long for the causes she took up; died in 1973.

Lenn, Miss Dorothy, was an early organiser for the Women's Labour
League. She travelled, lectured and organised, especially in those
areas where Labour Candidates had been adopted.

Longman, Miss Mary, one-time secretary of Women's Labour League;
first worked with Dr Marion Phillips, but when during First World
War Dr Phillips was unable to handle all her commitments, Mary
Longman took over the Women's Labour League; later she resigned
at the time of her marriage.

Louis Lévy, Marthe, came to London with her husband, a well-known
French Social Democrat, when Paris fell to the Nazis; they returned
to France to take up Social Democratic activities as soon as the
termination of war made this possible. Meanwhile she told British
Social Democratic women much about aims and methods of their
French colleagues.

Lowe, Mrs Eveline, the first woman in 50 years of its existence to
become Chairman of the London County Council; her first public
service was membership of Bermondsey Board of Guardians; later
she represented Bermondsey on the London County Council; great
interest was education; served as Chairman of Education Committee;
was made a Commander of the Legion of Honour by President
Lebrun.

Luxemburg, Rosa, born in Poland, but worked for Socialism in both
Poland and even more in Germany; became Leader of extreme left
wing of German socialism, but though on the left, always
firmly believed in democratic methods; was a victim of the
revolution of 1918 — she was killed by assassin's bullet on 15
January 1919.

McKay, Mrs Margaret, Member of Parliament for Wandsworth Clapham
1964-9. Member of Transport and General Workers' Union; Chief

Woman Officer of Trades Union Congress; author of *Women in Trades Union History*.

Manning, Mrs Leah, an educationalist and past President of National Union of Teachers; Member of Parliament for East Islington February-October 1931 and for Epping Division 1945-50.

Mosley, Lady Cynthia, wife of Sir Oswald Mosley and daughter of Lord Curzon of Kedleston; joined Labour Party in 1920; Member of Parliament for Stoke-on-Trent 1929; in 1931 stood down in favour of her husband fighting for his New Party — he was beaten.

Nodin, Mrs Minnie, foundation Member of Women's Labour League and one-time treasurer; attended the weekly sewing parties for the League and the Baby Clinic until her health broke down; then she continued to raise funds by holding sewing parties and sales among her friends in Tadworth, where she lived. Her husband, Philip, was Treasurer of the Baby Hospital for some years before it was taken over by the National Health Service in 1947.

Noel-Buxton, The Lady (Lucy) Member of Parliament North Norfolk 1930-1, and for Norwich 1945-51; the first peeress to sit in the House of Commons.

Pethick Lawrence, Mrs Emmeline, 1867-1954; fought for the emancipation of women and for world peace; in these causes she and her husband were a great team; up to 1912 she supported Emmeline and Christabel Pankhurst, enduring imprisonment and hunger-striking, but then broke with them because of the increasing militancy of the campaign; she wrote her memoirs *My part in a changing world.*

Picton-Turbervill, Miss Edith, of well-to-do family but devoted her life to the poor and needy; carried on an active campaign for women's rights; joined Labour Party 1918; Member of Parliament for Wrekin Division 1929-31; had been Vice-President of YWCA; spent six years in India working for Indians and Eurasians; author and broadcaster.

Pollak, Marianne, wife of the well-known Austrian writer and politician, Oskar Pollak, had been a leading figure in Austrian and International Socialist circles in the days of the Vienna Working Union, a group which had split off from the Second International during the First World War, and was reunited with the International at the Hamburg Conference 1922 to form the Labour and Socialist International. Came to Britain when Hitler invaded Austria.

Quale, Mary, 1886-1958, born in Dublin; worked as waitress in Manchester; through Manchester Trades Council did pioneering organisation among women; became National Woman Organiser of

Transport and General Workers' Union 1922-33; Member of General
Council of Trades Union Congress 1923-6.

Rackham, Mrs Clara D., 1898 gained Classical Tripos Newnham College,
Cambridge; 1901 married H. Rackham, Fellow of Christ's College,
Cambridge; served on Board of Guardians; active in women's
suffrage campaign; Founder and President of Cambridge Cooperative
Women's Guild; 1915 Temporary Factory Inspector in Lancashire;
1919 transferred to London; 1919 member of Cambridge Borough
Council; 1929 Cambridge County Council; 1935 fought Saffron
Walden Constituency as Labour Candidate.

Salter, Mrs Ada, was the wife of Dr Alfred Salter, Labour Member of
Parliament for Bermondsey 1922-35 with a short break 1923-4.
They lived in the Borough and she was a member of the London
County Council and of the Borough Council; theirs was a great
political and humanitarian partnership.

Short, Mrs Renee, Member of Parliament for Wolverhampton North East
since 1964; active cooperator and in local government; member of
British Delegation to Cuba 1963; special interest, health and
welfare problems.

Slater, Mrs Harriet, won Stoke-on-Trent North Division in by-election
1953; was first Labour Woman Member of Parliament to be
appointed a Whip; greatest interest lay in Cooperative Movement.

Sloan, Ms Isabel, organiser for Federation of Women Workers, but she
left trade union work when the Federation amalgamated with the
General and Municipal Workers' Union. She is believed to have taken
up work for the Ministry of Labour at that time.

Smith, Ms Constance, civil servant; appointed as adviser to government
delegation to the Washington Conference 1920.

Summerskill, Rt. Hon. Edith, (Baroness since 1961), Member of
Parliament 1938-61; physician since 1924; Parliamentary Secretary,
Ministry of Food 1945-50; Minister of National Insurance 1950-1;
Privy Councillor 1949; founded 'Women for Westminster' in
1930.

Summerskill, Dr Shirley, medical practitioner; Member of Parliament
for Halifax since 1964; Parliamentary Under-Secretary of State,
Home Office, with special responsibility for sex discrimination;
daughter of Baroness Summerskill.

Swanwick, Mrs H.M., was the first British woman appointed a delegate
to the League of Nations 1924; she had been an ardent propagandist
for world peace and an advocate of women's emancipation since
the early years of this century.

Symons, Madelaine, an officer of Federation of Women Workers; after amalgamation of Federation with General and Municipal Workers Union worked for short period in that Union; later married and, as Mrs Robinson, was magistrate; in that capacity worked hard for establishment of juvenile courts.

Thorndike, Sybil (Dame), the well-known actress of the twentieth century was one of the founders of Equity, the actors' trade union; supported many good causes, especially the Middleton-MacDonald Baby Clinic.

Treves, Maria, was the widow of the Italian Socialist Leader Claudio Treves. She came to London with her two sons as a fugitive from Mussolini's Italy.

Zetkin, Clara, was one of the earliest pioneers of International Socialism among women; lived and worked in Germany, she was in touch with the Women's Labour League almost from its inception.

NOTES ON CONTRIBUTORS

Sheila Lochhead, JP, is the youngest daughter of Margaret and
  J. Ramsay MacDonald, and has had wide experience of social work
  both in the United Kingdom and abroad.

Sheila Ferguson, is Head of History Department, Peckham
  Comprehensive School, Joint author of Studies in Social Services
  Official Civil Histories of the War, HMSO and Longmans Green.

Margherita Rendel, Fellow of Royal Society of Arts. Author and
  University Lecturer and Barrister at Law. Member of various groups
  concerned with status of women, Parliamentary Equal Rights, etc.

Mary Walker, is a Borough Councillor, former Secretary of International
  Socialist Women's Bureau and former Secretary and Chairman of
  London Fabian Society. She is Chairman of Croydon North East
  Constituency Labour Party.

Dame Anne Godwin, has had vast experience of Trade Union Movement
  from Branch Secretary to the first General Secretary of a Union
  catering for both sexes. Member of General Council of Trades Union
  Congress 1949-63; Chairman of Trades Union Congress 1961-2;
  President of Trades Union Congress.

Jean Gaffin, is a Lecturer in Social Policy and Administration,
  Polytechnic of the South Bank; Parliamentary Candidate 1974; has
  wide knowledge and experience of the Cooperative Movement.

Oonagh Anne MacDonald, MP, is Member of Parliament for Thurrock
  Constituency; Lecturer in Philosophy, Bristol University; author
  and editor; has done much voluntary work in Labour and trade
  union movements.

Margaret McCarthy, is married to Lord McCarthy, and is a Borough
  Councillor, housewife, former Lecturer in trade union studies. She
  holds the Oxford University Diploma in Economics and Political
  Science, Ruskin College.

Maeve Denby, author and lecturer, has fought three Parliamentary
  elections and is a former City Councillor. She has travelled widely.

INDEX

Acland, Alice 113-14, 117
Adamson, Jennie 90, 178, 180
aims of women in TUC 170-3
Anderson, Marie 90
Annakin, Ethel *see* Snowden
Anomolies regulations 148
anti-discrimination provisions 184
  see also under equality; equal
  discrimination; Sex Discrimination
  Act
apprentice schemes, 171
Arts Council, women serving on 155
Asquith, Herbert Henry 29, 60, 63,
  68, 72, 73, 77, 82
Attlee (Earl) Clement 178, 181
Ayrton-Gould, Barbara 90, 107, 179

baby hospital and clinics 30, 44-7
Bacon, Alice 92, 179, 183-4
Baker, Jennie 85
Balance of the Sexes Bill
  (1975) 155-6
Barker, Dame Sara 157
Barnes, George 33
Barton, Eleanor 132, 138
baths at pit-heads 53-5
Battle, John 75-6
Bell, Mrs Harrison 89
Bentham, Dr Ethel 30-1, 42, 43,
  44-5, 79, 88
Bentwich, Helen 154
Besant, Annie 22, 96
bibliography 191-3
Billington-Grieg, Theresa 79
birth control 54
Black Clementina 120
Bondfield, Margaret 23, 28, 30, 36,
  44, 47, 52, 62-3, 67, 72, 79, 87,
  89, 97-8, 103, 108, 129, 176-7
Booth, Charles 17, 39
Boothroyd, Betty 185
Boyd Orr, Sir John 144
Braddock, Bessie 179-80
British Labour Party:
  administration for, names of
  women in 203; start of 13, 23;
  today's party 144-60; women
  chairmen of 202; Women's

Labour League becomes a part
  of 28
British Nationality Act 1948, 148
Brown, W.J. 107
Brussels Women's International
  Conference 89-90
Butler, Joyce 182

Carlin, Mary 90
Castle, Barbara 149, 171, 179-80,
  183, 185
Cawthorne, Mrs 25
Cecil, Lord Robert 74
chairmanships, names of women
  holding posts of 202
Charter for Women (TUC's) 171-2
childbirth and employment 87, 90,
  108, *see also under* maternity
children, social services for:
  baby clinics 44-7; employment
  54; food for needy 41-2;
  medical inspections 42-4;
  milk at school 51, 54;
  nursery schools 48-50
Child welfare, working for
  improvement in 147
Chinn, Vera 95
Chipchase, Ethel 20
Christian Socialists 116-18
Civil Service 106-8, 162
Clinic, foundation of memorial
  29-30, 44-7
Coal Mines Act 1911 53
College, TUC's, courses for
  training at 166
Colman, Grace 157
Colquhoun, Maureen 155
Conciliation Bills 68, 71, 73
Congress, Women attending
  Trade Union Annual 167-9;
  see also under Trade Unions
Constituencies, do women get
  undesirable? 187
Contributors, notes on 215
Conway, Katherine St J. 22
Cooper, Mrs 61-2
cooperation, women's part in
  international 16, 113-41

216